THE ACADEMIC POSTMODERN AND
THE RULE OF LITERATURE

David Simpson

THE ACADEMIC POSTMODERN AND THE RULE OF LITERATURE

*A Report on
Half-Knowledge*

THE UNIVERSITY OF CHICAGO PRESS
Chicago & London

DAVID SIMPSON is professor of English at the University of Colorado, Boulder. His many books include *Romanticism, Nationalism, and the Revolt against Theory*, published by the University of Chicago Press, which won the American Conference on Romanticism Book Prize in 1993.

The University of Chicago Press, Chicago 60637
The University of Chicago Press, Ltd., London
© 1995 by The University of Chicago
All rights reserved. Published 1995
04 03 02 01 00 99 98 97 96 95 1 2 3 4 5

ISBN 0-226-75949-0 (cloth)
ISBN 0-226-75950-4 (paper)

Library of Congress Cataloging-in-Publication Data

Simpson, David, 1951–
    The academic postmodern and the rule of literature : a report on
half-knowledge / David Simpson.
        p.   cm.
    Includes bibliographical references (p.   ) and index.
    1. Postmodernism (Literature) I. Title.
PN98.P67S57   1995
809'.045—dc20   95-1972
                                                        CIP

♾ The paper used in this publication meets the minimum requirements of the
American National Standard for Information Sciences—Permanence of Paper for
Printed Library Materials, ANSI Z39.48-1984.

For Michael Oruch

"The Eye Altering Alters All"

*He that hath liberty to define, i.e. determine the significa-
tion of his Names of Substances (as certainly every one
does in effect, who makes them stand for his own* Ideas, *)
and makes their Significations at a venture, taking them
from his own or other Men's Fancies, and not from an
Examination or Enquiry into the Nature of Things
themselves, may, with little Trouble, demonstrate them
one of another, according to those several Respects, and
mutual Relations he has given them one to another;
wherein, however Things agree, or disagree, in their own
Nature, he needs mind nothing but his own Notions, with
the Names he hath bestowed upon them.*

John Locke

An Essay concerning
Human Understanding

CONTENTS

ACKNOWLEDGMENTS

This book has benefited significantly from conversations with Margaret Ferguson, Gerald Graff, John Guillory, Mary Poovey, Bruce Robbins, and H. Aram Veeser, and from the published essays of Alan Liu and Joel Fineman. Audiences at the universities of Chicago and Colorado and at the British Association of Romantic Studies conference (Strathclyde, 1993) have proved both testing and helpful. I thank my hosts on these occasions: John Comaroff, Dennis McGilvray, and Tom Furniss. Two recent books have been especially forceful in helping me formulate my thoughts: John Guillory's *Cultural Capital* and Bruce Robbins's *Secular Vocations*. It is gratifying that their authors were the two readers assigned to this manuscript by the University of Chicago Press. They supplied exceptionally thoughtful and generous reports, and have significantly assisted me in preparing the final draft. I thank Colleen Anderson for prompt and meticulous help in preparing this manuscript. Dean Charles Middleton of the College of Arts and Sciences has been very helpful and supportive in mitigating the pressures of my four years of departmental administration, and I thank him warmly. Although this book is not about art, art has been a big part of my life, and for his huge contribution to that, and for his thoughts about the artistic postmodern (and even more for his paintings), I thank Michael Oruch, my good friend these many years. Margaret Ferguson remains my most stringent, insightful, and generous reader, my ideal audience, and my constant companion in mind, spirit, and person.

Earlier versions of chapter 5 appeared in *Critical Quarterly* 35, no. 3 (1993) and in *Raritan* 14, no. 1 (1994); and a version of chapter 4 appears in *Feminism and Postmodernism,* edited by Margaret Ferguson and Jennifer Wicke (Durham and London: Duke University Press, 1994). Permission to reprint is gratefully acknowledged.

Introduction

THE ACADEMIC POSTMODERN?

I am not sure what *postmodernism* is, although I do know a good deal about the arguments surrounding that term. None of the world-scale or even national modelings of the postmodern leave me entirely comfortable. An industry of definition and subdefinition has grown up around the question of the postmodern, so that there is already a need for a history of usages; and, fortunately, at least one such history is available. [1] Looking at the range of debates about the postmodern, one might say, with Jennifer Wicke and Margaret Ferguson, that the term functions best at its simplest, as a description of "the way we live now, " and as an "umbrella term for the cultural, social and theoretical dimensions of our period." [2] To speak about the postmodern is then to make a claim for immediate attention to contemporary concerns.

I am a little more confident that I know what *academic postmodernism* is. The major contention of what follows is that the academy, which now mostly means the university, provides us with a very traditional set of terms within which to nest most of what we have to say about postmodernity, and that those terms come principally from the institutional vocabulary dealing with literature and literary criticism. This is what I mean by the "rule of literature." Thus, as we celebrate the new centrality of localism, autobiography, anecdote, and so forth—the paradigms that are the subjects of this book—we mostly fail to perceive or acknowledge their ancestries in the long-durational process of modernization (a process ongoing since at least the seventeenth century), and specifically in the "literature" that took on its very defini-

1 Margaret A. Rose, *The Post-Modern and the Post-Industrial: A Critical Analysis* (Cambridge: Cambridge University Press, 1991).

2 Margaret Ferguson and Jennifer Wicke, eds., *Feminism and Postmodernism* (Durham and London: Duke University Press, 1994), 1, 3.

tions during that same period, as well as in the "literary criticism" that grew up to describe it as if from the outside, and by the application of a supposedly unaffiliated, free intelligence. As we pronounce for and against the postmodern, and for and against various definitions of the postmodern, I suggest that we risk mistaking the internal migration of terms and priorities among the disciplines inside the academy for a radical redescription of the world outside the academy. What can look like a completely new configuration of knowledge can also be understood rather more modestly as a result of the exporting of literary-critical categories into disciplines that had previously resisted them by being more confident of the sufficiency of their own. This confusion is encouraged by the rhetoric of the postmodern and about the postmodern, which indeed, as Fredric Jameson tells us, "looks for breaks" and imagines that, for instance, "the modernization process is complete and nature is gone for good."[3]

In other words, when we say or imply that, for example, the world does not provide us with a foundational reality, or that we live within the realm of the spectacle, or that it is impossible to authenticate any form of knowledge as truth, or that all knowledges must be understood as productions of particular, situated minds and therefore as incommensurable with the knowledges of differently situated minds—and all these are familiar if deliberately trivial examples of a recognizably postmodern ethos—we are indeed trying to make a good-faith statement about the way the world now seems to be; but we are also (most of us) speaking from within an institution (the academy) in some parts of which these insights are familiar to the point of being banal. And when we get excited, and begin to proselytize for these views as views of the world, then we are responding as much to an internal redistribution of institutional capital as to any outside motivation. What we are sensing as new is not, or not necessarily, the world in general, but rather the degree to which "radical" philosophers, social scientists, historians, anthropologists, historians of science, and even some scientists are prepared to accept the traditional vocabularies of literary criticism as viable for their own descriptive tasks.

When enough disciplines are prepared to agree on a common vocabulary, as has happened with the migration of literary-critical priori-

---

3   Fredric Jameson, *Postmodernism, or The Cultural Logic of Late Capitalism* (Durham: Duke University Press, 1991), ix.

ties into other fields, then it is very tempting to propose that the world has indeed changed. And perhaps it has. For there has to be some explanation other than mere coincidence for this commonality of method and purpose to emerge in the way that it does. But I am convinced that we must address the topic of the internal migration before we can have any kind of informed access to what is outside it, or working within it from the outside. The following chapters attempt this task. Their spirit is intended to be cautionary rather than accusatory. They call into question the claims we might make or the desires some of us might have for the radical effectivity of what we are doing when we define or project the postmodern, but they do not deny those claims or desires. I hope above all to contribute to a history, or careful historicizing, of a body of work that takes as one of its major initiatives the subsumption of history itself.

I therefore hope that there is a useful politics to this, though it is not that of purifying the disciplines, of putting each set of methods and priorities back in their proper boxes and next to the other boxes on the shelf. Habermas laments the collapse of the boundaries between philosophy and literary criticism, which he blames on Derrida, in terms of philosophy's consequent loss of "seriousness" and "productivity": "the false assimilation of one enterprise to the other robs both of their substance."[4] For him it is as if the question of adjudicating the relation of the academy to the world can be solved simply by making sure that the philosophers (though not Derrida) rather than the others get to define it. The whole problem is then reduced to one of getting philosophy back into shape. This might indeed have the function of consolidating philosophy departments into purposive unanimity (and most of them to this day would be reluctant to hire Derrida), but the local, intrainstitutional gains to be had from this hardly constitute a politics, or indeed a knowledge. No, if there is a politics to be had here, I hope it will be more like that recently evinced by Masao Miyoshi in his arresting critique of the academic predilection for the postcolonial, which he sees as a "sanitizing" reaction, at the service of "pedagogic expediency," to a global economy of "intensified colonialism."[5]

4 Jürgen Habermas, *The Philosophical Discourse of Modernity*, trans. Frederick Lawrence (Cambridge: MIT Press, 1990), 210.

5 Masao Miyoshi, "A Borderless World? From Colonialism to Transnationalism and the Decline of the Nation-State," *Critical Inquiry* 19 (1992–93): 750–51.

Miyoshi suggests that the academy is as often engaged in deflecting as it is in reflecting the world. It does so by its invocation of its own internally established traditions, and not just by acts of outright bad faith. That is why it is useful to know what those traditions are and how they work.

The confidence with which we scholars (as Nietzsche called us) talk about the postmodern is, I suggest, significantly derived from our inhabiting an institutional subculture that offers us some very familiar vocabularies for carrying out the analysis. Jameson has argued that in all definitions of the postmodern there takes place an "inaugural narrative act" that decides in advance, for instance, whether we are dealing with "historical originality" or "simple prolongation."[6] He understands that we are dealing with some degree of both, but chooses to take seriously postmodernism's claim to originality. My own focus on the academic postmodern requires the opposite emphasis, since I am less interested in the general social and cultural functions of the concept (Jameson's interest) than in the location of our inaugural narrative act within a rather narrow tradition of narrativization, that of the academy and specifically of the literary academy. This tradition can betray us into all sorts of hypotheses about origins, many of them with comforting intradisciplinary landmarks. Gianni Vattimo, for example, claims that "the scattered and often incoherent theories of postmodernity only acquire rigour and philosophical credibility when seen in relation to the Nietzschean problematic of the eternal return and the Heideggerian problematic of the overcoming of metaphysics."[7] Such statements partake as much of reproduction as they do of discovery. After tossing upon the seas of historical confusion that make up the ocean of the "postmodern," we beach ourselves, exhausted and relieved, upon the familiar proper nouns anchored to the received disciplines.

To invoke the specter of reproduction, as I have just done, not only strikes terror into the would-be academic activist and offers reciprocal relief to the academic quietist; it also conjures up another proper name, that of Pierre Bourdieu, by now just as familiar as the others and perhaps just as suspicious. Bourdieu's work, long familiar to sociologists, has been making its wider way into the anglophone academy

6   Jameson, *Postmodernism*, xiii.

7   Gianni Vattimo, *The End of Modernity: Nihilism and Hermeneutics in Postmodern Culture*, trans. Jon R. Snyder (Baltimore: Johns Hopkins University Press, 1991), 1.

very much as a sobering corrective to the assumptions we associate with the "sixties," assumptions that endorse models of academic behavior as radically effective for positive political change. Those who still believe that to change the classroom is to change the world, or that the truth has only to be pronounced in order for it to be believed and to have global consequences (like the flap of the proverbial butterfly's wing) are those most in need of the shock therapy that Bourdieu's work makes available. In brief, Bourdieu suggests that the principal business of the educational apparatus is that of reproduction and accreditation. The content of our classes then becomes significantly less important than the grades we give, the role models we project, and the advantages we preserve for ourselves and our successors as the preservers and disseminators of cultural capital. Education is less an outreach or response to the wider world than a mechanism for reproducing inherited social and class distinctions. As Evan Watkins puts it, the familiar "ideologies of the new" may be not just ineffectual but even "dangerous" insofar as they disguise the degree to which the specific working conditions and social functions of our profession have not changed, even as we think we are introducing a brave new world at the level of content. [8] The class now discusses Madonna instead of Milton, but it is the same old class. This is what Bourdieu and Passeron call "the ruse of academic reason" whereby "the institution leads the teacher to serve it by disposing him to make use of it." [9]

Academic disciplines are, according to this position, principally in the business of disseminating various forms of (variously marketable) literacy and culture. Whether linguistic, scientific, or professional, their social function is one of separating the few from the many, the right sort from the wrong sort, the As from the Fs. (Some of the current panic about grade inflation may be attributed to the perceived failure of this function.) John Guillory's *Cultural Capital* presents, among other things, a powerful analysis and history of this syndrome for the educational culture of literature and literary language, and is to the best of my knowledge the major adaptation to date (outside sociology) of Bourdieu's work for an anglophone readership and an Anglo-American

8 Evan Watkins, *Work Time: English Departments and the Circulation of Cultural Value* (Stanford: Stanford University Press, 1989), 27–28.

9 Pierre Bourdieu and Jean-Claude Passeron, *Reproduction in Education, Society, and Culture*, trans. Richard Nice, 2d ed. (London: Sage Publications, 1990), 125.

tradition. [10] The emphasis of Guillory's argument falls upon the degree to which virtual radicalizations of and by English teachers (canon reform, attention to theory, and so forth) are symptoms of real reproduction. Change is driven less by the fact of response to a changing "world," conceived of in the largest ethical and political sense, than by the need to preserve some viable place for the profession of the literary academic in a period of *professional* crisis. John McGowan has similarly attributed the symptoms of postmodernism to "a heightened anxiety about what impact intellectuals have on a world that appears increasingly inimical to the values promoted in the arts and in intellectual work."[11]

Veblen long ago gave us the terms with which to begin theorizing this predicament. He saw the "higher schools" as reactionary rather than vanguard institutions, responding slowly to changes in the world rather than anticipating them. The function of higher learning in the developed consumer society is to display the kinds of expertise that can be "conventionally recognised as evidence of wasted time," and hence open to patronage within a culture of conspicuous consumption. The humanities, precisely because of their disconnection from the technological base of industrial society, are most adequate to this task. Thus its practitioners serve as shamans for the ritualized intimidation of the general public, respected for their aura of the occult even as they lower the collective economic efficiency of the whole. [12] This of course puts the intellectual, especially the humanities intellectual, in a very uncomfortable position. On the one hand, according to Veblen, our very social function is premised on our uselessness. On the other hand, we are constantly under pressure to be useful and to explain ourselves according to institutionally alien models of productivity. Veblen does not himself pursue this paradox, but it seems pertinent to an un-

10   John Guillory, *Cultural Capital: The Problem of Literary Canon Formation* (Chicago and London: University of Chicago Press, 1993).

11   John McGowan, *Postmodernism and Its Critics* (Ithaca and London: Cornell University Press, 1991), 1. See also Peter Bürger, "The Disappearance of Meaning: Essay at a Postmodern Reading of Michel Tournier, Botho Strauss, and Peter Handke," in *Modernity and Identity*, ed. Scott Lash and Jonathan Friedman (Oxford: Blackwell, 1992), 94–111. Bürger too wonders whether the articulation of the postmodern is a symptom of shifts in academic priority rather than in literary production itself.

12   Thorstein Veblen, *The Theory of the Leisure Class: An Economic Study of Institutions* (New York: Macmillan, 1899), 380, 396, 366.

derstanding of our present situation, the one within which we have our arguments about the postmodern. In our predicament we strive simultaneously to serve two discursive masters, and they are themselves in conflict in the larger sphere inhabited by us all, and cyclically related as residual and emergent components of that sphere. This tension was very evident in Britain during the Thatcher administrations. Conservative intellectuals who thought that a radical Tory government would continue to patronize the intellectual subculture for its very traditions, its visible participation in the representation of the reactionary (its robes and furred gowns), found to their surprise that government scrutiny was not restricted to the leftists but applied to all intellectuals and was exercised according to explicit criteria of productivity. This itself was a symptom of the radical refiguring of the Tory party, whose own "organic" intellectuals, to use Gramsci's term, were committedly utilitarian, and corresponded neither to the familiar Right nor the familiar Left in the preexisting academic subculture of traditional intellectuals.

The situation in the United States, while less easy to typify through the exemplary political personality of a single figure like Margaret Thatcher, is not dissimilar. There is a larger acceptance of pure professionalization, divorced from content, as useful in itself; but there is also a growing cynicism, fuelled in part by the local tax revolts and by the perceived runaway costs of higher education, about the values and efficiency of the universities. At best we are respected for our disinterest and our efforts to teach the habit of critical thought, but we are also critiqued for that same disinterest. Both in Britain and in the United States, humanities intellectuals are particularly vulnerable, because of our association with those very qualities Veblen attributed to us, qualities of the occult and the liminal. This shared anxiety must be part of any comprehensive explanation of our current turn to cultural criticism, which paradoxically provides us with a rhetoric of referentiality, a posture of speaking about the world, even as we admit that the world is made up largely of representations. Cultural studies, as we now see it, is a form of survivalism, and those who deplore its incursion into the universities would do well to reflect upon the degree to which it ensures their own continued existence. [13]

13 For some pertinent remarks on the role of populism in the postmodern, see Bruce Robbins, *Secular Vocations: Intellectuals, Professionalism, Culture* (London and New York: Verso, 1993), especially 110, 122–23, 180, 203–8. There is of course an extensive de-

But that is not all it is. It does not seem quite convincing to suppose that we might as well teach entomology as postmodernity. This would be true if our task were merely and entirely that of accreditation, of selecting out a few sheep from a horde of goats. The subculture of professional humanists and social scientists, which requires debate and discrimination in order to fulfill some of its institutional functions, has never operated with a completely arbitrary content to those debates. The cultural capital we possess, or aspire to, depends upon an arguable reference to the social whole, so that even the self-reproduction of the guild requires an effort at what is now called outreach. Thus we are caught somewhere between vanguard and rear guard. In a world where people feel that Shakespeare is important to the traditional culture, it pays us to study Shakespeare. At the same time feminism, multiculturalism, and gay-lesbian studies, for instance, have emerged as topics of concern because they are academically inflected formulations of changes taking place in and around the academy. And global culture is a topic of concern because there is an apparent decrease in autonomy of nation states (though this is a process Marx noted as early as 1848 in *The Communist Manifesto*). [14] Debates about romanticism or virtue, which are intrinsically interesting to some of us (for what is virtue, and where does romanticism begin and end?), do not function as efficiently, because they are not intuitively or epistemologically related to larger questions being addressed in other subcultures, in what is called society at large.

John Guillory's strong application (in *Cultural Capital*) of some of Bourdieu's ideas to questions of literacy and canonicity in literary education thus needs to be qualified by a recognition that the *content* of that education is not, for humanists, completely arbitrary, as he sometimes seems to suggest that it is. As a corrective to the delusions of content-based pedagogical would-be revolutionaries, Guillory's work is ex-

---

bate about the social functions of intellectuals. An up-to-date sampling can be gained from *Intellectuals: Aesthetics, Politics, Academics*, ed. Bruce Robbins (Minneapolis: University of Minnesota Press, 1990). See especially the essays by Robbins, Aronowitz, Radakrishnan, and Ross.

14   Karl Marx, *The Communist Manifesto*, in Karl Marx and Frederick Engels, *Collected Works* (New York: International Publishers, 1976), 6:488: "In place of the old local and national seclusion and self-sufficiency, we have intercourse in every direction, universal inter-dependence of nations. And as in material, so also in intellectual production."

tremely timely, and those who think that all we have to do to produce a better world is to teach Toni Morrison should be told to read it. But the theorization of the social functions of intellectuals and professional academics calls for an expanded analysis. Alvin Gouldner's important book *The Future of Intellectuals and the Rise of the New Class* might serve as a place to start. Gouldner understands the "new class," which includes university teachers along with educated technicians and professionals, as significantly engaged in pursuing its collective self-interest. But because that process depends upon the use of a "culture of critical discourse" with theorizing and generalizing powers, and because the new class is itself historically positioned as struggling with alienation and "blocked ascendence" even as it expands, it lives the experience of contradiction and can therefore carry the energy of social transformation. [15] Gouldner does not just exonerate the intellectuals (and the new class in general) from the suspicion of complete moral and political turpitude; he sees them as "the most progressive force in modern society" and a "center of whatever human emancipation is possible in the foreseeable future" (83).

Gouldner wrote soon after 1968 and the antiwar movement; Guillory writes after Reaganism and after a period of incremental loss of faith in the academy and its values. Gouldner sees the intellectuals as (among) the best we've got, and points to their leadership of some important historical revolutions. Guillory's message is pitched as a corrective to the lazier spirits (left and right) who take their own significance for granted, as it also partakes of a generational cynicism or despair about an end of history with capitalism triumphant. In the (seemingly) more modest context of the postmodernism debate, an openness to various judgments works best. The interrogation of the postmodern does function efficiently within the academy as an urgent interdisciplinary inquiry, and this is because it *is* visibly related to more general social concerns about the economy, about demography, about the condition of the developed or the emergent nation-state, and so forth. (Jameson is therefore correct in taking seriously some of postmodernism's claims to originality.) To some degree, this can certainly be reduced to a legitimation process: because it is out there, we had better talk about it and pass an opinion, lest we be regarded as mere

15 Alvin W. Gouldner, *The Future of Intellectuals and the Rise of the New Class* (Oxford and Toronto: Oxford University Press, 1982), 28–29, 62, and throughout.

scholars of dead poets and expired cultures. But it is also a consequence of one of the best and most persistently declared ambitions of the academy, and one that is fundamental to its "culture of critical discourse": the effort to reach an audience beyond the ivory tower, somewhere in the nebulous public sphere (whose existence or disappearance is also compulsively debated); the effort, as we used to say, to make a difference, and to exercise a critical function. [16]

The dialectic between internal reproduction of colleagues and students and public "outreach" can be seen in the phenomenon of the academic "star system." Every so often we produce, or allow to be produced, a small number of persons who make the transition from internal to external recognition. They are never entirely approved of by their less visible colleagues, but they are also celebrated and defended by those same colleagues, because they do provide a distinct professional legitimation, and they are felt to address issues other people find important. Any profession employing an estimated 800,000 people in the United States alone, as does higher education, is going to require some kind of positive visibility. Lawyers, doctors, and engineers seem to us to acquire this by virtue of the content of their jobs, though this has not protected the first two from the attentions of a highly suspicious public with whom they are engaged in intense struggles for respect and self-respect. The scientists reasonably feel that they are the heirs of Newton and Darwin (if also of Nobel and Teller), and their survival and expansion has at least until recently been relatively well assured by the perceived priorities of the state apparatus. Humanists and social scientists similarly aspire to become worthy upholders of the traditions of Hegel and Marx, Newman and Arnold. At the same time, we accept as inevitable the radical changes in the condition of the intellectual in relation to the public sphere. The debate about the postmodern is one of the ways in which we are rehearsing the questions raised by this recognition. It is a symptom of our "new class" agenda of self-reproduction and expansion, at a time when the historical expectation of that expansion (ongoing through at least the last half century) is no longer confident. The world we speak about, in the vocabulary of the postmodern, is the world that may be leaving us behind. The urgency is thus doubled. We want to interpret the world, in

16   Robbins, *Secular Vocations*, 90–95, makes the case that professionalism traditionally requires ethical self-consciousness and public approbation as part of its very existence.

terms of our traditional commitment to enlightenment, and we more than ever need to interpret it if we are to maximize our own chances of survival. What we may be seeing, in other words, is a disaggregation within Gouldner's "new class," whereby the interests of one sector (for example, humanist intellectuals) are no longer simply congruent with those of other sectors (scientists, computer experts, and so forth). The appeal of some sort of unified field theory (the postmodern) for the humanities and social sciences may then be understood as at least in part (though only in part) the result of a perceived need among humanists for a more powerful lobbying position aimed at the preservation of our collective piece of the cultural-economic pie.

Readers who have come this far will already have noticed my saying two seemingly different things. On the one hand, I have said that the existence of an academic postmodern seems to me clearer than that of the general postmodernity that it often purports to describe. On the other hand, I have argued for a wider and larger state of affairs beyond the academy, to which the academy definitely responds and which it may even affect. Analysis is best served, it seems to me, by trying to have this both ways: we are indeed responding to a world, but there is no guarantee that our habits and inherited models give us a clear image of it. This is why, quite apart from the in-house pleasure of a little joke at Lyotard's expense, I have subtitled this project "a report on half-knowledge." The key concept is, again, *mediation*. We are now quite used to hearing this term and its attendant methodologies decried as some sort of hangover from a mechanical-Marxist past. It does after all seem to presuppose a dialectic between two established entities, whole and part, entities whose existence is now commonly called into question within the very rubric of the postmodern itself. For this reason the accounting for and investigation of the processes of mediation must somehow, now, be carried on without any prior certainty about what the whole might be that is mediated into the part, and what the part "is" that is available for totalization. To admit that this poses enormous difficulties need not lead us to declare it improper. There is a long tradition, exemplified in the work of Hegel but not unique to it, and indeed apparent even in the perceptions of those who might otherwise accord no respect at all to the Hegelian project, which identifies the analysis of a work of art with that of its total historical moment. This confidence is no longer felt to be deserved, even as we cannot afford to give up on the notion of some at least local historical significance to the expressive forms to which we choose to attend. (This is, after all, the common ground of cultural studies and traditional literary history.) The same tentative methodology applies to the analysis of the academy. It does not image the greater world, in any merely reflective way, but neither is it completely independent of that world. So we may at least start with this assertion: that the existence of an academic subculture within which the debate about the general postmodern takes place *requires*, if it is to claim any intellectual honesty, a recognition of the traditions governing even the spontaneities uttered within the academy about the world in which it functions. Bourdieu's notion of "field" is very helpful here. The field is distinguished from the Althusserian "apparatus" by its refusal of "pessimistic functionalism" and its projection of a scene within which "agents and institutions constantly struggle" in a "structured space of social forces and struggles."[17] Serious things happen when fields and component subfields come into coherent conjunction: Bourdieu uses this model to account for the events of May 1968.[18] But the determinants of field formation and reformation must also include extrinsic energies ignored by Bourdieu; international Maoism and the Vietnam War come to mind for 1968, which cannot be read as just the result of demographic adjustments in the education system. If it is not convincing, after Bourdieu and others, to speak from the academy as if there were no glass in the windows through which we peer at the world, then it is equally unconvincing, despite Bourdieu and others, to imagine that all our windows are paned with a reflecting surface on which we see only the image of ourselves.

This may be the point to say something about the limitations of what is called discourse theory, the model that seems now to do the work that mediation once did. Discourse has largely taken over from structures and homologies as the latest preferred alternative to the loudly disavowed base-superstructure model of early cultural Marxism (though why this model had to be represented in its most reductive and absurd forms even by those sympathetic to Marxist methods has

17   Pierre Bourdieu and Loïc J. D. Wacquant, *An Invitation to Reflexive Sociology* (Chicago and London: University of Chicago Press, 1992), 102, 243.

18   Pierre Bourdieu, *Homo Academicus*, trans. Peter Collier (Stanford: Stanford University Press, 1988), e.g. 128–29, 163, 173.

never been clear to me).[19] Its function has often been to flatten the analysis into near-complete synchronicity. If everything that makes us what we are is in "the discourse," then there is no need to set it against other discourses, or against any kind of protoempirical history (in the economy, in demography, in material life). Recourse to discourse at the expense of mediation as the means of cultural analysis has mostly worked to limit the number of terms and possibilities one works with, and thus as a strong inhibition on totalization. That this is not the single application opened up in the work of Foucault himself, the major merchandizer of discourse, is another story.[20] But there is little doubt that the popularity of discourse, or at least the mind-set that its popularity represents, has made it easier for us to talk of single subcultural units such as the corporation or the school or the university as effectively imbued with the determining powers of a social whole. (Perhaps this is one more fantasy of self-importance.) In this way, for instance, what we "reproduce" is entirely and only the academy, which is either completely at one with or completely different from the rest of the social-historical configuration we inhabit. My own account will inevitably seem to fall into this trap, if only because I am looking more or less exclusively at the academic postmodern and am not much interested in (or capable of) proposing definitive relations between the academic postmodern and a more general condition, postmodern or otherwise. At the same time I obviously hope that what I have to say here will be useful to anyone setting out on that larger analysis.

I have assumed so far that there is a good chance of being able to say something plausible about the academic postmodern from within the academy, because that is the subculture I inhabit and know something about. Bourdieu makes just this case for the scientific power of sociology, even as he more than anyone has alerted us to the power of self-deception within the guild.[21] Thus the exact opposite could be

19   On the base-superstructure model, see Terry Eagleton, "Base and Superstructure in Raymond Williams," in *Raymond Williams: Critical Perspectives*, ed. Terry Eagleton (Boston: Northeastern University Press, 1989), 165–75.

20   See my remarks on discourse in "The Moment of Materialism," in *Subject to History: Ideology, Class, Gender*, ed. David Simpson (Ithaca and London: Cornell University Press, 1991), 4–5.

21   Bourdieu and Wacquant, *Invitation to Reflexive Sociology*, 187–88.

supposed. It could be argued that the more *interested* we are, the more wholly we inhabit a subculture, the less we can know about it, owing to our inevitable subservience to the pressures of its operative ideologies. By this logic we academics might conclude that we have a better chance of understanding global-economic categories than our own local institutional formations. But of course they are not distinct, and any distinctions we might make are matters of immediacy and emphasis. The inevitability of working with models of mediation and totalization renders this too a falsely absolute dichotomy.

And this is why I have opted not to write explicitly about "myself" in the pages that follow. This decision might seem perverse, especially at those points where I claim the privilege of criticizing others who do write about themselves, and who thereby claim some kind of epistemological integrity in so doing. One could as well write about the postmodern academic—who suffers from the very thing she or he analyzes while replacing one obsolescent computer after another—as about the academic postmodern. I do not mean to plead the familiar "death of the subject" in order to license my silences about my personal investments and perspectives. It seems to me that the subject never really died, but was merely put on hold for a while as an attempted corrective to an entrenched tradition of liberal expressivity. That tradition is back with a vengeance, I will later argue, so that it sometimes seems that the attack on "theory" is but a code for the reinstatement of the organic individual and of the identity politics that comes with that restatement. The project of objectifying subjectivity—or, better put, of setting forth on its totalization—seems to me to be of the utmost urgency in the light of this reactionary trend. And such a project must be implicated with (though it need not "depend" upon) the historical-biological idiosyncrasy of the self that is doing it—in this case, me. I cannot simply and smugly dismiss those (and they are many) who are busily writing about themselves in variously authorized "transgressive" modes, since (as I will argue in chapter 3) they are the bearers as well as the fools of our common history. But I am not going to tell you my life story in this book, and if I am everywhere in what follows, as I must be in serious as well as trivial senses, then it will be in disguise. And if thus I signal my interim allegiance to some notoriously Enlightenment-sounding declarations of faith—*larvatus prodeo*, and *de nobis ipsis silemus*—then it is with the aspiration not to replicate those moments (this could only be nostalgia) but rather to invoke the limitations of a propaedeu-

tic method, and to prepare the way for all of us to set about our engage-
ments with what may be (precisely for historical reasons) the most
confusing question of all, the one through which all others seem to
flow, and which has been ignored by the Marxist tradition very much
at the expense of its credibility within the liberal cultures of the developed world (if not so seriously elsewhere): the question, precisely, of
how each of us speaks or ignores the element of "myself."

I will also be avoiding any precise adjudication of the chronology
of the postmodern, though my focus on the residual or traditional components of what is *called* the postmodern will involve long-durational
models almost by definition. Any casual inspection of the literature on
this subject will make clear that there is no substantial consensus about
where the postmodern begins. Much depends upon whether one thinks
one is defining a postmoder*nism*, a break from the aesthetic formations
of the early twentieth century, or a postmoder*nity*, a break from the
entire culture of modernity and modernization in place since at least
the Enlightenment and perhaps before. The first definition is usually
discussed in terms of works of art and items of culture; the second in
reference to global-economic categories of the most momentous kind.
One also notices the predictable academic habit of using items from
the first context as evidence for changes in the second. So that perhaps
the most familiar version of the distinction is the implicit reluctance to
make it a distinction at all. In this way a painting or a building comes to
"represent" some seismic shift in the spirit of the age, with no very precise accounting for all the things that might mediate between a thing
and the world in which and for which it is made.

Versions of these distinctions, half distinctions, and identifications
—themselves the symptoms of our half-knowledge—can be tracked
across much of the literature discussing the chronology of the postmodern. Vattimo concurs with the idea of the passage from *Ulysses* to
Finnegans Wake as a "key event" in the evolution of the postmodern, a
status he also accords to a similar and earlier "break" in the work of
Nietzsche. [22] Baudrillard specifies the critical moment as the passage
into monopoly capitalism, sees a critical juncture in the crisis of 1929,
and associates the emergence of the political economy of the sign with
the Bauhaus. [23] Lyotard speaks of significant changes occurring "since

22   Vattimo, *End of Modernity*, 106, 164–65.
23   Jean Baudrillard, *The Mirror of Production*, trans. Mark Poster (St. Louis: Telos Press,

the end of the nineteenth century" that have been figured into the
postmodern "since at least the end of the 1950s."[24] Edward Soja looks
to the late 1960s in general and then specifically to the global recession
of 1973–75 as the moment of the emergence of the fourth modernization of capitalism and thus of postmodern spatiality.[25] This is also the
emphasis of David Harvey's *Condition of Postmodernity* and of Jameson's
Postmodernism, though here the moment of 1973 is embedded in a complex, dialectical, and unevenly developing model of the "American
century" of 1945–73 (of which the postmodern is the expression), and
referred not to a fourth but to Mandel's "third stage" of capitalist evolution.[26] Andreas Huyssen offers further refinements in approving a general postmodernity after World War II, while specifying a shift between
the 1960s and the 1970s, a shift further particularized in different national cultures.[27] Huyssen also quotes Charles Jencks's refreshingly
precise identification of the end of modern (and the beginning of postmodern) architecture at 3:32 P.M. on 15 July 1972 in St. Louis (186).
Most have required more gradual explanations, even as they emphasize certain exemplary moments, and Jameson in particular has a very
complex account of the persistence of the modern in the postmodern,
and of the anticipatory postmodernisms within the modern.[28] Others
have joined the hunt for the first use of the term *postmodern*, in hopes of
settling the issue on the terrain of historical etymology.

1975), 124, 127, 144; Baudrillard, *For a Critique of the Political Economy of the Sign*, trans.
Charles Levin (St. Louis: Telos Press, 1981), 144.

24   Jean-François Lyotard, *The Postmodern Condition: A Report on Knowledge*, trans. Geoff
Bennington and Brian Massumi (Minneapolis: University of Minnesota Press, 1984),
xxiii, 3.

25   Edward W. Soja, *Postmodern Geographies: The Reassertion of Space in Critical Social Theory*
(London and New York: Verso, 1989), 15, 39, 182.

26   David Harvey, *The Condition of Postmodernity: An Enquiry into the Origins of Cultural
Change* (Cambridge, MA, and Oxford: Blackwell, 1990), 141–72; Jameson, *Postmodernism*, xx.

27   Andreas Huyssen, *After the Great Divide: Modernism, Mass Culture, Postmodernism* (Bloomington and Indianapolis: University of Indiana Press, 1986), e.g. 188, 191, 195–96.

28   For good summaries of the varieties of postmodern chronologies, see Steven Best
and Douglas Kellner, *Postmodern Theory: Critical Interrogations* (New York: Guilford Press,
1991), 5–16, 277–80, and throughout; and Zygmunt Bauman, *Legislators and Interpreters:
On Modernity, Post-Modernity, and Intellectuals* (Ithaca: Cornell University Press, 1987),
117ff.

The establishment of chronologies is of course not infrequently a tactic for the publication of values. Stephen Toulmin's *Cosmopolis* proposes a history whereby the rationalist project of Descartes displaced the humanist particularism of Montaigne, forcing European culture away from the "particular, concrete, transitory and practical aspects of human experience" whose proper recovery is the task of an authentic postmodernity.[29] One could dispute this history of Western culture both for its illusory coherence (for the rationalist paradigm was never hegemonic) and for its reductive modeling of the turn to theory as the result of traumatic national and international conflict (the Thirty Years' War and World War I). And this is history backwards, of course, history written to justify the author's perception of the needs of the present, which he sees as requiring the recovery of a carnivalesque pre-Cartesian past: tolerance and skepticism, a "practical concern for human life in its concrete detail" (x, xi, 168). Toulmin sees us as adrift in a sea of doubt and indecision, "stranded and uncertain of our location." His solution is to "try to recapture the practical modesty of the humanists, which let them live free of anxiety, despite uncertainty, ambiguity, and pluralism" (3, 105).

Toulmin's preferred categories are visibly coincident with those of the literary tradition, and thus his historical narrative is an exemplary instance of what I am calling the rule of literature in the academic postmodern, as well as of the half-knowledge it produces. Whenever one locates the exemplary emergence of the postmodern in history or in the world, it is important to remember to look first for motivations in the academy, the location from within which that world is described. Toulmin pronounces philosophy, for instance, as at a "dead end" and therefore ready again to take up "the practical issues sidelined by Descartes' *coup d'état* some 300 years ago" (168). But we cannot really be dealing here with a simple return to a fork in the road and a road not taken; such a notion affords the intellectual an unbelievable capacity for clear vision, and supposes a direct intuition and transmission of the energies of history. I am suggesting, again, that there is an academic postmodern, which mediates even though it does not completely falsify what academics come up with when they attempt to describe the world. The compounding of knowledge and half-knowledge that in-

---

29   Stephen Toulmin, *Cosmopolis: The Hidden Agenda of Modernity* (Chicago: University of Chicago Press, 1992), 76.

forms our position needs to be addressed even if it cannot be definitively resolved.

The academic postmodern of which I am writing here is, I should
admit, not the *only* academic postmodern. The range of different chronologies I have been describing should itself suggest that we are still in
the business of choosing between varieties of postmodernisms and
postmodernities. They are all made from within the academy, but they
are not all the same. I have chosen to focus on the conservative, "establishment" incarnations, those that have achieved a certain prestige and
reproductive power in the academy: the writings of Geertz and Rorty,
the new historicism, and so on. In particular, I am interested in the rule
of literature, the efficient transfer of literary and literary-critical mo-
dalities into other disciplines, which then seem radically new. To say
even this much seems to go against John Guillory's strong argument
that the category of literature has become "institutionally dysfunc-
tional," lingering only as the embattled cultural capital of the old bourgeoisie within an educational system that threatens to supersede it
completely.[30] The turn to narrative that characterizes the academic
postmodern might then seem less a return to literature than an effort to
reach out and imitate or absorb the formal features of mass culture:
popular rather than literary stories. Certainly, the cultural studies version of the academic postmodern seems on the surface to have little to
do with the high cultural claims of what we otherwise think of as "literature." But the relation between that literature and the mass culture
from which it sought to distinguish itself has always been thoroughly
dialectical. Despite the rigors of (for instance) modernism and theory,
literature has never quite managed to set itself off from the demotic
narratives that provide its not-so-binary antagonists. Good novels and
romances are measured against bad novels and romances; good poetry
against doggerel; redeeming irony against reductive belief.[31] It is not
so surprising, then, that when the academy, the repository of high literary culture, seeks to take in the popular mode, there should be some
anticipatory familiarity to its models. So, if there is yet some tension
between the proponents of literary narrative and the apostles of popu-

---

30   Guillory, *Cultural Capital*, x.

31   Thus Fredric Jameson, for example, has argued for the popular romance as the historical context for Conrad's *Lord Jim*; see *The Political Unconscious: Narrative as a Socially
Symbolic Act* (Ithaca: Cornell University Press, 1981), 206–80.

lar culture, there is also a deep common tradition uniting them. Furthermore, one could extend and apply Guillory's case to account for exactly the dissemination (and not the disappearance) of "literature" by supposing that the proliferation of literary models in other disciplines speaks for the range and energy of the rearguard action carried out by those he calls the "old bourgeoisie." And if one goes this far—as I would—then we might wonder if the old bourgeoisie is indeed as disabled as Guillory supposes. Has it perhaps found a new lease on life in the apparently renovated but deeply conventional languages of the academic postmodern?

To suppose so is to take seriously, as I do, Richard Rorty's claim that the "literary culture" has been "putting the other disciplines in their places," even as it is to question Rorty's further claim (akin to Toulmin's) that this event is as radical a shift as that evinced in the supersession of religion by science in an earlier age.[32] This putting in place has had the effect of refiguring the boundaries between the (humanities) disciplines, mostly by abolishing them. Sometimes it can seem as if "literature" itself has also changed, becoming less hostile to technological and theoretical languages than previously. The academy is thus at once more unified internally, and more able to present a coherent account of itself in the face of some of the challenges that Guillory and others describe; and also more potentially limited by that very coherence in its abilities to describe and analyze a world outside the academy and playing, somehow, upon it.

Again, in writing exclusively about this version of an academic postmodern, I am definitely indulging in some degree of reification. First, it is not at all clear that the importation or migration of literature and literary criticism into other disciplines is the only such migration. Literary study itself has become more interdisciplinary than ever (for instance, in the form of "cultural studies"), and has borrowed new forms of description from sociology, anthropology, political science, and psychoanalysis, among others. But, notwithstanding the apparent intellectual climate of eclectic entrepreneurial authorization, I would still argue for a pattern in what we might call the new general method in the humanities and social sciences: a pattern whose major features are traditionally literary. Thus what literary critics import back from

32 Richard Rorty, *Consequences of Pragmatism: Essays, 1972–1980* (Minneapolis: University of Minnesota Press, 1982), 155.

such writers as Geertz and Rorty is often what they themselves previously exported, reappearing with acquired surplus value. Reciprocally, the nonliterary disciplines are gradually being colonized by their own radicals' recirculation of literary methods.

Second, I am undoubtedly guilty of ignoring the contestations mounted by others for possession of the vocabulary of an alternative (authentic?) postmodern, with more radical exponents and more radical effects than the conservative version I am calling the academic postmodern. If I do not talk about these initiatives, for instance in ecofeminism, technoculture, queer theory, or cultural studies generally, it is not with the aim of making them even more marginal than they already are, or of implying that they are necessarily one with the varieties of the postmodern I do talk about. The academy also has its local conflicts between its "traditional" and its emergent-organic intellectuals, who fight fiercely with each other over content, and thus over one kind of content-based attitude to the world, even as they continue to share the same workplace, which they occupy in contrast to the rest of the world. The currently emergent postmodernisms and postmodernities are very much in formation, and I do not personally have enough knowledge or perspective even to describe them thoroughly. If my comments have anything to contribute to these formations, then it will probably be as cautionary remarks asking for some articulation of their relation to the traditions I am describing: a relation that, I would expect, ought to be one of difference, if incomplete difference. A little history may help here, offered in the face of Nietzsche's very postmodern declaration that "an excess of history is harmful to the living man."[33] I do not, in other words, intend this argument for the unperceived dominance of the residual to preclude the plausibility of something else emerging. On the contrary, I would hope, if anything, to assist in that emergence by exorcising some familiar if artfully packaged compound ghosts. I think that these ghosts have tremendous appeal, not least at a time when we may be facing a downturn in the academic economy and a disaggregation of Gouldner's "new class" into mutually competitive sectors. (This is one of the important symptoms I take Guillory's *Cultural Capital* to be illuminating.) The turn to the personal (autobiography, confessional pedagogy, anecdote, conversa-

---

33   Friedrich Nietzsche, *Untimely Meditations*, trans. R. J. Hollingdale (Cambridge: Cambridge University Press, 1983), 67.

tion) and to the aesthetic (surfaces and simulacra, style and position) carries an immense appeal in the face of these pressures. I must admit that I myself respond to these symptoms of the academic postmodern when they come in the brilliant incarnation of, for instance, Byatt's *Possession*, discussed at the end of this book. The regressive temporalities of the postmodern, so visible in the exemplary forms of architecture (fragments shored against our ruin?), add extra energy to literature's traditionally conserving and vocalizing functions. The desire to speak with the dead, which I see as one of the leading preoccupations of the academic postmodern, can be either celebrated as an enduring human need or dismissed as an immense nostalgia for a world we have lost. Perhaps a profound sense of the history that works in and through us will decide that there can be no clear difference. It is, at least, no surprise to find that literature and its criticism, in their traditional modern forms, are ready and waiting for us as we invent the (academic) postmodern.

One

THE RETURN OF THE STORYTELLER AND THE CIRCULATION OF "LITERATURE"

I begin with Walter Benjamin, who opened his great essay "The Storyteller" by evoking the mood of nostalgia.

> [T]he art of storytelling is coming to an end. Less and less frequently do we encounter people with the ability to tell a tale properly. More and more often there is embarrassment all around when the wish to hear a story is expressed. It is as if something that seemed inalienable to us, the securest among our possessions, were taken from us: the ability to exchange experiences. [1]

Suppose we could rewrite history. Suppose Benjamin had been smuggled across the border into Spain in 1940, and had found his way to America. One hopes that he would have survived the McCarthy purges and that a well-deserved distinguished chair (probably in California) would have come his way. And if it had done, then we might just have seen him, born in 1892, as a presiding sage at some of the early conferences on the postmodern. Imagine the curious colleague standing up in the question period: "Professor Benjamin! You wrote many years ago that the age of storytelling was coming to an end. What has happened?"

How we must wish to have heard his answer. What indeed has happened? Benjamin was writing about the end of an oral tradition whose fullness we have certainly not recovered. Nonetheless, it now seems that everyone is telling stories, and professing the ability to exchange experiences. Perhaps the aged distinguished professor would have opined that we are here engaged in an enormous gesture of com-

1 Walter Benjamin, "The Storyteller: Reflections on the Works of Nikolai Leskov," in *Illuminations*, ed. Hannah Arendt, trans. Harry Zohn (New York: Schocken, 1969), 83.

munal nostalgia, seeking to live again in false consciousness what we have lost as historically authentic. (Had he said so, he would have been offering another definition of the postmodern.) Is this why people stand up at one conference after another and tell stories, often about themselves? Books and articles made up of stories pour off the presses, in literary criticism, ethnography, sociology, cultural studies, and philosophy. Literature, whose essence is storytelling, seems to rule the day. It is hard to say exactly when this began, but storytelling now looks like an orthodoxy even as its narrators may continue to claim to be engaged in a radical initiative. In his important *Metahistory* of 1973, a study roughly coincident with the incursion of French post-structuralist theories into the anglophone academy, Hayden White argued that the style of the historiographer could be "characterized in terms of the linguistic protocol he used to prefigure the historical field prior to bringing to bear upon it the various 'explanatory' strategies he used to fashion a 'story' out of the 'chronicle' of events contained in the historical record."[2] The destabilizing of such terms as *chronicle, story,* and *explanation,* and their proposed commonality as prefigured, tells us that we are in the realm of the literary. And since 1973, at least, the literariness of making history has become a commonplace, even if it is still contested by cliometricians and other social- science-based historians inside the discipline. Natalie Zemon Davis dedicates her *Fiction in the Archives* to Lawrence Stone, historian but "storyteller too," and looks at the historical record as evidence of "the crafting of a narrative," all the more carefully crafted for the fact that the teller might well have been "saving his neck by a story."[3]

The historian's interest in the techniques of storytelling may well derive from the permission granted by the literary mode to fudge or to make a virtue of the confusion between what is real and what is imagined. On the one hand, the rhetoric of fiction is a way of bringing to life the otherwise potentially tedious details of past lives. On the other

---

2   Hayden White, *Metahistory: The Historical Imagination in Nineteenth-Century Europe* (Baltimore and London: Johns Hopkins University Press, 1975), 426.

3   Natalie Zemon Davis, *Fiction in the Archives: Pardon Tales and Their Tellers in Sixteenth-Century France* (Stanford: Stanford University Press, 1987), 3, 15. Linda Colley has astutely described Stone's ability to transmit (or create) "the magically preserved voices of long-dead individuals caught fast in moments of extreme stress" in "Vengeful Susan," *London Review of Books,* 22 September 1994, 17.

hand, it thereby discourages any effort at the analytical distance
whose achievement (however illusory) remains the goal of traditional
history. Laurel Thatcher Ulrich's prize-winning book *The Midwife's Tale*,
a historical study of the life of an eighteenth-century midwife, is full of
the paraphernalia of presence. It uses the format of the diary entry, and
consistently proposes a vocalic intimacy with its subject in such
phrases as "as Martha would be quick to add" and "she was probably
unaccustomed to saying."[4] Here the reader is critically unsure how to
judge or interpret the legitimacy of this speaking for and with the
dead. And, if this is the predicament of all historical writing, then
what typifies Ulrich's kind of historical storytelling is its willingness to
inhibit the emergence of this truism to the point of anxious self-
consciousness, and to provide instead the pure pleasure of familiarity.
Simon Schama's virtuoso "historical novellas" are much more explicit
about the nature of historical storytelling and the identity of all inquiry with "the telling of stories."[5] They are the historian's analogue of
A. S. Byatt's dazzling novel *Possession*, which I will discuss in my last
chapter. Schama takes for granted the historian's "unavoidable remote-
ness" from the past, and the "teasing gap separating a lived event and
its subsequent narration" (320), and uses it to create a mesmerizing series of multiple presences whose different reality effects are largely
functions of rhetoric. The mode is confidently rather than covertly literary, and encourages what Coleridge famously characterized as the
willing suspension of disbelief that constitutes poetic faith.[6]

The same interest in narration, or storytelling, as the brave new
paradigm for defining one's discipline can be found among philosophers—for instance, as we shall see, in the work of Richard Rorty—
and ethnographers (or, as they used to be called, anthropologists).
James Clifford neatly sums up the passage of "writing" from the margins
to the center of his trade in explaining that "literary processes—
metaphor, figuration, narrative—affect the ways cultural phenomena
are registered, from the first jotted 'observations,' to the completed
book, to the ways these configurations 'make sense' in determined acts

4   Laurel Thatcher Ulrich, *A Midwife's Tale* (New York: Vintage, 1990), 170, 172.

5   Simon Schama, *Dead Certainties (Unwarranted Speculations)* (New York: Knopf, 1991),
322, 325.

6   Samuel Taylor Coleridge, *Biographia Literaria*, ed. James Engell and W. J. Bate
(Princeton: Princeton University Press; London: Routledge & Kegan Paul, 1983), 2:6.

of reading."[7] These are instances—and there are many others—of what Christopher Norris has called the "narrative turn" in contemporary academic writing, and what I am describing as an epidemic of storytelling.[8] In literary criticism itself, from whence so much of this inclination to storytelling comes in the first place, there is an understandable urge to go one better. Thus we are here in an era of autobiography, of the most personal storytelling, telling about oneself. Literary critics (as I will discuss in chapter 3) are busier writing about themselves than they have ever been before, to the point that the award of tenure now seems to bring with it a contract for one's autobiography. Sometimes the author tells his or her story in desired conjunction with some unarguably major topic or series of events; sometimes it is enough that it be about him- or herself. The anecdotal mode of writing history or criticism (which is the subject of the next chapter) is often a constituent of the autobiographical moment: we pick an event in the past whose very quirkiness and apparent isolation dramatizes its status as something *told*, something *we* are telling and have discovered, something whose significance is unfolded as a story, in the realm of the voice, even as its residue is written, as a text. If the storytelling mode is still rare in the natural sciences, and perhaps still radical in the social sciences, where the objectivist models drawn from the natural sciences continue to have a strong hold on the disciplines, it has become commonplace in the humanities, to the extent that it should soon become impossible for anyone there to continue to claim a radical effect in telling us, again and again, about themselves and where they are coming from, either as an end in itself or as a prelude to the story of the day. It is time to think about this seemingly compulsive telling of tales, which is producing less and less of the embarrassment that Benjamin noticed, and more and more of a sense of déjà vu. What does the fashion for storytelling tell us about ourselves, and about the academic postmodern that we inhabit?

Let us return to Benjamin, who located the high point of storytelling in the "trade structure" of the middle ages (85), a culture of undivided labor that allowed for the continuation of a tradition of fab-

---

7 James Clifford and George E. Marcus, eds., *Writing Culture: The Poetics and Politics of Ethnography* (Berkeley and Los Angeles: University of California Press, 1986), 6.

8 Christopher Norris, *The Contest of Faculties: Philosophy and Theory after Deconstruction* (London and New York: Methuen, 1985), 19–46.

ulation "woven thousands of years ago in the oldest forms of craftsman-
ship" (91). People told stories as they worked, and about their work,
masters and men (and women and men?) together. Modernity put an
end to that, with its divisions of labor and disciplinary organizations of
time, creating the "solitary individual" whose art form is the novel: it
displaced narrative from a "living speech" and ensured that only the
mere facsimile of that speech could now be represented. Such representation can only ever be nostalgic, and it henceforth appears in fiction and as fiction (87).

Benjamin's account asks some fairly demanding questions about
the recrudescence of storytelling within the postmodern. To tell a
story today, if we follow his diagnosis, would either be to offer a heroic
resistance to modernity, and to make a pitch for a new version of the
old authenticity, or it would be to replicate an ideological nostalgia
within modernity, and to attempt the very thing we cannot genuinely
perform. Can we talk about ourselves, in the mode of explicit autobiography that has for some time been the coming thing in the humanities sector of the universities, without giving way to this false
consciousness? Can we tell stories about the past or about the "other,"
in the mode of history making that implicitly or contingently admits
the autobiographical moment as somehow constitutive of inquiry itself, without a similar lapse? Postmodern theory asks this question of
itself when it foregrounds the incidence of the spectacle and the simulacrum. But any tendency of that theory to produce a confident critique of the specular (as specter) is undermined by the familiar and
profound antifoundationalism that prohibits the imagining of a place
to stand, from which such critique might be mounted. The sheer emotional and rhetorical difficulty of remaining in a state of constant
suspension—and this *is* the discipline that much of the strictest contemporary theory seems to demand—seems to have made a place for a
headlong retreat from theory and from the dissatisfactions it seeks to
prescribe. So storytelling is presented not so much under the guise
of stoical obligation—I can no other—as within a torrent of self-
enthusiasm and self-projection. It is all the harder to refuse permission
for this in the light of the doubts sown by even the most elementary
psychoanalysis, which we all now acquire with our mother's milk,
about preserving any defensible distinction between the two. Which
in turn renders all the more lonely the now so very evident loneliness
of Louis Althusser, whose autobiographical memoir depends upon the

structure of the family story even as it declares that "'not to indulge in storytelling' still remains for me the one and only definition of materialism."[9]

Is postmodern storytelling, then, a symptom of ideology, of false consciousness? What would it mean to make that claim, for a generation radically skeptical about being able to step outside (what used to be called) ideology and false consciousness? Adorno's *Minima Moralia* (which embodies in its own fragmentary form precisely the syndrome, signaled in the subtitle *Reflections from Damaged Life*, whose constraints a utopian method would most wish to supplant), tells us that what we see in seeing ourselves cannot be taken at face value:

> He who wishes to know the truth about life in its immediacy must scrutinize its estranged form, the objective powers that determine individual existence even in its most hidden recesses. To speak immediately of the immediate is to behave much as those novelists who drape their marionettes in imitated bygone passions like cheap jewellery, and make people who are no more than component parts of machinery act as if they still had the capacity to act as subjects, and as if something depended on their actions. Our perspective of life has passed into an ideology which conceals the fact that there is life no longer.[10]

One can see why the harsh convictions of the war-torn Frankfurt School have gone somewhat out of style, obscured by the glow of the postmodern. Adorno here supposes and critiques a relation between the belief in a self and a faith in the "capacity to act," in positive agency. And this agency is very much what is claimed or hoped for, both by the affirmative postmodernists who employ identity as the basis for recognition (for example, in minority rights movements) and by the more academicized, skeptical postmoderns who forswear identity as a bourgeois fiction but still retain a commitment to positive social change as the proper emanation of contestatory discourses within the self and between the self and others. Adorno suggests that the subject becomes *more* visible in the cultural scene, as ideology, exactly as its

9 Louis Althusser, *The Future Lasts Forever: A Memoir*, trans. Richard Veasey (New York: New Press, 1993), 221.

10 Theodor W. Adorno, *Minima Moralia: Reflections from Damaged Life*, trans. E. F. N. Jephcott (1974; reprint, London: Verso, 1985), 15.

historical authenticity declines: "Compared to the patriarchal meagreness that characterizes his treatment in Hegel, the individual has gained as much in richness, differentiation and vigour as, on the other hand, the socialization of society has enfeebled and undermined him" (17). If storytelling has something to do with the return of the subject, and of the subject as organically individual, then we may well be in the business of nostalgia rather than that of radical critique.

Adorno's passage brings us to Marx, and to that text of Marx that the postmodern has acutely selected as an important site for its own self-knowing: *The Eighteenth Brumaire of Louis Bonaparte*. For was not Louis Bonaparte, according to Marx, exactly one of those novelists draping marionettes in "imitated bygone passions" and convincing them that they still had a "capacity to act as subjects"? The second Bonaparte, for Marx, was a "conjurer . . . springing constant surprises."[11] Or, we might interpolate, a good storyteller, albeit one whose narrative is jerky and inelegant enough to signify its essence as pastiche (farce). Louis Bonaparte's recourse is to low literature, but to literature nonetheless. He too, in his "world historical necromancy" (104), wants to speak with the dead, or bring the dead to life, his "borrowed language" an atrophied variant of empathy inviting the willing suspension of disbelief. Marx proposes that any authentic nineteenth-century revolution must "let the dead bury their dead" (106). The prescription seems even more utopian now than it might have in 1852, burdened as we are with an extreme consciousness of the situatedness of everything and everyone, and of the power of what is there before us. At the same time, the rhetoric of the postmodern, like that of all promotional movements, is one of radical innovation, which at times seems to suggest that the dead really have been left behind. The academic postmodern is, as will become clearer throughout my narrative, especially adept at having it both ways.

For, of course, it is often by way of a confession or advertised acceptance of one's limits that the storytelling genre is elected, only then to permit passage to unskeptical narrativization. Precisely because I can no longer confidently offer the grand theory, the master narrative, the outline of the social-historical totality, I resort to telling about myself as an individual, or as a representative of a small subculture, or as

11   Karl Marx, *The Eighteenth Brumaire of Louis Bonaparte*, in Karl Marx and Frederick Engels, *Collected Works* (Moscow: Progress Publishers, 1979), 11: 197.

the maker of the history I transcribe. But having admitted this much by way of cautionary prologue, I am unstoppable! In 1984, writing for an audience then somewhat more under the spell of Derridean and Althusserian stringencies than that of today, Fredric Jameson introduced the English translation of Lyotard's *Postmodern Condition* by suggesting that our collective discrediting of "narrative or storytelling knowledge" was not as complete as it had often, for polemical purposes, been said to be.[12] It has proved quite useful for certain takers of positions of all kinds to represent the Enlightenment and its legacy as an efficient compound of abstract logic and scientific method, an iron cage that we need desperately to escape. Jameson saw, under the incumbent rubric of the postmodern, a visible efflorescence of "small narrative units" taking the place of the discredited master narratives, which then made a "passage underground" (xi–xii). They may have disappeared from sight, and thus from critique, but they remained active while unseen.

Now, ten years later, master narratives are even more out of fashion, and thus perhaps even more deeply underground. Small narratives are back with a bang, as a key component in the postmodern critique of modernity and Enlightenment as repressive, instrumentally rational movements. Grand narrative is out of style, with its rhetoric of truth and progress and its covert corollaries of masculinization and Eurocentrism. Grand narrative is the unacceptably reified form of storytelling. But storytelling itself is everywhere, and cannot be expunged even from scientific communication. It is at once what is demystified and eschewed, when it appears as grand narrative, and what is affirmed and declared, when its limits are confessed. Hence we have the privileging of the "little narrative" (*petit récit*), which according to Lyotard produces dissensus rather than consensus, and even encourages "blind spots" instead of "insights."[13] But, to take again and repeat Jameson's insight, we would be foolish to pretend that little narratives are true alternatives to grand ones, rather than chips off a larger block whose shape we can no longer see because we are not looking. What, we might wonder, is the grand narrative behind the compulsive appeal of little stories?

Lyotard's account of the onset of the postmodern is itself often quite nuanced. The predicament of dissensus is not always celebrated,

12   Fredric Jameson, introduction to Lyotard, *Postmodern Condition*, xi.

13   Lyotard, *Postmodern Condition*, 60–61.

and in his description of narrative as "the quintessential form of *custom-ary* knowledge" (19, italics mine), Lyotard may be taken to signal the merely reproductive potential in the fabric of all narrative, grand or little. What Lyotard calls the postmodern is often presented as the inevitable format of a way of life rather than as a hyperbolic, ethical preference. But in his punchier, more exoteric and therefore better-known appendix, "What Is Postmodernism?" he does end with the sort of flourish against totalization and "terror" that has permitted many of his readers to believe that they are part of a crusade for creativity and compassion. This is to forget, as Lyotard seems himself to forget, the incidence of the "blind spots." Jameson has shrewdly if acerbically referred to the current methodological carnival as the "delirious non-stop monologue" of "so many in-group narratives."[14] And indeed there is nothing whatsoever about our participation in little narratives, our own or those of a few natural hearts or professional colleagues or fellow sufferers, that guarantees an avoidance of the blind spots or even of critical errors. Telling one's own story, or the story of one's imagined group or subculture, with an implicit or explicit reliance on the dubious category of "experience," has in itself no more or less authority than the grandest of grand narratives.[15] And in a culture like that of the United States, where the liberal individual has seldom been offstage at all, he or she is always lurking in the wings waiting for the supplementary acts to falter and exit, left, in a hurry. In other words, there is a tendency for the tellers of little tales to smuggle back, behind the rhetoric of modesty or of radical alternative, precisely the most uncritical and traditional formations of self and subject, along with the unacknowledged grand narratives that surreptitiously maintain them.

At issue here, among other things, is the question of the relation between the world we inhabit and the way we theorize it or represent it. If the world were indeed organized according to the mandates of instrumental reason, then the crying of the little narrative might indeed project a critical function, and sometimes it can seem that way. My own zeal for dissent from the current fetishization of the little narrative and of storytelling itself requires restraining. It is not simply imaginable but quite evident, for example, that in certain times and

---

14 Jameson, *Postmodernism*, 368.

15 For some important cautionary arguments about the rhetoric of "experience," see Joan Scott, "The Evidence of Experience," *Critical Inquiry* 17 (1990–91): 773–97.

places the commitment to the little narrative really is a critical and even radical recourse. It would be fatuous to suggest to a torture victim or a truly beleaguered minority of however many that the story of their suffering is somehow contaminated and rendered incredible by virtue of its being part of a postmodern ideology of miniaturization. To give but one example of the power of the little narrative, let me produce Martin Gilbert's *Holocaust*, a text of over eight hundred pages that is little more than a telling, person by person, of recorded experiences of and from victims and survivors, almost completely without extended generalizations or interpretations and devoid of attention to Nazi motives and Nazi personalities.[16] It would be possible to suggest, and a dogged negationist probably would suggest, that the texts are forged and the memories corrupt. But it is against that tendency that the little narratives are themselves produced, as fragments shored against forgetting, and powerful by virtue of their sheer number and variety. This is not, I think, a place where one would want to critique the integrity of little stories, and there are many other, if less world-historical, examples in the fabric of daily life in less barbarous places.

But it is all a matter of place and time. The world that we academic postmoderns most densely and consistently occupy, as a collective (notwithstanding individual circumstances and overlaps), is not that of the ghettos and the gas chambers. It has arguable connections with a great deal of what does happen and has happened in the wider world, but it is not itself simply the image of that world, or worlds. Academic culture, especially in the humanities, seems so far from corresponding to the imaginary monolith of classical reason (and its technological criminalities) that one might sometimes wish it were more rational than it is. The currently fashionable dismissal of "theory" (in its association with reason) as having wrought all sorts of bad things from Auschwitz to Australia may be well meant as a critique of large events in world contexts; but it is hardly a radicalization of a *profession*, that of literary criticism, whose traditional subsistence has been by way of intuition and imprecision, and almost always "against theory."[17] At least, there is no clear license for our autobiographical literary critics and

16 Martin Gilbert, *The Holocaust: A History of the Jews of Europe during the Second World War* (New York: Holt, Rinehart & Winston, 1986).

17 For a history of this predisposition, see my *Romanticism, Nationalism, and the Revolt against Theory* (Chicago and London: University of Chicago Press, 1993).

exemplary storytellers to bestow upon themselves the rare and special virtue called courage as they launch into an extended account of themselves and where they are coming from. [18] Even without our ingesting the rigorous medicines of Marxist and poststructuralist critiques of individualism, we should be able to recognize that the literary academy has always encouraged (even as it appears to censor) the image of self-confident selfhood. Courage, for most of us, is scarcely the issue. Indeed, those whose model of repression assumes that mere willpower is an effective remedy for that repression are already so comfortably lodged in life that they can hardly require much bravery.

Storytelling, then, is the mode of literature, and increasingly of that profession of literary criticism whose terminologies and priorities are migrating into other disciplines and thereby creating—I am suggesting—so much of what we in the academy recognize as the postmodern. There is no undisputed point of origin for what I am describing, and in this chapter and the following chapters I will be invoking various (if mostly long-durational) chronologies. Much of the apparent novelty of the storytelling mode in literary criticism comes from a perceptible weakening or even collapsing of the boundaries between writing literature and writing about literature, for there have been times when the critics have sought the authority of objectivism for their reflections, as a way of setting themselves off from the creators of "primary" texts. But the distinctions have never been secure or long-standing, and the general syndrome of literature within modernity looks very compatible with the profile of the academic postmodern. I will now look briefly at some exemplary moments in the evolution of that syndrome.

The first of them is Sir Philip Sidney's *Apology for Poetry,* which appears at an early point in that evolution, and which for our purposes might be read as a vindication of storytelling. Sidney makes a firm distinction between poetry—which we would now call literature—and the contiguous disciplines of history and philosophy. The historian is tied to "example," to "the particular truth of things and not to the general reason of things." The philosopher, on the contrary, moves by

---

18   I am thinking here of Jane Tompkins's now widely circulated remark that (academic) "people are scared to talk about themselves . . . they haven't got the guts to do it." See "Me and My Shadow," in *Gender and Theory: Dialogues on Feminist Criticism,* ed. Linda Kauffman (New York and Oxford: Blackwell, 1989), 123.

"precept," so that his knowledge resides at the level of the "abstract and general."[19] The poet incorporates both. He is the "right popular philosopher" (109) and the moving spirit of history, as soon as the historian moves beyond the dry assembly of "mouse-eaten records" (105). The poet works by "moving," which is "the cause and the effect of teaching," and "with the end of well-doing and not of well-knowing only" (112, 104). He is a storyteller and "cometh unto you, with a tale which holdeth children from play, and old men from the chimney corner" (113).

Above all, like a god or a magician—though ideally not like the "conjurer" Louis Bonaparte—he experiences and generates a freedom of thought and reference, an escape from the quotidian restraints of empirical life, with his "high flying liberty of conceit" and his "freely ranging only within the zodiac of his own wit" (99, 100). Because he is not dealing in empirical verifications, "he lieth not" (124). That poetry has been the product of Sidney's own "idlest times" (95) marks it as leisure activity, but it maintains a high moral purpose within its commitment to delight. Its very existence seems to be premised on Sidney's *not* being a man of action or a slave to fact, even as it is argued to improve and purify one's active life. There is an incipient instability in its attributes of idleness and enticement—an incipient feminization, indeed, that is marked by poetry's status as "the companion of the camps" (127), which seems to allude to women as camp followers even as it means to declare a primarily masculine militancy. Sidney himself always aimed to be the aristocratic man of action, and could thus perhaps seem to afford the detour through poetry without complete loss of social identity and masculine purpose.[20] He has specified poetry as free from the more recognizable precisions of history and philosophy, even as he claims for it a superior kind of knowledge, that to be achieved by "freely ranging." In today's terms we may see Sidney as shaking off the trammels of both fact and theory in the cause of good

19   Sir Philip Sidney, *An Apology for Poetry, or The Defence of Poetry*, ed. Geoffrey Shepherd (Edinburgh and London: Thomas Nelson, 1965), 107.

20   On this question, see Margaret W. Ferguson, *Trials of Desire: Renaissance Defenses of Poetry* (New Haven and London: Yale University Press, 1983), especially 158–62. For an account of the tension between fact and fiction in the period, see William Nelson, *Fact or Fiction: The Dilemma of the Renaissance Storyteller* (Cambridge: Harvard University Press, 1973); and, for a later moment, Lennard Davis, *Factual Fictions: The Origins of the English Novel* (New York: Columbia University Press, 1983).

literature, a literature underpinned by a clear moral function. He thereby specifies one of the enduring appeals of the literary mode: its capacity to seem to mediate between mere generalities and dogged empiricisms. Generations of literary critics have applauded the power of literature to humanize abstraction while generalizing the particular. [21] What happens when the justificatory moment migrates from an aristocratic to a middle-class milieu can be seen in *The Spectator,* and above all in Addison's essays on "the pleasures of the imagination."

Addison further refines the function of imprecision as defining the literary experience, this time with an emphasis on response, as befits the expanding readership of the early eighteenth century. The faculty of good taste is first positioned between nature and nurture: it is "in some degree" born with us, but it can also be cultivated by an acquaintance with "polite" culture. [22] In this way Addison heads off a radicalized post-Lockean extension of the cultural franchise to all and sundry: if cultivation were everything, then all might pursue it. Taste is for this reason an imprecise attribute, and not simply the product of an efficient pedagogy. It is also antiprofessional and seeks its proper vocabulary in the "Works of Nature" rather than in the specialized terminologies of the "Arts and Sciences" (no. 421, p. 402). The imagination avoids the "knotty and subtle Disquisitions" of the understanding, which require "Dint of thinking," and are "attended with too violent a Labour of the Brain." But at the same time it is not to be compared to a merely "sensual" delight, bringing "Negligence and Remissness." It stands between hard work and complete inaction, "like a gentle Exercise to the Faculties," and serves to "awaken them from Sloth and Idleness, without putting them upon any Labour or Difficulty" (no. 411, p. 370).

Addison's "imagination," destined for readers of the middling sort, here mediates between a strong Puritan component, according to which only hard labor could keep us from sloth, and a strong aristocratic inclination, wherein all effort would be construed as interfering

21   The same appeal is being discovered by the inhabitants of other disciplines newly sensitive to the circulation of literature. Martha Nussbaum, for instance, celebrates exactly this blending of "concrete features" with "common passions" in her "Literary Imagination in Public Life," *New Literary History* 22 (1991): 903.

22   Joseph Addison, "The Pleasures of the Imagination," in *Selections from "The Tatler" and "The Spectator" of Steele and Addison,* ed. Angus Ross (Harmondsworth: Penguin, 1982), 366, no. 409.

with the good life. Addison also seeks to break down, by recourse to the sphere of the aesthetic, the psychological burdens of a culture of divided labor, in which most of us have to pursue some or other specialization, some one or other among the "Arts and Sciences," in order to make our way in the world. Thus is it that, at one of the high points of incremental urbanization in British social history (most evident, at first, in London), Addison stresses the desire for nature and for space. In "the wide fields of Nature, the Sight wanders up and down without Confinement, and is fed with an infinite variety of Images, without any certain Stint or Number" (no. 414, p. 378). At precisely the point of emergence of a readership with very little property or none at all, Addison plays up the property of the imagination, which gives us, without the awkward necessity of ownership, "a kind of Property" in everything we see: "a spacious Horison is an Image of Liberty" (nos. 411, 412, pp. 369, 371).

Of course, many of Addison's imagined readers would not have had the actual or frequent experience of spacious horizons. And literature emerges as a more than compensatory alternative: well-chosen words can give us "more lively Ideas than the Sight of Things themselves" (no. 416, p. 387). Roaming around the countryside can be not only displaced by but enhanced in the reading experience. And reading protects as it substitutes. Descriptions of sublime horrors leave us "not a little pleased to think we are in no Danger of them," and representations of suffering "teach us to set a just Value upon our own Condition" (no. 418, pp. 393–94). Sidney, still thinking to address a monarch and an aristocracy, could think that tragedy might have the function of making kings fear to be tyrants; Addison is clear that it works to make ordinary people glad not to be kings. His middle-class reader hates mere symmetry and strives always for some element of formative power and control, resisting what we have since come to call the constraints of "instrumental reason"; but she or he is also encouraged to expend these energies in art and literature instead of in empirical life. The revolt against urban space carried out in the Addisonian imagination is also a revolt against the compressions of professional space, against the habit of being tied to a single expertise in a single place, and contiguous to only a few other such places.

I suggest, then, that there is a visible connection between the late twentieth-century rhetoric of postmodernity and the details of Addison's account of the pleasures of the imagination. Already, in the capacity of the literary aesthetic to break the constraining efficiency of work discipline, we can see an anticipation of its current appeal among professional, academic disciplines as a breaker of boundaries and crosser of categories. Addison's polite reader, exercising freedom in the sphere of representations but not in the workplace (or only in contained ways, since limited freedom is indeed also a workplace ethic in an entrepreneurial culture), bears comparison with the academic postmodernist, projecting changes in the world system or in knowledge production from within an institutional setting whose own mediating determinations all too often disappear from sight and fail to come to consciousness as we describe our models of imagined experience. I say this not just to debunk the academic postmodern, but to highlight the degree to which its explanatory terms and preferred conventions are themselves the product of that same culture of "literature" and "taste" of which Addison produced the exemplary formation. This culture located the expertise of the critic or ideal reader in his or her ability to cope with the unpredictable, and to respond unpredictably. Theory could not foresee its pronouncements, and mere method could not replicate their genesis for others.

It is in this respect above all that Samuel Johnson, though hardly a complete candidate for the title of first postmodernist, remains the exemplary man of letters of the modern period, and thus an important measure of the degree to which the rhetoric of contemporary academia has and has not moved beyond its inherited infrastructures. In the "Preface to the English Dictionary" Johnson epitomizes the role (or the fate) of the critic who seeks to produce some order out of the chaos of human lives and languages, and who attempts precision in the inexact domain of culture. Employing an infinitely variable combination of "experience" and "analogy," induction and ratiocination, the dictionary maker remains ever alert to both rules and exceptions, unable to control the materials he describes, which are indifferent to his praises and censures. [23] All of the trenchant pronouncements for which Johnson is so famous, and which Boswell certainly magnified and occasionally invented, may be contextualized as Canute-like gestures in response to a cultural chaos that Johnson seems to have both celebrated and feared. He does not disavow method, but he is aware that it is not

---

23   Samuel Johnson, "Preface to the English Dictionary," in *The Complete Works of Samuel Johnson*, ed. Arthur Murphy (London, 1824), 2:32.

enough, and that nothing can be enough. His mode is thus that of irony, which both allows and undermines the well-known Johnsonian self-confidence. Commerce and translation modify our language in uncontrollable ways, but they are hardly to be stopped from making themselves felt in "the boundless chaos of a living speech" (41). The task of the critic is thus one of constant vigilance marked by an inevitable inadequacy. But this is also the guarantee of his continuous employment: improvement is always possible and necessary, and there is always more to do (55). Johnson professed nothing but scorn for the shelter of the "academic bowers" he had not himself ever enjoyed (66). But in his exemplary effusions against the idea of a national academy as incompatible with "English liberty" (64), he set forth the very rhetoric of principled independence that academicians themselves would draw upon to obscure their increasing dependence upon institutions (principally, the university). The agile adjudication between fact and theory, particular and general, exceptional and typical, would become the designated function of the professional literary critic. It would be carried out with a sense of absolute urgency, and in defiance of any limiting relation to disciplinary limits: this itself would, in other words, become the defining characteristic of the discipline.

Johnson is not comfortable with himself in the character of a storyteller, but his highly dramatized heroic failures do display the impossibility of methodological mastery and thus point the way to storytelling as an available alternative, one already latent in the concept of literature. They also record the emergence of a strongly *personal* voice, one crafted by both Johnson and Boswell to sound like no other, and thus to stamp the seal of personality (and autobiography) on the business of interpretation. After Addison and Johnson the definition and redefinition of literature and literary criticism goes on for two centuries in much the same terms. It can be traced in Burke's account of the sublime, where words, once again, are often more powerful than the experience they purport to describe; in Wordsworth's obscure attempt to place active imagination between the increasingly polarizing tendencies of work and leisure brought on by "the increasing accumulation of men in cities";[24] and in Shelley's radical claim for the power of

24   William Wordsworth, preface to *Lyrical Ballads*, in *The Prose Works of William Wordsworth*, ed. W. J. B. Owen and Jane Worthington Smyser (Oxford: Clarendon Press, 1974), 1: 128.

poetry as the energy behind cultural change. Literature, which for Addison still has explicit functions of differentiating the polite from the vulgar, and of compensating the moderately affluent for their lack of complete luxury, becomes more and more the thing that can save us, and more and more obscurely related to its roots in social appeasement, discipline, and control. Within literature, it is poetry above all whose transforming powers are played up, for, as Adam Smith put it, prose "is naturally the Language of Business; as Poetry is of Pleasure and Amusement." And "as it is intertainment we look for from the Poet as well as the storyteller, so we make them the same concessions."[25] Literature (or at least its description) also becomes, from the end of the nineteenth century, more and more the property of an institution—the university—and of a subculture within the university—English departments. The reemergence of this property from an exclusively departmental base, and its circulation among the humanities and social sciences in general, is the process I am calling the academic postmodern, which I take to be a very large part of what we are describing when we speak of the postmodern in grander and more general terms.

How can I make this claim, at a time when some of the most astute commentators on our contemporary condition are describing a move *away from* the literary as most urgently definitive of a postmodern condition? Jameson writes of literature as "the ideologically dominant paradigm" of the modern period, now being displaced by video as the signature of the postmodern.[26] And John Guillory observes a "capital flight" from literary culture as most characteristic of a condition in which literary critics and theorists are floundering in the canon debate as if in a desperate fantasizing of their continuing power and influence.[27] The contradictions are, I think, only apparent. Culture is not a monolith, and the academic postmodern is only one among the contestants for the title of the (imaginary) authentic postmodern. There are indeed stresses on the traditional dominance of the category of literature within the culture of modernity as the healer of wounds and the bearer of salvation. But this may be exactly why the *academic* postmodern is what it is, a retrospective embrace of the methods and prior-

25   Adam Smith, *Lectures on Rhetoric and Belles Lettres*, ed. J. C. Bryce (Oxford: Clarendon Press, 1983), 137, 120.

26   Jameson, *Postmodernism*, 68.

27   Guillory, *Cultural Capital*, 45.

ities of literary criticism, a pseudorevolution within the institution that seeks to cope with and hence to defend against a threatened eradication of the entire traditional project of humanist knowledge. Veblen, we remember, saw the universities as reactionary, behind history instead of ahead of it. If this is so, then we should not be surprised to see the excitable pouring of old wine into new bottles and to sense the familiar taste of old vines behind the labels promising new wineries. Hence Vattimo can claim that in a "radical fashion" the "application of the techniques of rhetorical analysis to historiography has shown that our image of history is completely conditioned by the rules of a literary genre; in other words, history is much more of a 'story' or narrative than we are generally inclined to admit."[28]

The dubious word here—and we all use it—is *shown*. One could defend it, but one could also wonder if *that* alone is what is shown, rather than or as well as the responsiveness of a stressed subsystem to a possible new nutrient. Vattimo's observation can be taken as an admission that the literary critics were right all along; that the hitherto benighted historians, philosophers, and social scientists should now admit the errors of their former ways and get the message about storytelling. It is as if the traditional weakness of literature and literary criticism, seen as such from a scientific-objectivist affiliation, has now become a strength, and the key to all mythologies. The instabilities that so concerned Samuel Johnson, and to which Coleridge and other prototypical literary theorists sought alternatives, have now become the proud signatures rather than the dirty little secrets of "literature" and literary criticism. But the turn to the literary happens within an institutional formation where the literary *already* has a place, and where the same anxieties about which Johnson was so dramatically public are themselves the guarantee of a relatively *stable* institutional role for the traditional academician. Thus, before we pronounce upon the new world dynamics brought about by global exchange, multinational corporations, postcoloniality, and so forth, we might usefully look at the import-export trade between the disciplines within the institutions from and through which we view the larger world. Here the return of the storyteller is a phenomenon that remains open to the critique to be derived from Marx and Adorno, as well as from Bourdieu. It is at once an acknowledgment of and acquiescence in the fragmentary

---

28 Vattimo, *End of Modernity*, 8.

and disjointed image of culture projected by Eliot and Pound and the high modernists, and also an effort at sealing up the fragments into newly confident narratives. Thus we move almost immediately from confessions of solipsism (speaking for ourselves) to celebrations of identity and continuity. The passage from necessity to virtue happens with the speed of light—as if by magic, or conjuring. Some of the confidence with which we do this is, I think, derived from the disciplinary and institutional identity of literature, an identity that has been in place for a long time and that affords us a very traditional posture of radical intent. In our moments of heroic dissent, we replicate the terms and traditions of our trade.

Among the various examples of the recourse to literature and literary criticism for the postmodernization of other disciplines, I will be discussing, in some detail, the work of Richard Rorty in philosophy and of Clifford Geertz in anthropology, who either practice or endorse the methods or results of storytelling in a high enough register to appear exemplary. In my next chapter I pursue the anatomy of storytelling in its specific commitments to anecdote and conversation.

Two

ANECDOTES AND CONVERSATIONS: THE METHOD OF POSTMODERNITY

Anecdote and conversation are the tools of storytelling as we now do it, if we are liberal intellectuals laying claim to the novelty of a postmodern commitment. As I have said before, I do not mean to suggest that there might not be, somewhere else, a mode of postmodernity that could be theorized as effectively radical, in a way that I do not find academic storytelling to be. Indeed, some such modes arguably depend upon the negation of storytelling, drawing instead upon technological-computational models with specifically antiorganic, antihumanist formations. But for all the lip service to these alternatives among humanist academicians, and admitting even a wholehearted enthusiasm for them among some of us, they are not as yet typical of the subculture of established professional humanists, which will be the object of my inquiry here. This subculture, I suggest, is most commonly preoccupied with the rhetoric of anecdote and conversation, now most familiar in their associations with, respectively, the new historicists and the philosophy of Richard Rorty, both exemplary versions of postmodern method. [1]

Anecdote and conversation bring with them interesting and complex histories, histories largely repressed in discussions of the import of the postmodern. Indeed, Fredric Jameson has proposed that the "disappearance of a sense of history" is a generic marker of the postmodern itself. [2] This may be especially true for an academic subculture

---

1 Rorty, I suspect, would be more willing to accept a designation as the exponent of some of the potentially positive components of modernity, in its liberal aspirations, than to allow me to call him a postmodern. But in his preference for the model of conversation, I find him to be exemplary and indeed formative of the kind of academic postmodernity I am addressing here.

2 Fredric Jameson, "Postmodernism and Consumer Society," in *The Anti-Aesthetic: Es-*

visibly implicated in a legitimation process marked by a rhetoric of novelty, with its "new" this and "post" that. Anecdote and conversation are tied together in an extended history that is coincident with that of literature in its modern sense. They are both important to storytelling, and as such they are both embedded in the effort at vocalization and making present that storytelling represents. Good stories and good conversations make telling use of anecdotes. And, if stories are incipiently monologic, good anecdotes make them seem more dialogic, more conversational. The conversation is the story we assemble together, and functions as such in the rhetoric of the academic postmodern.

I begin with the term *conversation* and its conceptual attributes. This is, as I have said, the signature word for the widely circulated philosophy of Richard Rorty. In his first major book, *Philosophy and the Mirror of Nature*, Rorty argued against the idea of the mind as able to represent anything in a "real" world, anything outside its own modes of behavior. Any "certainty" to be achieved then becomes "a matter of conversation between persons, rather than a matter of interaction with nonhuman reality." In this way "conversation replaces confrontation" as the procedure of philosophy, and hermeneutics displaces epistemology as its most adequate technique. [3] Much of Rorty's subsequent work is taken up with the elaboration of this notion of conversation and its implications. In *Consequences of Pragmatism* he makes the familiar case against method: "The idea that in science or philosophy we can substitute 'method' for deliberation between alternative results of speculation is just wishful thinking." To try to avoid conversation for the sake of some objectified reality now becomes a failure of moral courage or a sign of existential despair, an urge to "find something ahistorical and necessary to cling to" and to forget that conversation with "our fellow-humans" is "our only source of guidance" (164–66). And in *Contingency, Irony, and Solidarity* Rorty turns to the literary analogue and precedent —so dominant throughout the postmodern—for a description of cultural evolution. Offering us Harold Bloom's model of culture as "an ex-

---

says on Postmodern Culture, ed. Hal Foster (Port Townsend, WA: Bay Press, 1983), 125. This disappearance of a sense of history is of course also one of the major arguments of Jameson's *Postmodernism.*

3   Richard Rorty, *Philosophy and the Mirror of Nature,* corr. ed. (Princeton: Princeton University Press, 1980), 157, 170, 318.

panding repertoire of alternative descriptions" (though failing to note the Shelleyan and other precedents upon which it is based), Rorty invites us into an appreciation of the playful and creative imagination as the agent of good conversation.[4]

Rorty claims to be the successor of Wittgenstein and of the American pragmatists, and the translator—and he is a gifted one—of the more obscurely articulated concepts of Heidegger and Derrida.[5] But he is also the heir of a much larger tradition, one contemporaneous with the foundation of modern notions of "literature." These notions take on intensified forms in the eighteenth century, but they can certainly be traced in earlier periods and thus attributed to the generic ideology of modernity itself. Rorty's immediate and substantial precursor, acknowledged but underacknowledged in that compulsive academic way we are all so good at, is Michael Oakeshott, whose essay "The Voice of Poetry in the Conversation of Mankind" anticipates most of Rorty's concepts and some of his elaborations of them. Oakeshott, perhaps because of his different position (in England, closer to the end of World War II) has a somewhat darker prognosis for the future of the poetic mode of inquiry founded in conversation. Like Shelley, he sees the poetic as only "intermittent" in its effects, and as a "sort of truancy," confined to moments "abstracted and rescued from the flow of curiosity and contrivance."[6] Oakeshott is concerned about addressing the perceived hegemony of a scientific, technological worldview, and he sees the poetic-conversational mode as a positive but frail alternative. Rorty, operating within a more confident liberalism, which may or may not be deserved, disavows the question of the relation between

4   Richard Rorty, *Contingency, Irony, and Solidarity* (Cambridge: Cambridge University Press, 1989), 39–40.

5   The affiliation with Derrida, at least, should not go undisputed. Christopher Norris, in *The Contest of Faculties*, has made the case against Rorty's use of Derrida as "a halfway house on the road to pragmatist wisdom" (165), and in *The Truth about Postmodernism* (Oxford: Blackwell, 1993), 37–54, he makes the same objections against Rorty's use of Foucault. Stephen Tyler, in *The Unspeakable: Discourse, Dialogue, and Rhetoric in the Postmodern World* (Madison: University of Wisconsin Press, 1987), 57, is eloquent against any association of Derrida with Gadamerian dialogue: "Derrida's distaste for sound, his suspicion of communication, his speechlessness, his affair with the unspeakable chokes off dialogue." Hence, perhaps, the degree to which Derrida remains so threatening to a wide assortment of academic disciplines.

6   Michael Oakeshott, "The Voice of Poetry in the Conversation of Mankind," in *Rationalism in Politics and Other Essays* (London: Methuen, 1962), 247.

philosophy and the social whole as any necessary part of philosophy's analysis, though he is certainly well aware of possibilities, hopes, and implications.[7]

Oakeshott is also and I think significantly explicit about the relation of the conversation model to a doctrine of *politeness*. He is not sure that we can head off the barbarians, but he sees that the key to conversation, or good conversation, is to be able to "differ without disagreeing" in a context where there is no "hierarchy" and no "winner," and with a willingness to participate in an "unrehearsed intellectual adventure" (198). What makes us most usefully human is the inheritance of this conversational tradition, and an ability to participate in it (199). What ruins the conversation is "the bad manners of one or more of the participants. For each voice is prone to *superbia*, that is, an exclusive concern with its own utterance . . . And when this happens, barbarism may be observed to have supervened" (201). For Oakeshott the currently threatening barbarisms were those of "practical activity" and science (202).

For Rorty and for the American sphere for which he speaks (and this is not simply limited to the United States), the barbarisms are different: they would certainly include Marxism, fundamentalism, and "theory" in many of its incarnations. Rorty is less explicit about the relation of the conversational ideal to a culture of politeness, though he can sometimes sound as if he is briefing the household for an important dinner party: the task is to "keep the conversation going" and its failure (and that of philosophy) would be "to close off conversation" (*Philosophy and the Mirror of Nature*, 377). But the culture of politeness is indeed one of the long-durational components of the conversational ideal, and one form of response to the problems it has commonly sought to address. Politeness is what we try to resort to in difficult situations, but it has always been a limited and limiting recourse. It is fairly useless if you are dealing with someone outside the subculture whose ideals have composed the model of what is polite, or with someone who simply will not recognize them. And it depends, as Roy Bhaskar has noted, on leisure and on the absence of disruptive pain.[8]

---

7   The relation to Oakeshott, which is, as I say, underacknowledged according to my reading of Rorty, would bear more extended attention by way of the effort to specify Rorty's *nationalism*, an effort begun by Michael Billig in "Nationalism and Richard Rorty: The Text as a Flag for *Pax Americana*," *New Left Review* 202 (1993): 69–83.

8   Roy Bhaskar, *Reclaiming Reality: A Critical Introduction to Contemporary Philosophy* (Lon-

Oakeshott is not Rorty's only twentieth-century precursor in the circles of good conversation. Hans-Georg Gadamer, in his monumental *Truth and Method*, first published in 1960, modeled hermeneutics as "a conversation with the text" and thus described interpretation as containing within it "the original meaning of conversation and the structure of question and answer."[9] Here the associations of writing with passivity, immanence, finality, and even death are vivified by conversion to the living dialectic of speech, so that textual exegesis—the conversion of written marks into understanding—becomes a form of speaking with the dead (to repeat that famous remark by Stephen Greenblatt). Gadamer is faithful to the incipient poststructuralist moment in his recognition that this conversational understanding has nothing to do with identity. Neither in reading nor in speaking does one speak for or about oneself. Using a language is not preparatory *to* understanding, to some inner act of postlinguistic synthesis, but is itself coincident *with* understanding (347–50). We are already in language, and there we remain. But we are not therefore trapped in writing as a negatively "alienated speech" (354), so that Gadamer restores some of the comforts of the same identity whose nonexistence he has previously admitted. The alienation is positive, because "writing has detached itself from the contingency of its origin and made itself free for new relationships" (357). Language is not just ideology but a "generative and creative power," which would, were it not for the fact of death, enable us to participate in "a truly infinite conversation" (498, 493). We don't, in other words, need identity when we are never alone or uncomfortable.

Gadamer's highly technical hermeneutics, densely situated in the traditions of German romanticism, is less available to anglophone readers than Rorty's elegant and easeful intellectual brilliance, but shares with it a liberal commitment to positive reform by means of intelligible conversation. The model of absolute reproduction, whereby language can only repeat itself and all of us within it, which leads either to the prognosis of containment or revolutionary change, is es-

---

don and New York: Verso, 1989), 170. Bhaskar, in proposing the case for "transcendental realism," has a fully argued critique of Rorty's attack on epistemology (146–79). See also Sabina Lovibond, "Feminism and Pragmatism," *New Left Review* 193 (1992): 56–74.

9 Hans-Georg Gadamer, *Truth and Method* (New York: Seabury Press, 1975), 331, 333.

chewed in favor of the possibilities for polite attention. In the eighteenth century the aspiration to politeness can be traced as one of the various efforts of a bourgeois literary culture toward adopting the codes of an aristocratic precursor and of shoring up a new middle-class formation against what is outside and "below" it. The appropriation of the rhetorical property of social-economic superiors was all the more energetic because other, empirical appropriations took place more gradually, or not at all. The prerequisite of the polite was *leisure*, freedom from the exigencies of work and in particular from the psychological distortions accruing from divided labor and from affiliation to some or other (vested) interest. Politeness was thus preprofessional, prior to the emergence of divisive expertise and lexical obscurity of the sort that today's apologists of common sense like to call jargon. And, as such, it was analogous to and inscribed within the evolution of "literature." Addison's prescription for the acquisition or cultivation of taste was that one be "conversant among the Writings of the most Polite Authors" and engage in "Conversation with Men of a Polite Genius." This was conceived as a pluralizing and mind-broadening exercise: everyone "forms several Reflections that are peculiar to his own manner of Thinking; so that Conversation will naturally furnish us with Hints which we did not attend to, and make us enjoy other Mens Parts and Reflections as well as our own." So powerful is this conversational energy that it explains, for Addison, why "Men of great Genius" tend to occur in the same times and places, as "Friends and Contemporaries."[10]

The need to be encouraged to enjoy parts and reflections other than our own comes, of course, from the increasing sense of the power of an economy founded in divided labor to force us into mutually unintelligible languages and psychologically alienated personalities. John Davison, in the nineteenth century, offers "common conversation" as the yardstick distinguishing civilized persons from barbarians: "look into the huts of savages and see, for there is nothing to listen to, the dismal blank of their stupid hours of silence; their professional avocations of war and hunting are over; and, having nothing to do, they have nothing to say." In "improved life," on the contrary, conversation becomes "a very active agent in circulating and forming the opinions, tastes, and feelings of a whole people." But its topics must not belong to "any particular province" of the sort that the culture of divided labor

10   Addison, "Pleasures of the Imagination," 366–67.

will inevitably proliferate. [11] Conversation does here function to allow the civilized person to define himself against the primitive; but the ungainly reference to hunting as a "professional avocation" betrays the degree to which the real enemy of Davison's liberal education is the enemy within: the brutalized working class and the alienated philistines of the commercial middle class.

The appearance of the conversational ideal in postmodern culture thus asks to be read as nostalgia *for* the preprofessional, at exactly the moment when professionalism (also sometimes called theory) is under such heavy attack. Bruce Robbins has astutely noted that Rorty's belligerent antiprofessionalism and literariness may in fact function as a new lease on life for professional philosophy, and this kind of import-export trade between the disciplines is very much a part of what I am calling the academic postmodern. The banner of "rhetoric," Robbins suggests, makes the claim that philosophy will now speak the language of its hearers, and not the arcane jargon of special interests, since "rhetoric" governs us all. [12] And Cornel West has proposed that Rorty's neopragmatism is less "an earthshaking perspective for the modern West" than "a symptom of the crisis in a highly specialized professional stratum of educational workers: those in the philosophy departments of universities and colleges." [13] Being a good conversationalist presupposes having enough education to have something to say that is worth hearing, but not so much as to make one into a bore or a pedant, or indeed a professor. It presupposes being at least a middle-class speaker, since the ordinary folk, as Coleridge opined in his case against Wordsworth, are supposed to be unable to speak in connected sentences. [14] And it assumes that one does not have any awkward con-

11   John Davison, cited in John Henry Newman, *The Idea of a University*, ed. Martin J. Svaglic (Notre Dame, IN: University of Notre Dame Press, 1982), 130.

12   Robbins, *Secular Vocations*, 20–21, 112. A similar commitment to the ordinariness (and literariness) of philosophy informs the work and reputation of Stanley Cavell; see Michael Fischer, *Stanley Cavell and Literary Skepticism* (Chicago and London: University of Chicago Press, 1989), 3.

13   Cornel West, *The American Evasion of Philosophy: A Genealogy of Pragmatism* (Madison: University of Wisconsin Press, 1989), 206–7. See also Zygmunt Bauman, *Legislators and Interpreters*, 143, who argues on behalf of a larger-world demand for intellectuals who can translate between interests and disciplines, who are adept at "the art of civilized conversation."

14   Coleridge, *Biographia Literaria*, 2:52–53.

victions that might put an end to talk: that one is not a sectarian in religion or politics.[15] Good conversation has also traditionally performed a certain mediation between the genders, since polite women might join a conversation—and do so in countless novels and diaries and salons of the eighteenth century—but it kept out women of the lower orders, and opinionated feminists. The circulation and reading of literature performed very similar functions. And, according to Lorraine Daston, even Baconian science took on historical energy from its participation in "humanist attempts to polish academic manners."[16]

Much of the best literature of the eighteenth century and beyond has thus been imaged as conversation, or as some kind of analogue to the conversational mode. Great talkers, like Samuel Johnson, Samuel Taylor Coleridge, and Henry James, have gained reputations or had reputations made for them as just that, as talkers. John Keats's letters, with their renderings of a personal voice, their intimacies, and their casual intellections, are taken as seriously as his poems for designation as "literature." Poetry comes more and more to adopt the vocative manner in its titles—Cowper's "Table Talk" and "Expostulation," Coleridge's so-called conversation poems—either as it represents dialogue between persons or engages in such with the willing reader. Cowper's poem "Conversation" is a precursor to Oakeshott and Rorty in its delineation of the pros and cons of the genre. Cowper makes clear that mere "talking is not always to converse," and that much depends "on culture, and the sowing of the soil." We are to avoid "a duel in the form of a debate" and to discourage those who "suppose *themselves* monopolists of sense." For Cowper, what is to be repaired in the "true bliss" of "hearts in union mutually disclos'd" of good conversation is nothing

---

15   Here is John Lucas, *England and Englishness: Ideas of Nationhood in English Poetry, 1688–1900* (Iowa City: University of Iowa Press, 1990), 3: "Epic virtues are potentially dangerous . . . they are intimately associated with the difficult task of making a nation . . . Pope's dismissal of epic is his contribution to the suppression of radical republicanism. The verse epistle comes to stand as the typical poetic utterance of the time, its Horatianism at the service of those civilising values of friendship and a common cultural inheritance without which discourse becomes impossible."

16   Lorraine Daston, "Baconian Facts, Academic Civility, and the Prehistory of Objectivity," *Annals of Scholarship* 8, nos. 3–4 (1991): 338. For an extended account of the importance of conversation in the establishment of early modern science, see Steven Shapin, *A Social History of Truth: Civility and Science in Seventeenth-Century England* (Chicago and London: University of Chicago Press, 1994).

less than the Fall.[17] More secular instincts sought only to displace or disguise the evidence of serious social conflict or social-intellectual difference. Coleridge, it seems, often failed spectacularly to turn his talk into conversation. De Quincey called his habit that of *"alloquium, or talking to the company,"* rather than of *"colloquium, or talking with the company."* Coleridge himself may have seen the problem, in accusing himself of delivering *"oneversazione"* instead of *"conversazione,"* and the first editor of his *Table Talk* took on the task of making strategic emendations to make the delivery seem more interlocutive than it actually was.[18]

If the genre of printed table talk was designed to offer its readers a more relaxed introduction to the great man's thoughts than what was available in his more formal writings, then it succeeded only marginally if at all in the case of Coleridge, whose conversation was at least as intimidatingly dense as his written prose, and often more so. But the genre, which began with Luther's *Tischreden* and remained very popular throughout the eighteenth and early nineteenth centuries, was not just designed to provide a ready and easy way to great ideas.[19] It also carried with it an implication of authenticity, of lived experience, of ideas coming alive in the context of everyday existence. In other words, it communicated an ideal relation between ideas and ordinary life, in a way that inscribed at once sincerity and identity. It assumed, as we might now say, a reconversion of writing to speech, of the dead letter to the living spirit. The Protestant imperative toward the personal verification of all proper principles is here combined with a social-historical incentive specific to a developing culture of modernity, whereby the facsimile of speech and intimate contact is nothing less than a compensation for a deepening sense of alienation and social diversification. The spate of table talk, biography, and autobiography that appears more and more characteristic of eighteenth-century and romantic literature at once familiarizes a subjectivity we are to recognize as ordinary—a man speaking to men, in the Wordsworthian formula— and at the same time threatens, in its very focus on irreducible partic-

17 William Cowper, *Poems*, 3d ed. (London, 1787), 1:212, 216, 243, 246.

18 Samuel Taylor Coleridge, *Table Talk*, ed. Carl Woodring (Princeton: Princeton University Press, 1990), 1:lx, lv, xci–xcii.

19 For an account of the publishing history of various table talks, see F. P. Wilson, "Table Talk," *Huntington Library Quarterly* 4 (1940–41): 27–46.

ularity and detail, to remove the individual subject from sure repose within any simple model of general nature. The gesture toward representational familiarity is, in other words, indistinguishable from the inscription of interpretive crisis. Or, one might say, the desired representation of self during this period comes to consist in seeming at once akin to but finally not quite like anyone else, and as such beyond complete interpretability.

Perhaps no eighteenth-century man of letters was as unlike any other in his commitment to general nature as was the Samuel Johnson memorialized by James Boswell. Boswell's self-imposed task was to record everything, the "innumerable detached particulars, all which, even the most minute, I have spared no pains to ascertain with a scrupulous authenticity."[20] Boswell's determination not to exclude any record may be taken as a recognition of the potential interpretability of anything and everything in Johnson's life, and as an anticipation of the needs for future restorations of it. It also works to bring Johnson to life. The blend of the general career outline with the private incident is a mode "by which mankind are enabled as it were to see him live, and to 'live o'er each scene' with him, as he actually advanced through the several stages of his life" (22). The very redundancy of many of the recorded incidents works toward *vraisemblance*, toward realization. Why else are we being told something that seems not to matter, unless it is because it really happened, and can happen again for us as we read? The biographer's modesty, which painstakingly records everything it cannot presently make sense of in case others might someday do so (the exemplary summation here is the Freudian scene of analysis, where nothing is to be assumed redundant), is at the same time massively immodest in its claim to transcribe (and encourage the resuscitation of) the real. At this point the "real" has come to be defined, indeed, as that which cannot be completely interpreted, and therefore requires an infinity of future attentions.

I am arguing, then, that it is no accident that the literary critic Stephen Greenblatt was led to announce his famous intention: "I began with the desire to speak with the dead."[21] The very model of

20 James Boswell, *Life of Johnson*, ed. R. W. Chapman, corrected by J. D. Fleeman (London: Oxford University Press, 1970), 4.

21 Stephen Greenblatt, *Shakespearean Negotiations: The Circulation of Social Energy in Renaissance England* (Berkeley and Los Angeles: University of California Press, 1988), 1.

literature (and of its criticism) we inhabit makes that desire almost inevitable, just as it commits us to a sense of incompletion in our interpretive efforts. For what is "living" cannot be completely deciphered, cannot be limited to a connection with some and not other elements in the social whole, cannot be closed off from an infinite number of possible interactions.[22] The dead are brought to life to show that the conversation has no limits. To admit to limits would be to accept absolute social divisions, which the Rorty paradigm is unwilling to do. But it would also—and this is the astuteness of Greenblatt's confession—be to accept and to prefigure death. It is at this point that the postmodern culture of presence can seem almost melancholic, a kind of methodological effort at cryonic preservation. We want to live forever.[23]

Or, at least, we want to keep the conversation going for as long as we are around to benefit from it. The humanities sector of academia has an interest in inconclusive knowledge, not just to keep itself employed, but because as a commentator on culture it must assess materials and relationships that are themselves unstable and in more or less constant evolution. But time has always passed and things have always changed, so that the empirical argument cannot alone or itself explain why it is that we are so enamored of incompletion and uncertainty. Since at least Friedrich Schlegel and Kierkegaard, we have had in place an ethic of incompleteness, a prioritizing of active interpretation and world making as the proper responsibility of romantic and Protestant personalities. This has often received positive codings, so that the knowledge thus produced becomes *authentic* for the self (and for its prospects of redemption) even as it necessarily strains consensus. Heroism and solipsism go together here. The culture of conversation seems to mitigate the threat of incommunication latent in this paradigm, and to offset the likelihood of mere obscurity or stubbornness. It

22 Brook Thomas, in *The New Historicism and Other Old-Fashioned Topics* (Princeton: Princeton University Press, 1991), 215, notes that "literary texts generate paradoxes . . . because they are constituted by a lack, a space of negativity allowing readers to participate in their discursive play." This is of course the great insight of deconstruction, as publicized by Paul de Man, for literary criticism.

23 Alan Liu, in his superb essay "The Power of Formalism: The New Historicism," *English Literary History* 56 (1989): 721–71, has noted exactly the connection between the primacy of the theatrical and the desire to suspend mortality in the new historicism: "Finality is only the possibility of theatrical revival, cultural determination a casting call for future improvisation" (725).

suggests that the humanistic alternative to scientific method need not be merely subjective, but can create consensus among at least a few people in some places. Lyotard puts this alternative knowledge in counterpoint with "scientific knowledge" and relates it to "ideas of internal equilibrium and conviviality." He sees it as empowering, as leading to an awareness that "legitimation" can only come from one's own "linguistic practice and communicational interaction."[24] But of course the experience of empowerment goes along with the onset of responsibility. At the very point where we accede to the power we so desperately desire, we become critically anxious about the implications of employing it. This is the uncomfortable dilemma that the culture of conversation is designed to supersede, as the affirmation of localized small-group cultures mediates between discredited master narratives (of race or nation) and paranoid idiosyncrasy. The rhetoric of conversation seeks to suggest that, as long as we talk to others in the same social circle, we can avoid radical concerns about the languages we do not understand, and we can negotiate some way of adapting to the new or the incoherent without social and psychological collapse. Literature and literary criticism have also traditionally offered this resource: the history of literature and that of polite conversation are deeply mutual. I. A. Richards, to cite a literary critic of enormous influence (which undoubtedly extended to Oakeshott), saw in literature (when read rightly) an opportunity for displacing "conflict" by "conciliation" in both social and individual (psychological) spheres.[25] The mind permits a conversation between its own various impulses in the reading of poetry, adjusting that mind to the point where it is less likely to enter into interpersonal conflicts deriving from dogmatic convictions. This theme runs through the mainstream history of literary criticism. It is there, for instance, in Edward Said's notion of "beginnings" as gestures "with aims non-coercive and communal," and Wayne Booth's search for a criticism that "tests our actual responses in conversation."[26]

24   Lyotard, *Postmodern Condition*, 7, 41.

25   I. A. Richards, *Science and Poetry* (New York: Norton, 1926), 42–47.

26   Edward Said, *Beginnings: Intention and Method* (New York: Columbia University Press, 1985), xiv; Wayne Booth, *The Company We Keep: An Ethics of Fiction* (Berkeley and Los Angeles: University of California Press, 1988), x. Booth uses the word *conversation* five times in his first two pages.

I now pass on to the second term for inspection: *anecdote.* Within the culture of conversation, the anecdote has always had a visible importance. Anecdotes function in conversation as one of the yardsticks for distinguishing competence from incompetence. The good or polite conversationalist does not allow an anecdote to go on for too long, but uses it to surprise, to instantiate, to illuminate the general point by reference to the immediacy of a lived incident. Nothing is more gauche, more revealing, than the formulaic or inept anecdote. Nothing seems more transparent than the politician's pitch beginning "Let me tell you about John Doe, who runs a small farm outside Peoria," and yet nothing is more generic in the rhetoric of would-be authenticity. For when it is well deployed, the anecdote serves to bring to temporary closure or summation the otherwise infinite possible series of interpretations that come with participation in the culture of conversation. It provides a temporary clincher, or landing place, which we know to be only provisional, and very much a function of the skill and tact of the teller, and hence itself dramatic, within the orbit of the voice. But it may be all that we have of certainty, and its very limits are part of its conviction and secret function within the rhetoric of the "real." It tells us that there is always more to come, for everyone and everything might generate an anecdote.[27] But it provides access to a sort of history, and by making no claim for itself as other than anecdotal, as contingent and verging on the insignificant, it perhaps aspires to diminish (though it can never avoid) the anxieties that go with trying to con-

---

27   Again, Alan Liu, in "Local Transcendence: Cultural Criticism, Postmodernism, and the Romanticism of Detail," *Representations* 32 (1990): 75–113, has made the extraordinarily astute observation that postmodernist rhetoric's predilection for synecdoche is intended to "redeem the *etc.* from the wasteland of endless syntagm" (86). There is always more to say, and to include, if we are serious about eschewing totalization and subordination. Taken literally, this would oblige us to endless listings and enumerations. The synecdoche thus appeals as a way of "transforming incompletion into the figure of fulfillment" (86), for avoiding (even as it invokes) a "crisis of incompletion" (90). The anecdote, I suggest, similarly suggests a larger unit that it refrains from specifying: whether a whole, or a list of parts. Frank Lentricchia, in *Ariel and the Police: Michel Foucault, William James, Wallace Stevens* (Madison: University of Wisconsin Press, 1988), 3–5, has some brilliant remarks on the consensus-building aspirations of the anecdote. For an effort at the methodological use of the anecdote, see Kenneth Burke, *A Grammar of Motives* (1945; reprint, Berkeley and Los Angeles: University of California Press, 1969), 59–61, 323–26.

struct anything called *history* from within the predicament of modernity, a predicament that has as one of its constitutive principles the impossibility of an unsituated knowledge.

Samuel Johnson, again as reported by Boswell, this time in Boswell's journal account of the trip to the Hebrides, pronounced himself fond of anecdotes: "I love anecdotes. I fancy mankind may come, in time, to write all aphoristically, except in narrative; grow weary of preparation, and connection, and illustration, and all those arts by which a big book is made. If a man is to wait till he weaves anecdotes into a system, we may be a long time in getting them, and get but few, in comparison of what we might get."[28] It is once again tempting to propose the unlikely Johnson as the first postmodern, a Nietzsche before his time, here declaring a distaste for the master narrative and the "big book."[29] I would not make the case in quite this way, but I do mean to suggest that there is a continuity worth pondering in this coincidence, and that it reflects, again, a continuous inhabiting of the culture of modernity, which includes among its resources and/or sleights of hand the very subculture of conversation I have been describing. Before his untimely death Joel Fineman had made an exemplary beginning to a history of the anecdote, stimulated by its occurrence as a standard resource in the new historicism that was beginning to be all around him. He had begun a history that was in turn formal and historiographic, and he had taken the case back to ancient Greece, at the same time highlighting its reinvention or reemphasis in the essay form perfected by Francis Bacon.[30]

Each of these origins is credible as part of the story, part of the

---

28   *Boswell's Life of Samuel Johnson, Including a Journal of His Tour to the Hebrides etc.*, ed. John Wilson Croker (London: John Murray, 1839), 4:31.

29   For Nietzsche's case against Hegelian history and grand narratives, and his preference for a "loving absorption in the empirical data," see *Untimely Meditations*, 92–93.

30   Joel Fineman, "The History of the Anecdote," in *The Subjectivity Effect in Western Literary Tradition: Essays toward the Release of Shakespeare's Will* (Cambridge: MIT Press, 1991), 59–87. Fineman's thesis is in many ways an exact anticipation of mine. He too, for instance, offers the anecdote as "the literary form that uniquely *lets history happen* by virtue of the way in which it introduces an opening into the teleological, and therefore timeless, narration of beginning, middle and end. The anecdote produces the effect of the real, the occurrence of contingency, by establishing an event as an event within and yet without the framing context of historical successivity" (72). His absence from further conversation, along with that of Benjamin, is deeply regretted.

required information. But, again, it is in the eighteenth century (or thereabouts) that the anecdote becomes a compulsive mode of representation, whatever its longer-durational emergence or residual presence might be said to be (I would not argue against and will indeed later endorse the Renaissance as a good place to begin to describe what I have been calling modernity). Anecdotes, or anas, as they were also called (hence *Thraliana, Johnsoniana*) were everywhere. The editor of Spence's *Anecdotes* has noted that, with the distinguished exceptions of Drummond and Selden, "attempts to record actual conversation had been rare in England before Spence began to do so about 1727," while between 1769 and the end of the century "the genre became a literary rage, and more than a hundred titles containing 'Anecdote' reached the public, several of them extending to five volumes or more."[31] John Nichols's *Literary Anecdotes of the Eighteenth Century,* published in 1812, ran to 6,580 pages.[32]

The eighteenth century also saw a major theorization of the anecdote: Isaac D'Israeli's *Dissertation on Anecdotes* (1793). D'Israeli relates the plausibility of the anecdote to the culture of subjectification: "Our hearts have learnt to sympathise," so that we look to history "as a son and a brother would turn over his domestic memoirs" and no longer as might a mere "dull antiquary."[33] The anecdote brings history to life: as we read the "minute circumstances" of Milton's life as collected by Richardson, "we seem to live with him" (56). We understand human nature not by its grand appearances, but by the "minute springs and little wheels" (30) that anecdotes reveal. And as we read them over, we ourselves are brought to life, given *presence.* We do indeed seem to speak with the dead, and in so doing bring ourselves to life: "A skilful writer of anecdotes, gratifies by suffering us to make something that looks like a discovery of our own; he gives a certain activity to the mind, and the reflections appear to arise from ourselves. He throws unperceivably seeds, and we see those flowers start up, which we believe to be of our own creation" (30). Wordsworth's "Anecdote for Fathers," perhaps

31   Joseph Spence, *Observations, Anecdotes, and Characters of Books and Men, Collected from Conversation,* ed. James M. Osborn (Oxford: Clarendon Press, 1966), 1:xviii, xxi.

32   John Nichols, *Literary Anecdotes of the Eighteenth Century,* ed. Colin Clair (Carbondale: Southern Illinois University Press, 1967), 17.

33   Isaac D'Israeli, *A Dissertation on Anecdotes* (1793; reprint, New York: Garland, 1972), 4–5.

the first major poem to use the word in its title, functions in exactly this way, by providing an account of an incident whose meaning can be supposed only after active deciphering in the mind of an alerted reader. We too come alive. The whole romantic enterprise of aggressively stimulating a reader's response may be understood as a larger version of the anecdotal moment.[34] Its ethical-aesthetic motivation is drawn from and expressed in the commitment to (Protestant) self-making—the same syndrome that Stephen Greenblatt has found in the Renaissance—and has its antecedent in the tradition of Puritan confessionals. To make significant meaning out of fragments or anecdotes is to make a self for ourselves in the very act of so making. In this way we individuate ourselves within a culture whose premises otherwise deny individuation (a denial reproduced in some versions of the notorious postmodern "death of the subject"). At the same time the anecdotal gesture is one of rendering its object familiar and ordinary. As D'Israeli says, when we look "for the characters of eminent persons in their domestic privacies" rather than "in their public audiences," then we see that these "eminent personages are not so remotely removed from the level of ordinary humanity as the vulgar conceive" (16). In its two functions, the one stimulating self-activity in the reader and the other imaging its object as familiar and companionable, the anecdote provides one of the major requirements of a middle-class ideology: a sense of difference in sameness. But the self-active reader is still offered an experience of upward mobility in encountering the anecdote, albeit a diminished and domesticated one. The object, after all, is still exceptional enough to be worthy of anecdotal memory, and as such offers us all the prospect that we too might, with a small step, achieve something worthy of similar recollection.

This gesture of making ordinary while preserving some vestige or prospect of exceptionality is, I suggest, comparable with (because elemental within) the entire enterprise of the aesthetic, and thus of "literature," within modernity. The aesthetic was theorized most precisely in Kant's *Critique of Judgment*, where its definitional integrity consists in an absolute freedom from empirical interest; as such it is available in

---

34 On this topic, see my *Irony and Authority in Romantic Poetry* (London: Macmillan, 1979) and, on the Wordsworth poem, "Public Virtues, Private Vices: Reading between the Lines of Wordsworth's 'Anecdote for Fathers,'" in *Subject to History: Ideology, Class, Gender,* ed. David Simpson (Ithaca and London: Cornell University Press, 1991), 163–90.

the same way to everyone from prince to pauper. It is a special experience, not part of the common flow of daily life, but it creates, when it occurs, a community of taste among those who participate in it. Literature works in a different way, but to the same end of social accommodation and adjustment. It is not free of interest, since it encourages a desire to be someone or experience something else: it works through fantasy. But its form of interest is sympathy; that is, it stimulates an interest that draws together rather than separating persons of different social rank. (This is brilliantly operative in Byatt's *Possession*, discussed in my final chapter.) The result is the same: to provide an imaginary alternative freedom to the unfreedoms of everyday life. The accommodationist outcome of the anecdote is made clear by D'Israeli when he remarks that by its means the reader "discovers that, like himself, the sublimest geniuses have frequently stretched the bow without force, and without skill" (31). At these moments, which anecdotes reveal, they are just like us. There is nothing to envy, and everything with which to sympathize. But D'Israeli also signals an awareness of the fantasy fulfillment implied in the anecdote: "Are we not all desirous of joining the society of eminent men?" (50). Their works might be too abstruse to allow us to do so, but their "conversations" are more accessible and often, says D'Israeli, "more genuine" (51). They tell us that "genius is not above the little consolations of humanity" (59); that we too can live, for a time, with genius.

If one of the major tasks of eighteenth-century Britain was to come to terms with the continued existence of residual and emergent elites—and if this had always been a fact of social life, one might suppose it to have been more excessively so during a century of commercialization and empire building—then one can perhaps regard the anecdote, along with the literary mode of which it was a part, as playing a significant role in this coming to terms, in its work of making everyone seem ordinary and open to sympathetic identification, without diminishing the claim we would all like to make to potential exceptionality. Samuel Johnson recommended the incidents of private life as material for publication exactly because in them the empathic imagination works best: "we are all prompted by the same motives, all deceived by the same fallacies, all animated by hope, obstructed by danger, entangled by desire, and seduced by pleasure."[35] The writer of

---

35 Samuel Johnson, "The Rambler, no. 60," in *Essays from the "Rambler," "Adventurer,"*

anecdotes, D'Israeli tells us, must "possess a portion of that genius which he records" (82), just as does the reader finding meanings that feel as if they are his or her "own creation" (30). Everyone comes together under the happy aegis of the anecdote, as if within a well-rounded conversation. Significantly, the means for thus coming together are casual and unforced, emerging from the flow of natural spirits and not from the efforts of theory. D'Israeli writes that the "science of human nature, like the science of physics, was never perfected till vague theory was rejected for certain experiment" (27). Anecdote provides the experimental dimension that moral science might otherwise overlook. Very much in the spirit of D'Israeli's remark about physics, Lorraine Daston has argued that the appeal of "facts" in Baconian circles was dependent less on perceived fidelity to nature than on the desire to avoid the divisive effects of "theory."[36] Among the gentlemen of the Royal Society the imagined prerequisite for technological progress was a circle of convivial and mutually respectful experimenters in more or less constant conversation. In the sphere of inexact knowledges—the sphere of culture and literature—the same desiderata become the mechanisms for social and aesthetic consensus. Lacoue-Labarthe and Nancy see in the anecdote exactly what the Baconians, according to Daston, saw in facts: "the absolutely empirical essentiality of the empirical."[37]

D'Israeli's gesture "against theory" should seem familiar enough to observers of the postmodern, and critics of the new historicism have taken issue with its use of the anecdote on precisely these grounds.[38] Coleridge, in trying to rescue theory from its radical, revolutionary associations, and in seeking to present his own life as a systematically exemplary identity that was more than mere contingent personality,

and "Idler," ed. W. J. Bate (New Haven and London: Yale University Press, 1968), 111.

36   Daston, "Baconian Facts," 349.

37   Philippe Lacoue-Labarthe and Jean-Luc Nancy, *The Literary Absolute: The Theory of Literature in German Romanticism,* trans. Philip Barnard and Cheryl Lester (Albany: State University of New York Press, 1988), 60.

38   See, among others, Jean E. Howard, "The New Historicism in Renaissance Studies," *English Literary Renaissance* 16 (1986): 13–43; and Walter Cohen, "Political Criticism of Shakespeare," in *Shakespeare Reproduced: The Text in History and Ideology,* ed. Jean E. Howard and Marion F. O'Connor (London: Methuen, 1987), 18–46.

took issue with the culture of anas and of merely empirical verification in the sphere of the literary judgment. [39] *Biographia Literaria* is a prophetic recognition of the problems that literary criticism has subsequently had to confront when it aspires to any describable method: it cannot afford to bypass the fact of situatedness, of personality, even when it seeks to move beyond it. We may surmise that postmodernism's choice against theory is made, when it is thus made, within a general literary culture encouraging exactly such a choice and finding its long-durational persuasions, latent in modernity itself, reinforced by more recent anxieties inspiring a new turn to the literary culture for their articulation. The general culture, indeed, may be pervaded by the literary, at least in its nonscientific incarnations. Or at least we may say that it is hard to argue for absolute demarcations between the humanities "disciplines." Despite the strenuous differentiation of poetry from history made by Sidney and Shelley in invoking the power of imagination against the trammels of mere fact, our notion of literature has seldom been content with its purely arbitrary, unempirical status (hence the radical challenge of surrealism) any more than history has proved willing or able to abandon the embellishments of style and substance conventionally associated with the literary. This is especially apparent in the eighteenth century, when literature makes more and more efforts (led by what we call the novel, but not only in the novel) to describe the real lives of ordinary persons. Verisimilitude jostles against allegory for pride of place, and what emerges has to have, if it is to hope for any general acceptance, some relation to what is recognizable as "life," as well as an emblematic potential that is not merely circumstantial or trivial.

Literature, then, must have something of history about it, but it cannot wholly become history without losing its own generic identity or appeal. Hence we have the anecdote, the item of history that, as I have said, is convincing enough to come across as real at the same time as it dramatizes the act of telling and requires an act of interpretation or application. A similar series of pressures and potentials may be traced in the emergence of the aphorism as a viable technique for doing philosophy. Johnson, we recall, had proposed the aphoristic style as an alternative to the "big book." Friedrich Schlegel made it the mode of philosophy, very much in the spirit that Nietzsche and Wittgenstein

39 Coleridge, *Biographia Literaria*, 1:48.

would later reflect. This is the philosophy with which the postmodern spirit feels most compatible, and which it most commonly invokes as its own precursor. Lukács regarded the aphorism as the mode appropriate to a philosophy able to perceive a new social development "only in embryo" while still "striving for an intellectual grasp" of what is to come.[40] But its recent justification has been more affirmatively announced as subversive of some or other master narrative, and as a refusal of the goal Lukács had set for it. Adorno has remarked on the threat that the aphorism poses to a totalizing or dialectical method, which must abhor "anything isolated."[41] But it is not enough to choose sides, as if one could be for the aphorism, or anecdote, and against the master narrative, or theory. My argument here is intended to work toward a renewal of attention to the general, to the larger (whether or not master) historical model within which the postmodern can be made sense of, precisely by showing the historicality of our compulsive attention to particularities. Even Hegel, the great Satan against whom (or whose apparitions) so much postmodern righteousness is directed, saw the need for a concession to the norms of his (and our) age. In a system wherein "the share in the total work of Spirit which falls to the individual can only be very small," something must be offered to "the earnestness of life in its concrete richness."[42] The little guy must be acknowledged, and it is the kinds and consequences of such acknowledgment that drive the debate between particular and general, item and system, that dominates both the modern and postmodern rhetorics. In these times we are all little guys.

Anyone who has read this far is probably already aware that I am moving toward some sort of decision about the periodization of the academic postmodern by way of an account of its methods and their histories. I have suggested some continuities, within the long-durational period of modernity, between the postmodern and its

40   Georg Lukács, *The Destruction of Reason*, trans. Peter Palmer (Atlantic Highlands, NJ: Humanities Press, 1981), 323.

41   Adorno, *Minima Moralia*, 16. Compare Victor Shklovsky, *Theory of Prose*, trans. Benjamin Sher (Elmwood Park, IL: Dalkey Archive, 1990), 207: "A plot schema with a resolution is a rare thing in anecdotes. This is an accidental affliction of the material itself, which connects with the schema only at one point."

42   G. W. F. Hegel, *Phenomenology of Spirit*, trans. A. V. Miller (Oxford: Clarendon Press, 1979), 45, 3.

past—a past that it itself represses or disavows in order to lay claim to recognition as the new. [43] I confess that I cannot see much that is new in the articulation of this academic postmodernism, though as I have said there may well be others—in architecture or the visual arts—that require different terms of analysis than those I have offered here. This does not of course mean that there can be nothing new in the conditions within which the postmodern method is taking shape. It just means that, if there is such a shift in the conditions, then we have not yet caught up with them. All too often, history and the aesthetic (or, more to my point, the academic) are made to march together, as if we need not contemplate the possibility of an uneven development, or even an arrested development. Thus Fredric Jameson, one of the most persuasive theorists of an original component to the postmodern, looks for "a periodizing concept whose function is to correlate the emergence of new formal features in culture with the emergence of a new type of social life and a new economic order" and finds a "new postmodernism" expressive of "the inner truth of that newly emergent social order of late capitalism."[44] It may be that this correspondence of a new artistic form with a new historical reality can indeed be traced in the creative arts, and in a radical postmodern where pastiche replaces parody, and so on, in the sense that Jameson proposes. But the evidence for the academic postmodern of which I have been speaking is rather different. Here the history seems more constant, and if its present articulation is not wholly and simply a repetition—for it can seldom be that—then it is still dominantly contained within a set of methodological preferences long established within modernity.[45]

The storytelling and conversing and anecdotalizing that is going on across the academic profession and especially in its humanities departments is then, I am arguing, historically original only in its institutional intensity, and not in its intrinsic formation. But the endurance of

---

43 I am not the first or the only one to call for such a history. Joel Fineman began the task, and Alan Liu and Brook Thomas have also made exemplary contributions in their already-cited publications.

44 Jameson, "Postmodernism and Consumer Society," 113.

45 Even in arguing for a radical postmodernism, Jameson suggests that "radical breaks between periods do not generally involve complete changes of content but rather the restructuration of a certain number of elements already given" (ibid., 123). One might see academic storytelling as a return to latent traditions temporarily discredited by the heydays of New Criticism, deconstruction, and other impersonal theoreticisms.

this formation should suggest that it has served a definite function, one not simply to be scorned or wished away, since we do not yet have a solution to the problems they are designed to make us forget. In everyday life we function mostly without the need to distinguish knowledge from mere habit. But the intellectual, in the Enlightenment definition, is supposed to discriminate between knowledge and habit, truth and ideology, fact and fiction. Since we have widely accepted the inability of the professional intellectual to continue to apply these distinctions, we are left searching for other kinds of legitimation. (This acceptance is not universal, but it does characterize the majority of professional humanists in the United States and in some other anglophone contexts.)[46] Hence the storytelling mode, which is one such effort at compensation. To tell stories is to seek to reinstate oneself in a preprofessional culture, so that the recourse to anecdote and conversation may well be the academic postmodernist's version of the fiction of the "common reader"; it is at least a clear reaction against the kinds of professional impersonality applauded by the likes of I. A. Richards—who notoriously distrusted the appeal to biography—and Paul de Man.[47]

Above all, the turn to conversation is an alternative to a lonely effort at truth, an effort we no longer believe that we can make without error or frustration. This conviction is a sort of condition of inquiry, and its traces appear in much of the significant work that is being done now. To take but three among many possible examples: the editors of a recent collection devoted to the now massive publishing industry of autobiographical criticism see themselves as "identifying and initiating conversations" and hope "to call forth more voices out of the void."[48] There can be no whole, no totalized system, as long as we are dealing with real lives, and so the proper ambition is one of continual accumulation without closure. The anthropologist Ruth Behar expresses

46   For a strong statement of an alternative, see Aijaz Ahmad, *In Theory: Classes, Nations, Literatures* (London and New York: Verso, 1992), which declares a position quite outside the Anglo-American professional-metropolitan consensus about postmodernity.

47   Thus Cornel West, in *The American Evasion of Philosophy*, 199–200, stresses the force of Rorty's account of the dilemmas of "academic philosophy" as a disciplinary formation. This is not, I would add, to be construed as at all identical with the application of Rorty's model to a description of how things might be in the world.

48   Diane P. Freedman, Olivia Frey, and Frances Murphy Zauhar, eds., *The Intimate Critique: Autobiographical Literary Criticism* (Durham and London: Duke University Press, 1993), 10.

huge hopes for the conversational gesture: "At a time when the act of talking across a table with someone quite different from you and listening, really listening, has become so difficult, maybe this book about the encounter of two translated women can be a gesture toward peace." She concludes that such gestures can help us "get beyond the self/other division that has marked Western thinking" and are thus "the best hope we have for liberating anthropology from the legacy of its links to colonizing domination."[49] Rather more modestly Gerald Graff, in his *Beyond the Culture Wars*, looks to establish the habit of conversation in the classroom, a "cultural or disciplinary conversation, a process not unlike an initiation into a social club." Graff wants to replace the isolated reiteration of prepared positions with a more dialogic education. What can at best emerge from this is, as he describes it, a level of compromise and understanding of alternatives: a good conversation, where the loudmouths learn to listen and the shy to speak up.[50] Such recourses to conversation are now everywhere, and for very good reasons. As the storyteller tells his or her own story in hopes that it will be recognized by others, so the conversation is the place where all have a space to tell and to listen.

The impasse of speculation that these conventions (and that of the anecdote) are deployed to sidestep was elegantly and prophetically described by David Hume at the end of the first book of his *Treatise of Human Nature* (1739), as he took stock of the "leaky weather-beaten vessel" upon which he must navigate all philosophical seas.[51] Hume describes how the vocation of philosopher alienates him from his fellow men and provides him with an inward life made up only of "doubt and ignorance" (264). The insight into how much of our so-called knowledge is based in imagination, and thus "merely in ourselves" (266), seems to leave us only a choice "betwixt a false reason and none at all" (268). It is at this point that "nature" takes a hand and leads the philosopher's addled brain to amiable company: "I dine, I play a game of back-gammon, I converse, and am merry with my friends" (269).

49 Ruth Behar, *Translated Woman: Crossing the Border with Esperanza's Story* (Boston: Beacon Press, 1993), xi, 302.

50 Gerald Graff, *Beyond the Culture Wars: How Teaching the Conflicts Can Revitalize American Education* (New York and London: Norton, 1992), 77, 58–59.

51 David Hume, *A Treatise of Human Nature*, ed. L. A. Selby-Bigge (Oxford: Clarendon Press, 1973), 263.

No sooner has the social therapy run its course, however, than Hume finds himself inclined to philosophy once again, and the whole cycle repeats itself.

Conversation, then, is not quite enough for Hume, who images himself as still compulsively driven to solitary speculation in hopes of finding something true. The implication is that the realm of knowledge is best aspired to alone rather than in the negotiations of the conversation. In other words, Hume here replicates at once the alienation of critical thought and the compensatory pleasures of conversation, but without suggesting that the one is the other. He is not, at this moment, yet convinced of the essentially and entirely socialized constitution of important knowledge; he is not *content* with the model of conversation—and for him the model might well have been the eroticized one of the Socratic dialogue—as alone sufficient for its production. In this way he anticipates the contemporary culture of conversation without simply approving it. And he makes clear that the appeal of conversation is natural and social, that it is a means of mitigating alienation and of achieving (or at least briefly experiencing) identity.

The mitigation of alienation and the experience of identity, along with the deferral of the acceptance of death itself, may then be the desires whose admission might lead to some pertinent explanation of the contemporary culture of storytelling. Both of these preoccupations are significantly historical, however long-term the history might be, and however natural they might seem. (Exemplary moralizations within Greek culture, for instance, emphasize the effort at acceptance rather than avoidance of death.) As we academicians embrace once again what Benjamin thought had gone forever, the telling of stories, are we perhaps looking to create the public sphere whose disappearance another side of our inquiries tells us so much about? Ironies abound, of course, since our stories are usually intended for printed publication and seldom for the pure immediacy of oral consumption, although it is the name and addition of oral experience that is proclaimed. Within these limits, nonetheless, the gesture of storytelling often looks like familiarization, as if we were thus able to reach out even beyond (but definitely into) the lecture room and bring together all the different interests we know (by the critical act of *de*familiarization that is another part of our professionalized understanding) to be out there, our disbeliefs willingly suspended by the spell of fabulation. If this is so, then storytelling, while riding high on the back of the

postmodern endorsement of an undifferentiated culture (no high culture, no low culture), may also perform a covertly reactionary task for
those who tell and those who hear. The story empowers its hearers as
it—in Benjamin's phrase—lifts "the burden of demonstrable explanation" from the teller and makes space for "interpretation." But the listener, as long as his or her "relationship to the storyteller is controlled
by his interest in retaining what he is told" ("Storyteller," 96, 97), can
also pass on the task of interpretation to others. Listener becomes
teller in the act of retention for the purposes of repetition; interpretation is always deferred; and in the cycle of repetitions our own lives
become the story.[52] We voice ourselves into presence, against the
grain of a critical-historical analysis—Adorno's or Derrida's, for instance
—that tells us that we have no authentic access to such presence. The
performed mode of storytelling, in which the burden of meaning is
passed on for further passing on, then becomes an act of transference
or self-projection as much as an effort at consensus. Not for nothing,
perhaps, have we invented a category of so-called third-world literature based on magical realism—recall the extraordinary international-
anglophone success of García Márquez's *One Hundred Years of Solitude*
and of such novels as Salman Rushdie's *Midnight's Children*—whose narrative integrity is imagined to consist in its quality of storytelling.
Such literature is our desired other, and is used to create a paradigm for
domestic adoption as if we are truly taking something from the outside, from a world we have lost, and not from a facsimile we have con-
spired to help create.[53]

There is then a way in which the commitment to storytelling is at
odds with the culture of conversation in the general syndrome of the
academic postmodern. Both, as I have said, are images of vocalization,
of living speech in the place of dead letters. But if storytelling tends
toward charismatic repetition—one listens, spellbound, and then
repeats—conversation retains the aura of exchange and mutual rec-

52 Thus Ruth Behar, *Translated Woman*, 13: "I have tried to make clear that what I am
reading is a story, or set of stories, that have been told to me, so that I, in turn, can tell
them again, transforming myself from a listener into a storyteller." Thus the apparent
modesty of the confession of narrativity leads into the fantasy (an immodest one, in
today's world) of seamless inclusion and permissible authority: the authority of the teller
of tales.

53 See Ahmad, *In Theory*, 125–26.

ognition. Many professionalized academicians are rather poor con-
versationalists, in the classic sense. Few of us are good at strenuous
listening, though most of us are delighted to talk about ourselves, our
own work. There is about our professional exchanges a good deal of
what De Quincey found in Coleridge: *one*versazione. The zealous references to conversation as the "new" academic norm may well then be
fantasy formations about how we wish things to be, or still think that
they should be: preprofessional, prealienated, and immune to the limitations of the empire of the self. Dialogue as a literary-philosophical
genre more or less went out with the eighteenth century. Hugh Blair
was clear about the challenges it posed to the writer, "for it requires
more than merely the introduction of different persons speaking in
succession. It ought to be a natural and spirited representation of real
conversation; exhibiting the character and manners of the several
speakers, and suiting to the character of each, that peculiarity of
thought and expression which distinguishes him from another."[54] It
required, in other words, a genuine impersonality and disinterest, and
a Shakespearean immersion in the world of another: the ultimate conversational grace. The question remains, then, whether the contemporary commitment to conversation can be a genuine re-creation of
this vanished sacrifice to modernization, or whether it is, to use the
postmodern's own category against itself, mere pastiche, rather like
Frank Gehry's delightful notion, as reported by Jameson, of getting
"into a dialogue with the old house" (*Postmodernism*, 109).

But the culture of storytelling and of conversation, and of the autobiographical literary criticism that is so prominent within it at the
moment, along with the proliferation of anecdote, does hold together
as part of an effort at immersing criticism back into literature—into
the literature from which, I have suggested, it has never fully emerged
—often with that almost audible sigh of relief at the accompanying
retreat from "theory" that goes with a reidentification with what is
thought of as truly literary. I have suggested that literature as we know
it was constituted precisely to serve the needs of an emerging social
unit, one we might loosely call a middle class, and to mediate between
and make accessible the properties not previously identified with that
class. Bourdieu and Passeron describe the seventeenth-century French

---

54   Hugh Blair, *Lectures on Rhetoric and Belles Lettres* (Philadelphia: Troutman & Hayes,
1853), 411.

image of the *honnête homme* as an image of politeness, and as consisting in

> the disdain for specialization, trades and techniques, the bour-
> geois transposition of the contempt for business; the pre-
> eminence conferred on the art of pleasing, that is, the art of
> adapting oneself to the diversity of social encounters and con-
> versations; the attention devoted to nuances and imponder-
> ables, perpetuating the aristocratic tradition of "refinement" and
> expressed in the subordination of scientific to literary culture,
> and of literary culture to artistic culture. [55]

Norbert Elias has written even more pertinently on the evolution of bourgeois *civilité* from aristocratic *courtoisie* as critical to the precipita-tion of the modern from the medieval social hierarchy, a process that simultaneously creates a position for the independent intellectual and disciplines the otherwise potentially disruptive ambitions of others into a self-enforced code of polite behavior. [56]

In this general cultural project of accommodation, literature played a primary role. Castiglione's spokesperson Federico Fregoso, in a work that is itself a grand conversation, specified the courtier as one who "should know how to refresh and charm the minds of his listeners . . . in such a way that, without ever being tedious or boring, he is always a source of pleasure." The two modes of this pleasuring are, moreover, very close to those I have been describing as storytelling and anecdote: the "long narrative" and the recourse to "sayings," also called "dicta" or "quips." [57] Very similar categories are approved for po-etry in Sir Philip Sidney's *Apology for Poetry*, published in 1595. Not only is poetry prior to and constitutive of history and philosophy, but it is the norm to which they must approximate if they are not to bore us or divide us one from another according to the limitations of expertise. The historian is otherwise committed to "old mouse-eaten records" that make him "a tyrant in table talk" and a zealot of the merely empiri-cal from which we can draw "no necessary consequence." At the other

---

55   Bourdieu and Passeron, *Reproduction*, 130.

56   Norbert Elias, *The History of Manners: The Civilizing Process*, trans. Edmund Jephcott (New York: Pantheon, 1978), 1:70–84.

57   Baldasar Castiglione, *The Book of the Courtier*, trans. George Bull (Harmondsworth: Penguin Books, 1976), 151–52.

extreme the philosopher operates entirely by general precept and "bare rule," without the enlivening adornment of example. Thus "both, not having both, do both halt" (105–7). The poet or man of letters, is, in other words, a master of good conversation, and poetry as a genre here mediates between theory and instance in much the same way as does the anecdote in good conversation. Where historian and philosopher are confined by narrow method, the poet is "freely ranging only within the zodiac of his own wit" (100). He is the "right popular philosopher" (109) because he is a "homely and familiar" figure and, like Menenius Agrippa and Nathan the prophet, he is a storyteller (115). He breaks down the boundaries between specialized psychologies by making something we can all enjoy, at the same time leaving space for our self-makings and thus for our experience of the exercise of a certain sort of power.

All of this, and more, seems to me to be behind the currently popular academic culture of storytelling, with its deployment of the conventions of anecdote and conversation. I have said that there is in this embrace something deeply motivated, something that includes a desire to forestall death itself. This too, for all its apparent universality, is a historical condition. People have not always sought to deny death, or spent their time finding ways to outwit mortality. We have already seen Gadamer, in *Truth and Method*, imagining a "truly infinite conversation" (493) spoiled only by death (or perhaps not, for certain sorts of resurrectionists). Why should the apparent unacceptability of mortality signify so powerfully in the culture of conversation? Marx and Adorno might propose that the force of this component lies in our historical condition of death-in-life. And Marshall Berman has remarked on the urgency of conversation and dialogue as functions of a modern condition in which subjectivity is more isolated as it is more developed and rewarded.[58] Certainly such an analysis tells us much about the eviscerated solidarities of the academy, which linger on in ghostly form if they are apparent at all. And it perhaps helps explain (though it should not be thought of as a single or primary explanation) the *erotic* component of literature as a genre within modernity, which is committed to sympathy and connection, and the similarly erotic aura around the culture of conversation. The erotic component is never more than highly implicit in, for instance, the writings of Richard Rorty, but it is

58   Marshall Berman, *All That Is Solid Melts into Air: The Experience of Modernity*, 2d ed. (Harmondsworth: Penguin, 1988), 8–9.

latent nonetheless. One of the early senses of the term *conversation* was, until the eighteenth century, sexual intercourse, along with an extended sense of "living together, commerce" and of "conducting oneself in the world" (*OED* 3, 2, 6). The etymology of *anecdote* also, in its inclusion of the idea of secret knowledge and of access to what is intimate and unpublished, contains a distinct (though more domesticated) erotic implication. The metaphysics of modernity thus define themselves in terms of an individuated response—the erotic—for overcoming or working against the generic alienation of each from all that accompanies the political economy of that same modernity.

Might this general condition, within which it is hard to divide the metaphysical from the instrumental, the self-making from the self-dividing, help to account for the noticeable popularity of the conversational paradigm as a significant critical mode among our most distinguished literary critics? Bourdieu and Passeron have observed that the French educational system in general is marked by a "well-nigh absolute preponderance" given to "oral transmission" over "other techniques of inculcation or assimilation," and see in this, among other things, the "bourgeois transposition of contempt for business" revealed in the alternative preference for "the art of pleasing" and of "conversation."[59] Thus they are able to explain why it is that a form of communication as low on information as is literary pedagogy can still be so cherished and deemed functional (107–8).[60] The pedagogic effort in the arts is thus, from this perspective, designed to efface the appearance of effort itself. The high point of this tendency, particularly timely during a period of anxiety or insecurity about professionalism, is perhaps the noticeable popularity of the interview. To disavow the labor of the article or book for the immediacy of the interview is of course to put one on a footing with the rock stars and movie stars whose expressive norm in our culture is already that same interview, or printed conversation. But it is also access to presence and to voice, to the very things that Derrida told us long ago we were too much in love with, and must suspect if *critique* is to be possible. Roland Barthes himself, who did as much as anyone to disestablish conventional models of

59   Bourdieu and Passeron, *Reproduction*, 120, 130.

60   Bourdieu's *Homo Academicus*, 41, 44, shows that among all the disciplines the arts are the most narrowly reproductive; a higher proportion of arts professors are children of other arts professors than is the case in other disciplines.

subjectivity and authorization, made this clear in the volume devoted to his own interviews, in describing the place of the *"phatic* or inter-pellant function" in speech, whereby "we want our interlocutor to lis-ten to us." He supposed that speech (the interview) "is dangerous because it is immediate and cannot be taken back."[61] But in that danger is there not also a tremendous security, whereby by being thus in dan-ger one is real, important, not to be negated? (Jane Tompkins, we re-call, spoke of a "courage" involved in speaking of oneself.) To *write* the transcript of *speech*, as the interview does, is thus to have it both ways, to be available for posterity without any sacrifice to the pleasures and/or illusions of full presence. Its rhetoric of empirical confirmation can even promise a back way to the openly disavowed grand narrative, as it does for Ruth Behar in her interviews with Esperanza: "The book mirrors our movement through time and space. Every story and con-versation carries a date, for each telling took place on a particular night, not in a timeless vacuum, and was marked off in the flow of his-tory."[62] Even Bourdieu, who has specified the ideology of the inter-view in his critiques of reproduction, seems himself to have come round to its appeal as a pragmatic genre of (apparently) "provisional formulations."[63] The primacy of the spoken, of the interview mode, is indeed a reaction against technical definitions of the humanist's voca-tion (so that in America, for instance, it remains more prestigious in many universities to teach literature rather than composition). But it is also, and as such, an attempt to occupy living speech instead of dead letters. The bourgeois culture of preprofessional freedom, which I have been describing throughout this essay, is also to be seen within a general reaction on behalf of individuality against the scientific erasure of the observing subject, and against the modern and quite material alienations whose figure, made metaphysical, is that of death.

Barthes went one step farther than simply appealing to the voice. In his *Roland Barthes by Roland Barthes* he disavowed the conventional trap-pings of autobiography by invoking some of the convictions he had

61   Roland Barthes, *The Grain of the Voice: Interviews, 1969–1980,* trans. Linda Coverdale (Berkeley and Los Angeles: University of California Press, 1991), 4, 5.

62   Behar, *Translated Woman,* 14.

63   Bourdieu and Wacquant, *Invitation to Reflexive Sociology,* x, 222. The words are actu-ally Wacquant's, and may thus signify a certain pressuring of the question of the inter-view toward a confidence not fully authorized by Bourdieu himself.

made familiar: "Once I produce, once I write, it is the Text itself which (fortunately) dispossesses me of my narrative continuity. The Text can recount nothing; it takes my body elsewhere."[64] But whatever is written about text, in this text, is offset by the plethora of photographs, images that *present* Barthes with his family, on the beach, sitting in a seminar, and so on, and thus bring him to life. Nor is Derrida himself unmarked. For all its extraordinarily vertiginous attempts to dissolve autobiography in language, evolve it through language, Bennington's and Derrida's recent *Jacques Derrida* is also full of photographs, of facsimiles of presence. And however artfully we might want to undermine the authority of photography as offering any access to the real, these facsimiles remain effective as images of presence because of the contrast they provide to the ethereal intellectuality of the writing.[65]

Again, it is not then unreasonable for Stephen Greenblatt to wish to speak with the dead, and therefore to speak. I will return to this desire in my final chapter. Speaking with the dead may well be what literature teachers do, unless they are involved in cultural studies, which purport to speak with the living (and are thus in dialectical coexistence with their predecessors). Greenblatt goes on to explain, "This desire is a familiar, if unvoiced, motive in literary studies, a motive organized, professionalized, buried beneath thick layers of bureaucratic decorum: literature professors are salaried, middle-class shamans" (*Shakespearean Negotiations*, 1). Was Veblen right? Is he still right? I wonder if we are even this important, except to each other and thus to ourselves. Greenblatt recognized his term *negotiation* as a form of conversation, and he also came to see that among the voices he was hearing he had to hear his own (20). The bureaucratic decorum he claimed to find was already wearing thin when Greenblatt published his book, in 1988. Now it is hard to find at all. I suppose, in trying as I have done to suggest a history for the methodological choices of academic postmodernism, and thereby to correct that postmodernism's preference for forgetting or denying all histories, I am bringing up the dead in hopes of speaking with the living, who are otherwise, as the next chapter will show, speaking largely with themselves.

64 Roland Barthes, *Roland Barthes by Roland Barthes*, trans. Richard Howard (New York: Farrar, Strauss & Giroux, 1989), fourth page of unpaginated preface.

65 Geoffrey Bennington and Jacques Derrida, *Jacques Derrida*, trans. Geoffrey Bennington (Chicago and London: University of Chicago Press, 1993).

Three

Speaking Personally:
The Culture of Autobiography
in the Postmodern

The return of the storyteller to the spoken and printed discourse of the contemporary academy has been paralleled, as we have seen, by a renewal of the rhetoric of anecdote and conversation in the writing of professional intellectuals, especially those in the humanities. Story and conversation are not precisely the same. Listening to stories holds us passive, even spellbound, awaiting the evolution of a narrative that we do not want to interrupt, while the conversational mode contributes to our sense of equal participation and mutual narration, as does the anecdote, which requires, for its accreditation as *sense*, the hearer's affirmation of its tact or relevance. But this distinction is not absolute. As I have said before, we listen passively to the story (and indeed the anecdote) with the covert intention of passing it on, of becoming ourselves the storyteller. Storytelling is thus deferred conversation, or conversation one at a time and through extended time. And despite the differences of temporality and apparent reciprocity, storytelling and conversation share one very important characteristic: they both foreground the living voice of speech, and the metaphysics of "presence" it produces. Their current popularity thus suggests that speech and presence are very much back in style, and by way of reaction against the deconstructive stringencies of the 1970s and early 1980s, which emphasized the primacy of writing and language—metaphorically "dead" forms—over the apparent spontaneities of lived experience and expression. Much of the motivation behind postmodernism's declaration of itself as "against theory" may be understood in this context. Indeed, even the mentors of the avant-garde of twenty years ago, Barthes and Derrida, are not, as we have seen, themselves immune from the images of presence as they explore and deploy—or have others deploy on their behalf—the signatures of physical life, of being alive.

What is revivified here as if in all historical innocence is one of the time-honored preferences of literary criticism and scholarship. Hiram Corson, who became a professor of English at Cornell in 1870, believed oral delivery—the ultimate gesture toward presence—to be the only sure guide to the authentic meaning of literature. For him (and Bourdieu would love this) the teacher's job is to communicate his *"being . . . and not his brain,"* along with the being of the author he is presenting, by "vocal interpretation."[1] Corson here keeps alive the connection of literary criticism with elocution, which the subsequent professionalization of the discipline has eroded but never quite destroyed. Three years later, in his defense of the very philology denigrated by Corson, Albert Cook would still cast it as a life-giving expertise, a bringing back to life, an attempt to "relive the life of the past; to enter by the imagination into the spiritual experiences of all the historic protagonists of civilization in a given period and area of culture; to think the thoughts, to feel the emotions, to partake the aspirations, recorded in literature."[2] Cook too, it is clear, intends to speak with the dead.

The rhetoric of presence took on a prophetic and influential form in the work of I. A. Richards, wherein it also became professionalized and rendered acceptable to a pedagogic avant-garde no longer vulnerable to accusations of amateurism and belletrism. *Science and Poetry,* first published in 1925, contains an important account of the value of reading poetry aloud, in order to "give the *full body,* as it were, to the words," since "it is with the full bodies of words that the poet works, not with their printed signs" (20). Richards has a psychologistic theory of poetic effect whereby the sounds and rhythms of good verse play upon our "interests" without primary reference to whatever sense the words might make. The modification and restoration of equilibrium effected by poetry happens primarily (though not exclusively) at the physiological level, like Aristotelian catharsis, though it may be accompanied by, and should encourage, precise semantic discriminations. The power of this experience, for Richards, does away with any anxieties we might have about whether we are reading what the poet intended us to read. The power of sound and rhythm "directly reflects

1 Cited in Gerald Graff and Michael Warner, eds., *The Origins of Literary Studies in America: A Documentary Anthology* (New York and London: Routledge, 1989), 92, 94.
2 Ibid., 99.

personality" and is "not separable from the words to which it belongs" (50). Thus the words are "the experience itself," not thoughts about or attitudes to some prior experience that we have to struggle to apprehend by some or other hermeneutic process (35). The reader in this way becomes the poet. Provided that the original experience is real (as Richards would say), then the reader "will reproduce in his mind a similar play of interests putting him for the while in a similar situation and leading to the same response" (35).

The condition of satisfaction for this solution to (or avoidance of) the hermeneutic problem is that the reader's response is primarily non-semantic, not dependent upon the exact meanings of words. The meanings Richards wants us to apprehend are indeed highly precise, but they are selected in response to "interests" rather than mere dictionary definitions or etymological researches, and they are adjudicated relationally and formally, in terms of their place in the whole system of the poem. It follows from this that the point of literary scholarship and teaching is to create (and to recreate) presence, and the past in the present: not so much speaking with the dead, but speaking *as* the dead, by way of the replication of the experience of balancing interests.

Richards himself was passionately cosmopolitan. But for other critics the pursuit of presence has meant not just access to an individual personality, a Shakespeare or a Milton, but participation in a national or racial energy of life and feeling, a great tradition. F. R. Leavis reconstructed English literary history around a model of presence wherein John Donne could remain "obviously a living poet in the most important sense" by virtue of his "use of the speaking voice and the spoken language."[3] Leavis regarded the benefits of a literary education as coming "only by working and living into it"; and this presentism brought with it a celebration of vitalist imperfection, beyond theory, in favor of an education "necessarily full of incompletenesses and imperfections."[4] The emphasis upon imperfection may be read as an acceptance of mortality; literature and its criticism become a sort of memento mori for the secular mind, a going to dusty death with the maximum of imagination. The infinite incompleteness of reading and interpreting

3   F. R. Leavis, *Revaluation: Tradition and Development in English Poetry* (1936; reprint, Harmondsworth: Penguin, 1967), 18–19.

4   F. R. Leavis, *Education and the University: A Sketch for an "English School,"* new ed. (London: Chatto & Windus, 1948), 37, 59.

signifies the worm in the bud, the unavoidable imperfection of life itself. But if this analogy implies an acquiescence in the fact of death, then it is also and maybe much more a compensatory celebration of presence, of situated humanness. In literature no one dies, and every transcribed life is reanimated in every act of reading. Two hundred years of references to such categories as character, feeling, sincerity, and personality have supported these aspirations to presence. They are the same categories we look for in amiable conversation, as Adam Smith made clear in his description of the best "style" in both writing *and* "conversation" as that which is "natural and easy," and authentically expressive of an individual's "genius and temper."[5] No one, in these matters, wants to be deceived. We prefer living spirits to dead letters, and, moreover, spirits that do not change their shape.

There is, then, a long-standing tradition in literary criticism collapsing past and present, self and other, the "in itself" and the "for us," into a synthesizing moment of excited reverie or presence. (This is the dynamic of Byatt's *Possession*, as we will see.) Frank Lentricchia has written insightfully of the survival, by way of the literary, of the image of "free selfhood" throughout the period of apparent antihumanist hegemony in recent theory.[6] In its more patiently theorized forms this emerges as hermeneutic theory in the manner of Gadamer, who recommends, as we have seen, carefully monitored conversations with the past and its traditions as a lived and experienced solution to the problem of authenticating knowledge. More exuberant versions of presence are more typical of the Anglo-American liberal tradition (for which even Gadamer is too bound up in "theory") and especially of the literary critics within that tradition. If we have, as professionals, become more and more embarrassed about the publication of Addisonian taste and Arnoldian touchstones, then we are still and perhaps now more than ever very much persuaded by the propriety of speaking personally and speaking for ourselves, in despite of or against any limiting theoretical constraints that might be (and have recently been) applied to the very notion of the "self."[7]

---

5   Smith, *Lectures on Rhetoric and Belles Lettres*, 55–56.

6   Lentricchia, *Ariel and the Police*, 89, 101–2.

7   Christopher Lasch long ago identified "pseudo-self-awareness" as a besetting cultural condition, along with a compulsion to "mere self-disclosure." See *The Culture of Narcissism: American Life in an Age of Diminishing Expectations* (New York: Norton, 1978), 17, 71–99.

The profession of subjectivity is of course a perfectly respectable and indeed unavoidable response to the apparent instabilities of knowledge production in the humanities (which already deal with inexact determinations). We now take for granted that, as Linda Alcoff has elegantly put it, "a speaker's location is epistemically salient."[8] Everything said about something or somebody else is said by a person in place and time, a person subject to conscious and unconscious interests and affiliations that complicate any aspiration toward generality, let alone objectivity. This has been a condition of humanist knowledge for a very long time, though it has often been contested or avoided. But it does not in itself require the conclusion that everything claimed in the way of knowledge is by definition knowledge only for the person speaking during the time of speaking. There is a subjective condition, but it is not the only condition. So the energy with which the habit of speaking personally is now taking over professionalized academic discourse suggests, I think, a weariness with professionalism itself, but also a revival of a particular kind of literary professionalism. In the long-durational sense, and within the broad history of modernity, it has been literature and its criticism that have carried this charge, positioning themselves as alternatives to the respective reifications of science, history, and philosophy, and to the whole culture of specialization and divided labor by which modernization has been achieved.

This residual energy has recently been strengthened by the postmodern turn against theory and against its traditionally rational-scientific aspirations. But instrumental reason is not the only or even the major enemy for the new apostles of speech and presence. They are reacting also against the radical skepticism that was, for the 1970s, the most readily identifiable form of "theory" (loosely called deconstruction, but also Marxism) and that threatened the assumption of presence in an a priori way. If instrumental reason seemed to threaten to take away that presence by the force of its repressions, then deconstruction proposed the even gloomier notion that there was nothing there to take away. In the present moment the revolt against theory thus does double duty, or takes aim at two different targets: the rationalism traditionally associated with theory, and the skepticism publicized by poststructuralist theory in particular. Neither created much

---

8   Linda Alcoff, "The Problem of Speaking for Others," *Cultural Critique* 20 (1991–92): 7.

discursive space for the display of feeling or affirmed the integrity of speaking personally.

I am of course unable to defend my right to speak of a *cult* of autobiography, though that was the word I started with in setting forth on the topic here explored. To do so would be to claim for myself some exemption from the determinations of subjectivity and situatedness, like some nineteenth-century explorer going out into the world's dark corners with a rationalist faith in the primitive status of alien forms of life. The better word is *culture*, for that is the word that signals that we are all in this together. But, at the same time, no culture is a simple construction, and disagreements are inevitable both within it and about it. It goes almost without saying that as I set about a critique of the culture of autobiography, with its "mock lyrists" and "large self-worshipers,"[9] I press the button that calls into question my own situatedness and my own life story. As I have said before, I intend to dodge that question here, not because it is not important or interesting (to me it is of course fascinating, and it is at the very least "epistemologically salient"), but because I am attempting to chronicle a tradition, one that contains me up to a point but one from which I also differ.[10] That is, when one understands the compulsion to autobiography not as a proven universal but as a strong determination within a specific subcultural tradition, that of the liberal individual in general and in particular within the institution of literary studies, then it is *not* obviously an obligatory gesture (though it is bound to be a persuasive one), even when one cannot establish an alternatively foundational presupposition to put in its place (for this would be to accept foundationalism

9 *John Keats: Complete Poems*, ed. Jack Stillinger (Cambridge and London: Harvard University Press, Belknap Press, 1978), 366.

10 Compare Bourdieu's effort at a "fundamentally anti-narcissistic" form of reflexivity, which produces the humbling knowledge that what appears exceptional turns out to be "shared, banal, commonplace." Bourdieu sees the confessional mode as providing ammunition to those who would reduce everything to relativism, even as it seems to reward "egomaniacal postures" as "approved of and even rewarded by the intellectual institution, especially in France." See Bourdieu and Wacquant, *Invitation to Reflexive Sociology*, 72, 202–3, 213–14. That the autobiographical mode is indeed unusually prominent among French intellectuals is one of the theses of Michael Sheringham's *French Autobiography: Devices and Desires* (Oxford: Clarendon Press, 1994). If true, this context sheds an ironic light on Alice Kaplan's *French Lessons: A Memoir* (Chicago and London: University of Chicago Press, 1993), which claims (or assumes) for itself a transgressive privilege in its address to anglophone academic readers.

itself). In other words, the contemporary notion that all knowledge claims must be accompanied by or seen as consisting in a rhetoric of speaking personally and saying where one is coming from has not yet been proven to be an epistemological ne plus ultra. That it is taken as such by so many intellectuals in the humanities is itself the question, not the solution.

There are of course good reasons for this. An awareness of the problems of situatedness has not been invented out of nowhere. What we are seeing is a heightened anxiety (which can sometimes look like celebration) about a precondition integral to modernity itself and handled in different ways by different subcultures over the last three or four hundred years. Conventionally this awareness has been conformable with the languages of literature and antithetical to those of the sciences. In the twentieth century the unprecedented attributes of science, economic, social, and cataclysmic, have led many to look harder than before at the situatedness of objectivist traditions and practices, while the corresponding professionalization of literary studies (with the coming of "theory") has set going a corresponding reemphasis on its inexact legacies and personalist components. But wherever one cuts the historical cake—whether with Descartes, with Hume, or with Hegel—it is hard to construct a definition of the modern that does not recognize the emergence of subjectivity as a philosophical and methodological problem. This might be seen as the inevitable consequence of a process whereby state and society adapted themselves and their discourses to an entrepreneurial culture, a privatized theology, and a legal system recognizing significant spheres of personal responsibility. Macpherson's important book *The Political Theory of Possessive Individualism* argues for modernity's coming into being along with the notion of the individual's proprietorship of his own person, his ownership of himself (male gender intended). His citation of Richard Overton's *Arrow against All Tyrants* (1646) suggests that the Levellers might have felt quite at home on today's university lecture circuit: "I may be but an Individuall, enjoy my selfe, and my selfe propriety, and may write my selfe no more than my selfe, or presume any further; if I doe, I am an encroacher & an invader upon another mans Right, to which I have no Right."[11] This is not quite equivalent to our habitual "let me tell you

---

11   C. B. Macpherson, *The Political Theory of Possessive Individualism: Hobbes to Locke* (1962; reprint, Oxford: Oxford University Press, 1983), 3, 140.

where I'm coming from," but it is a stage along that same road. Failure and success, virtue and vice, innocence and guilt, being and nonbeing, all become critically subjective. And as soon as there is subjectivity, there is the problem of subjectivity. It is there in the dalliance with solipsism and performativism in Descartes's *Discourse on Method*, and it explains why models of universal psychology are always most vigorously proposed when they are already and visibly collapsing (witness the short cycle from Kant through Hegel to Marx, Nietzsche, and Freud).[12]

Foucault illuminates the situation most elegantly and economically in his account of the "analytic of finitude" as the defining condition of modernity. He explains that all knowledge is thus positioned as both knowledge "in itself" (all that we have of it) and knowledge *production* from within bodies and minds in times and places.[13] As soon as knowledge is thus created by a knowing and living subject whose physical life is part of the picture, while the knowledge itself is also in and of temporality, then we are compelled to an endless concern about whether what we know is also known to others, whether it is real or phenomenal, and whether we can know anything about ourselves (for the unconscious also appears within this configuration, and it has not yet left us). One might wonder whether the very notion of the "self" depends for its existence on these *problems*, rather than on any original intuition, since it is so often the pursuit of solutions that justifies the supposition of an entity responsible for the problems in the first place.

Foucault locates the emergence of the "analytic of finitude" at the end of the Enlightenment and the turn of the nineteenth century. But we need not agree about an exclusive chronology to identify the syndrome as latent within and even typical of a longer-term modernity evolving two hundred years earlier and articulating a subjectivist "vanguard" by way of the languages of literature and its criticism. These languages have overemphasized the subjective moment by responding not just to a general historical condition but doing so within a discipline differentiated from others precisely by virtue of a commitment to

12   For an (overstated) account of the solipsistic tendency in Descartes, see my "Putting One's House in Order: The Career of the Self in Descartes' Method," *New Literary History* 9 (1977): 83–101.

13   See Michel Foucault, *The Order of Things: An Archaeology of the Human Sciences* (New York: Random House, 1973), 303–43.

personality and to presence. The contemporary reaffirmation of the culture of autobiography takes place within this long-term tradition whose very traditionality is obscured by the intensity of a reaction against theory and against method (that is, also against professionalism), one that appears to license the gesture of speaking personally as, once again, radically original.

An exemplary instance of this gesture is Jane Tompkins's well-known and widely reprinted essay "Me and My Shadow," which makes a radical case for the importance of the personal and for the association of the personal with the feminine and the feminist. Tompkins writes as follows about her long-standing discomfort with what she feels to be the norms of academic propriety: "The problem is that you can't talk about your private life in the course of doing your professional work. You have to pretend that epistemology, or whatever you're writing about, has nothing to do with your life, that it's more exalted, more important, because it (supposedly) *transcends* the merely personal. Well I'm tired of the conventions" (123). So, apparently, are a great many others, who now seem to regard the really important work of the literary critic as the production of his or her autobiography. Tompkins's claim is fascinating and bears much attention. It would be much harder for her to claim that the perceived constraints are unreasonable were she another kind of professional, and not a literary critic and teacher. We would not take kindly to paying our doctors or lawyers by the hour to hear about their personal lives and how they impinge on the diagnosis or the legal advice. Students, of course, are paying too. But they are anticipating engaging with a subculture that, while certainly professional, is also traditionally personalized, even governed by charisma (according to Veblen), and dominated by the oral relationship (according to Bourdieu). There is thus no perceived contradiction. Students may not yet know the conventions of which Tompkins is so tired, but they know they are not supposed to obey them. They are paying, in short, for an experience of professionalized bohemianism, and for an initiation into professional antiprofessionalism.

But not all of them. When I first read Tompkins's essay I couldn't imagine where she located the model of dry objectivism and masculinized impersonality with which to repress herself. My own students, I thought, are far readier to talk about themselves and how they feel about a text than to try to understand it by way of impersonal, technical vocabularies. Indeed, it is a constant surprise to me that the first can proceed quite happily without the second, and even at its expense. Not a few critiques of (say) Milton's ideology are produced without any engagement with Milton's grammar, theology, or politics. Students are still quite comfortable opining about the meanings of literature on the grounds that they see it that way, or because life is like that. At the same time, I went on to realize, Tompkins does have a point when one thinks of graduate school, much of the time in many places. New Critics, structuralists, and deconstructors have all successively taught us to describe how an "it" works, largely without any reference to an "us" doing the analysis. Professionalized criticism in the academy has made heavy use of the objectivist rhetoric. It has done so in part tó keep up with the scientific Joneses, to the extent that "research," a science-based term, is now used to describe all nonclassroom activity in the university. But it has also done so, I suggest, because preprofessional pedagogy has made such heavy use of the rhetoric of subjectivity, personality, and presence. Theory and objectivism (though the second has also been an undergraduate teaching orthodoxy) have functioned principally to distinguish graduate school from the rest of the humanities education. In this sense Tompkins's cri de coeur represents not an alternative to the profession but a tension within it. Literary criticism as a social-educational complex is neither wholly objectivist nor wholly personalized, but subsists by a seemingly inevitable struggle between the two, between a masculinized professionalism and a traditionally feminized subjectivism. Adherents of one camp or the other have proven, by their very tenacity, unable or unwilling to see the setup.

By defining objectivism as the besetting norm, which it is not, Tompkins can offer the private voice as a radical alternative. In fact, literary theorists and would-be objectivists have just as much empirical justification for casting themselves as marginalized minorities. In 1949 Wellek and Warren made the claim that "literary theory . . . is the great need of literary scholarship today," [14] and one has only to talk to textual editors, bibliographers, and historians of the language to find out what is most marginal in the profession of literary studies today. For Tompkins, however, it is the personal voice alone that can lay claim to existential heroism: "people are scared to talk about them-

14   René Wellek and Austin Warren, *Theory of Literature*, 3d ed. (Harmondsworth: Penguin Books, 1963), 19.

selves . . . they haven't got the guts to do it" (123).[15] The issue has very little to do with guts, I think, and much more to do with the relations between those guts and the minds or selves to which they are apparently but problematically attached. Tompkins is looking for a foundational self through speech, and, in Gerald MacClean's words, a "self that is capable of self-knowledge."[16] She is also looking for a revolutionary pedagogy. In a related essay she proclaims that "the classroom is a microcosm of the world: it is the chance we have to practice whatever ideals we may cherish."[17] The second statement seems unexceptionable, the first, after Bourdieu and others, highly questionable. Tompkins describes her effort to get her graduate students to "feel some deeper connection between what they were working on professionally and who they were, the real concerns of their lives" (658). A striking assumption here is that there is a definitional incompatibility between the personal and the professional, between who you are and what you have to say and do. Tompkins does not quite *say* that all knowledge is situated knowledge, so that it is methodologically dishonest not to talk about oneself. To do so, after all, would rob her rhetoric of its radically oppositional claim, and involve her in the very labyrinths of theory she wishes to avoid, for it is through theory that the topic of situatedness is to be pursued. But it is the traditional acceptance of the situatedness of literary knowledge that makes her argument so affirmative and so credible to so many.

And credible it is. There is a virtual stampede into autobiography on the part of literary critics. One dissenter, Daphne Patai, has described the scene as a "cacophony of competing particularisms," but for many others it is a reaffirming burst of common and familiar humanity.[18] There is no place in this rhetoric for those oddballs who

---

15   Tompkins repeated this conviction in a subsequent interview in the *Chronicle of Higher Education* (Scott Heller, "Experience and Expertise Meet in New Brand of Scholarship," 6 May 1992, A9): "Self-indulgence is the charge made by people who are afraid of their own selves." One might say that fear of or skepticism about the self is the principal legacy of both psychoanalysis and poststructuralism (or "theory"); it is this above all that Tompkins seeks to supplant.

16   Gerald MacClean, "Citing the Subject," in *Gender and Theory: Dialogues on Feminist Criticism*, ed. Linda Kauffman (New York and Oxford: Blackwell, 1989), 141–42.

17   Jane Tompkins, "Pedagogy of the Distressed," *College English* 52, no. 6 (1990): 656.

18   Daphne Patai, "Sick and Tired of Scholars' Nouveau Solipsism," *Chronicle of Higher Education*, 23 February 1994, A52.

might find passion in intellection. The subsisting tension is *between* passion and intellection, between the "person" and the professionally alienated specialist. In an interview on the topic of the Duke writers group of which Jane Tompkins was a founder member, Alice Kaplan confides, "I didn't realize . . . what an intellectual I had become and how unused I was to expressing emotion."[19] Cathy Davidson declares herself freed by autobiography into being "both passionate and academic" (A18). The assumption is that the appeal to the "general reader" can only be by way of personalized writing, full of warmth and idiosyncrasy. And the assumption may well be correct, since such personalization brings criticism back to literature and as literature, with all the permissions literature extends in avoiding the icy waters of theory.

Alice Kaplan, whose *French Lessons* is one of the best-sellers among the new academic autobiographies, has a particular tale to tell, since her liberation into the personal voice came as a release from the spell of Paul de Man's teaching. De Man was of course one of the most stringent repressers of the personal dimension (for reasons about which we are now compelled to speculate in quite personal terms), but he was not, I would argue, typical of the literary-critical tradition. In other words Kaplan's release is a release back into the mainstream from which she deviated in graduate school. There is a pathos in the relation to de Man, of interest at least to us professionals, but there is also an extraordinary self-inflation behind Kaplan's mantle of epistemic humility (for she is not given to crude self-advertisement): "Now I'm helping my own PhD students write their dissertations, and I don't want to fail them the way that de Man failed me. How do I tell them who I am, why I read the way I do?" (174). The claim is moral and emotional; we are not to doubt that de Man *did* fail her, nor to offer the opinion that no one can help failing others in such respects, nor to suggest that de Man's openness about his secrets might have taught her precisely nothing. To do so, of course, would be to undermine the enabling conventions of Kaplan's own book, which supposes, it seems, that an honest confession of who she is and where she's coming from will somehow assist in the production of dissertations. And perhaps, in today's market, Kaplan is absolutely right.

19   Liz McMillen, "A Passion for French," *Chronicle of Higher Education,* 9 February 1994, A8.

With the emphasis upon public emotion as a way of displacing or supplementing public intellection, which Tompkins associates with holding onto "the fleshly, desiring selves who were engaged in discussing hegemony or ideology or whatever it happened to be," [20] we touch inevitably and explicitly upon that dimension of the erotic that has so often before appeared as a challenge *to* the literary establishment even as it emanates with a profound logic *from* the literary establishment. There have been strains in that establishment, moments when the balance has been tipped too dangerously away from what looks like common sense, so that the function of literature as a socially or nationally cohesive principle has been threatened. Thus at various points, from the Jacobin novel of sensibility in the 1790s to the debates around *Ulysses, Lady Chatterley's Lover,* and *Naked Lunch* in the present century, writers and critics have been divided among themselves about what can be tolerated and explained and what must be disavowed as authentically "literature."[21] The erotic finds its way into Tompkins's classroom, one reads, in an encouragement of hugging and crying. And it is finding its way into an increasingly widespread and complex variety of professional publication in which the autobiographical element appears as an erotic element either accompanying or even motivating whatever else one might be writing about.[22] The point is not that this is somehow wrong, or offensive, or inappropriate in reference to some absolute standard of behavior. What is interesting about it, I think, is that it is precisely *not* an occasion for outcries of unprofessional or shocking behavior; that it is an intensification or reinvention of a traditional component of the literary subculture. Even Derrida fails to signal this as he introduces the personal-bodily and "literary" dimension into philosophy as "the only philosopher who, accepted—more or less—into the academic institution, author of more or less legitimate writings on Plato, Augustine, Descartes, . . . will have dared describe

---

20   Tompkins, "Pedagogy of the Distressed," 658.

21   For a related discussion, see my *Romanticism,* 164–71.

22   See, for example, Jane Gallop, "Knot a Love Story," and Eve Kosovsky Sedgwick, "White Glasses," *Yale Journal of Criticism* 5, no. 3 (1992): 209–18, 193–208; and Nancy K. Miller's meditations on her father's penis in *Getting Personal: Feminist Occasions and Other Autobiographical Acts* (New York and London: Routledge, 1991), 143–47. The locus classicus of this new academic genre, and still one of its most thought-provoking instances, is Eve Kosovsky Sedgwick's "A Poem Is Being Written," *Representations* 17 (1987): 110–43.

his penis."[23] The only change is that the critics are now trying to match or outdo the writers. The association with the feminine is also, as we will see later, traditional to a literary subculture whose general role has been consistently feminized. The erotic, in the context of the present argument, may be seen as among the most powerful and persuasive vehicles for the experience of presence: speech intensified.

Presence, to say it again, is the object of Tompkins's "Me and My Shadow," as if the shadow can become the self, perhaps the only self there is. She does not of course intend to have this particular philosophical investigation; indeed, she hopes to render it supernumerary by the sheer density of realist rhetoric in her essay. Her meditations on and about going to the bathroom, or not, have become notorious in a minor way, and as a matter of casual gossip among fellow academics, who perhaps enjoy a whiff of the carnivalesque within the otherwise earnest routines of scholarly argument. But we are not, here, in the sphere of a Rabelaisian abandon: the author, after all, is "not going yet" (126). Notwithstanding the effort at minor impropriety, this is basically an instance of the *vraisemblable*. We are to relate its being mentioned to the fact of its really happening: why mention it otherwise? There is someone there, a real person: "I pee, therefore I am." Professionalism is not the issue. Almost none of us, after all, have jobs that prevent us going to the bathroom (though there are such workplaces for the working class). No, we are being told that we are speaking with the living, not reading a dead letter. We don't *become* Jane Tompkins, as we might become one with the poet as described by I. A. Richards, but we know she is there. The proposed shock is in the service of a quite traditional message. Ironically, even the graduate schools against which Tompkins's case might best be taken to be directed are becoming more and more the province of people just like her.

The gesture of making present, of bringing to life, tends to function, in Tompkins as elsewhere, as an alternative to methodological doubt, and as a celebration of living without that doubt. Analytical perplexity is displaced by incarnation. Wordsworth offers one of the exemplary articulations of the sort of doubt that presence seeks to displace:

> Hard task, vain hope, to analyse the mind,
> If each most obvious and particular thought,

23   Derrida, in Bennington and Derrida, *Jacques Derrida*, 115.

> Not in a mystical and idle sense,
> But in the words of Reason deeply weighed,
> Hath no beginning. [24]

The mode of romantic writing is one of transference and repetition: to wonder thus and with Wordsworth is to wonder about ourselves as we wonder. It is also to wonder, indefinitely and inconclusively, about what is mystical, idle, obvious, and particular, and about what it might be that reason can expect to weigh and measure. Thus to pose the problem is to ensure that there is no solution without changing the terms of solution itself. Presence and performance, the lived event in actual time, have for many taken the place of ratiocination, as they did for David Hume in those famous passages about playing backgammon in the *Treatise of Human Nature*. What we recognize as "literature" has been the major vehicle of this transition, and literary criticism has largely followed along. For this reason it is the literary that remains so readily available as the language for expressing the resistance to or exhaustion with theory. Indeed, so pervasive is this exhaustion, that the priorities of the literary are increasingly coming to redefine theory itself, so that what is now known by that term describes the very obscurities and personalisms traditionally associated with "literature" and once imagined as antithetical to "theory."

Tompkins's essays, and the tradition that they represent, offer one kind of solution to the hard task of analyzing minds: forget it, just be yourself. If situatedness is the problem, then speak loudly so that others know where you are. Literary critics and theoretically minded interpreters have long struggled with the paradoxes of situatedness, one of the dominant consequences of Foucault's "analytic of finitude." Tompkins and others respond with a doggedly declared faith in the personal voice, and hope thereby to conjure up a person. Stanley Fish, some years ago, fashioned a weakly socialized version of personalism in his model of "interpretive communities." He conceded that no reader stands (or reads) alone; that "solipsism and relativism" are "modes of being" that "could never be realized."[25] We all inhabit interpretive com-

---

24   William Wordsworth, *The Prelude*, ed. Jonathan Wordsworth, M. H. Abrams, and Stephen Gill (London and New York: Norton, 1979), 77 (book 2, lines 228–32).

25   Stanley Fish, *Is There a Text in This Class?: The Authority of Interpretive Communities* (Cambridge and London: Harvard University Press, 1980), 321.

munities, so that meanings are not governed by immanent codes in printed texts but are made and remade in time and place by those communities. But Fish used this insight to propose the institutional containment of the community, a subculture unto itself with no critical relation to the outside world and no consequences for it. This message proved a bracing alternative to some of the lazier prevailing radicalisms, but it left the debate pretty much where it was, with the person now replaced by the institution, the interpretive community, itself a self-sufficient whole with a single identity and an autonomous life. The gesture toward Bourdieu is made at the expense of what is most interesting in Bourdieu: the complex sense of dialectical relations between parts and wholes.

Fish's influential writings also tried to head professional discussion toward the here and now, rather than toward the effort at recovering an accurate model of the historical past, which he regarded as impossible and even dishonest. Meanings are not, he proposed, so much found in texts as put there by readers, giving rise to the need for a "reader response" criticism, a movement with which Jane Tompkins also had much to do. This too is a truism, but only up to a point. To say that meanings are "put" into texts—that dead letters are brought to life—is not to solve the questions raised by the complicated coexistence of past and present, recoverable and partly recoverable meanings, and so forth. That meanings are made or remade in the present does not tell us very much in itself. It might lead, quite properly, either to a critical interest *in* the present or to an effort to overcome its blindnesses and to recover something of the past. New historicism has flourished by promising to do both at once. Fish, on the other hand, sought to discourage both responses by describing a gesture of pure presentism offering no information about either past or present, beyond the tautological reproduction of the (autonomous) interpretive community. Reading, once again, becomes a version of speaking personally, since no critical distinctions can be made between different readings. All are equally true (to the present) and equally false (to the past).

Fish's arguments worked toward denying any social or political consequences to the "profession" of literary criticism by embedding all social reference within an isolated professional subculture. At the same time, the power and autonomy of the profession itself (as able to ensure its own reproduction) was reciprocally (if perversely) validated, as it was by Paul de Man. If there has indeed been a "capital flight" from literary studies, as John Guillory argues in *Cultural Capital*, then the move away from the traditionally preservationist ambition of literary studies—the recording and resurrection of a cherished past—toward the more technical expertise of interpretation and argument represented by critics like Stanley Fish asks to be read as a residual defense of the same professionalism decried by so many of the autobiographers. But the *point* of this professional expertise is purely self-reproducing; Fish agrees with one half of Alvin Gouldner's thesis about the new class, but denies the possibility of significant action for which Gouldner also contends. In this respect Fish describes the institution of the university as a communal version of the isolated self, uniquely situated and unable to communicate with other such selves. He is thus, implicitly, a participant in the culture of autobiography to exactly the degree that he negates it. He does not claim radical idiosyncrasy for himself, but for the profession to which he and others belong.

So dominant is this culture that its rhetoric can hardly be avoided or displaced, especially given the enormous difficulty of now conceiving a critical language that might convince us of its credibility as an alternative to speaking personally, or as a scientific explanation of the place of subjectivity within its larger situation. To make autobiography thoroughly historical and history convincingly subjective—enacted through the subject—remains for us the great task, as it was for Sartre and others. And it may be an impossible task, itself the symptom of a condition whose very historicality is contained in the erosion of a faith in being convincingly historical. Those of us working within and addressing ourselves to a culture whose dominant paradigms are liberal, individual, and expressive can perhaps not even think beyond those terms, which become the limits of our language. Or if we can think beyond them—and this remains the covert hope of all *critical* work— then it is likely that we will not find much of an audience for our alternatives.

Frank Lentricchia has advanced the claims of a "personal subject," which he refuses to dismiss as mere "bourgeois illusion," as a critical requirement for literary theory today.[26] After all, if subjectivity is the condition of our contemporary being, it does not make much sense to leave it out of any description of what we do. But the sheer difficulty of the task of *critical* subjectivity is such as to make it terribly tempting to

26   Lentricchia, *Ariel and the Police*, 23.

give up, and to slide back into the affirmative rhetoric of writing about oneself, just because it seems to be there. In 1886, in *Beyond Good and Evil*, Nietzsche scorned the "exaggerated manner in which the 'unselfing' and depersonalization of the spirit is being celebrated nowadays as if it were the goal itself and redemption and transfiguration."[27] Perhaps there was a time, in late-nineteenth-century Europe, when this might have been a serious concern. Perhaps it still is in the contemporary cultural whole wherein the priorities of "big science" are still arguably primary and where the effects of consumerism are, we are often told, hostile to any authentic individualism. But the rhetoric of individualism is not to be imagined as identical with authenticity; it may indeed, as R. Jackson Wilson has cogently reminded us, be in itself a fabrication of the literary marketplace, with definable historical origins and motivations, rather than an alternative to the determinations of history.[28] But, under the aegis of a declared postmodernism, that is exactly the sort of argument we are not supposed to be able to make. The assumption of distance, and of critical distance in particular, has, in the words of Fredric Jameson, "very precisely been abolished in the new space of postmodernism."[29] Even the magisterial Jameson, certainly our most astute and complex literary theorist of the postmodern, has registered the moment in the transformations of his own style. Ten years ago that style was brilliantly analyzed by Terry Eagleton as a balance of portentous "structural rigour and historical prognostication" with subtly personalized moments of "self-delight."[30] Eagleton saw here a countering of two antithetical tendencies, the obscurity of the European and the "anaemic transparency" of the Anglo-American (68). In 1991, in Jameson's *Postmodernism*, the style has shifted and evolved toward an *ironic* recognition of the personal voice, a rhetoric, infrequent to be sure yet clear and distinct, that acknowledges its author's private and professional personality in a series of reductive subjectivisms that reproduce even as they advertise, in good postmodern style,

---

27   Friedrich Nietzsche, *Beyond Good and Evil*, in *Basic Writings of Nietzsche*, trans. Walter Kaufmann (New York: Random House, 1966), 316.

28   R. Jackson Wilson, *Figures of Speech: American Writers and the Literary Marketplace, from Benjamin Franklin to Emily Dickinson* (New York: Knopf, 1989).

29   Jameson, *Postmodernism*, 48.

30   Terry Eagleton, "Fredric Jameson: The Politics of Style," in *Against the Grain: Essays, 1975–1985* (London: Verso, 1986), 66.

the egregious inevitability of the personal within the effort at the critical-professional. Such phrases as "I have visited the house myself," "according to me," and "if I may indulge in a personal note" would have seemed out of place even in Eagleton's earlier identified language of self-delight.[31] Some of this might be explained as the well-deserved acceptance of the role of mature intellectual, himself now the subject of a large secondary literature across a number of fields and national debates. It is also a tongue-in-cheek reproduction of the now besetting language of criticism itself, still visibly at odds with Jameson's principally critical effort even as it registers a change in the nature of that effort, and in the times themselves. And, once again, it is an image of a conversational Jameson, a presence, and as such an image of one simultaneously within time (and mortal) and beyond death (because always to be brought to life). Derrida expresses, as he writes of his dying mother, a fear of the biographer's closure, of being "deprived of a future, no more event to come from me."[32] Again, when Leavis invoked for literature the "courage of enormous incompletenesses," he hinted at the specter of death that literature at once acknowledges and defies.[33] This too has to do with the return of the storyteller, and of the compulsion toward speaking personally.

And there—if I may indulge in an impersonal note—you have it. Terry Eagleton, in critiquing the Hegelian component of Jameson's work, argued that "it is not clear that there is anything inherent in late capitalism which spontaneously selects such philosophical issues as the relation between subject and object as the order of the day, as opposed, say, to questions of the character of the state and its repressive apparatuses, problems of proletarian organization and insurrection, of the role of the vanguard party."[34] Perhaps not. But if you function within a literature department in an English or American university, there is a very strong likelihood that you are going to be more interested in (and better prepared to address) the problem of subject and object than that of the vanguard party. Jameson is exemplary in the breadth of his intellectual curiosity and in his control of more than one

31   Jameson, *Postmodernism*, 110, 116, 297.

32   Bennington and Derrida, *Jacques Derrida*, 30. See also Geoffrey Bennington's very apposite remarks on pages 52–56.

33   Leavis, *Education and the University*, 60.

34   Eagleton, "Fredric Jameson," 75.

expertise. But even he cannot escape the effects of coming at the topic of modernity and postmodernity through "literature" and literary criticism—hence, perhaps, the significantly brief chapter on economics (nineteen pages) and the enormous chapters on culture and theory in *Postmodernism*. Literature, as I have been arguing (now to the point of near-monotony), has always been in the business of placing and voicing the subject. Thus it is the fate of those of us who seek to do a different literary criticism to find a different place for the subject— perhaps a placing without a voicing. But for us, at least for the time being, the culture of autobiography is not going to go away.

Four

FEMINISMS AND FEMINIZATIONS
IN THE POSTMODERN

The renewed interest among professional literary critics in "speaking personally" must number among its causes and analogues the widespread incorporation of feminist criticism within the academy. Speaking personally is not the exclusive disposition either of women or of feminists. Indeed, I have been arguing that it is the overt or covert convention in literature and literary criticism as a whole. But the recent reemphasis on the personal voice and on the critical seriousness of autobiography has come largely from female critics, even as it is welcomed by many men. Judith Lowder Newton has argued with some conviction that the new historicism, which is one of the exemplary literary-critical incarnations of the academic postmodern, has come into existence by taking over the methods and assumptions of feminist criticism, depriving them along the way of any practical political application and converting them to masculinized and professional ends. The process she observes is a familiar one: the masculine appropriation of female labor.[1] From the long-durational perspective, this can be read as a locally gendered struggle for position in what has always been the generally feminized role of literary criticism within the culture of modernity. In that culture both women and literature have been allocated the functions of sensibility, expressive personality, and authenticity. Both have claimed (or been accorded) the privileges of methodological quixotism and imaginative surprise as alternatives to the dry rationalisms of theory. Both have been imaged as the preservers of polite consensus and emotional flexibility against the alienating energies of modernization. And both have incurred a coun-

---

1   Judith Lowder Newton, "History as Usual? Feminism and the 'New Historicism,'" in *The New Historicism*, ed. H. Aram Veeser (New York and London: Routledge, 1989), 152–67.

tercriticism that figures them as the icons of luxury and leisure, distracting and even, sometimes, dangerous. The "narratives" that are the fabric of literariness are, for Lyotard's man of science, accordingly cast as "fables, myths, legends, fit only for women and children."[2]

Insofar as feminist literary criticism censures the deviation into protoscientific or masculinized varieties of theory and method—as it often does in its postmodern celebration of speaking personally—then it may be seen as a very traditional literary criticism. It may still register as locally radical, because it is the signature of a demographic shift within the profession, which has in the last twenty years become much more open to the inclusion of women academics and feminist priorities. Thus we now see women doing confidently and openly what they have been told women do well, while their male peers either follow along with them or look halfheartedly for alternatives. The new fashionability of the personal voice has in turn given rise to a countercurrent among others competing for recognition as feminists of a different kind. Thus there is a growing number of feminist and mostly female critics (the work of Gayatri Spivak is exemplary here) who do not endorse the priorities of traditional literary (feminist) criticism as I have described them, and who make it their business to discriminate between their own feminisms and the replication of inherited and femin*ized* cultural roles. They understand feminization as a historical component of modernity (apparent perhaps before modernity but exaggerated within it), one that creates a licensed alternative by imagining the properties of women and literature as empathic and personal but always subservient to a containing power that is not theirs. This process of feminization includes most women, in different degrees measured by class and subculture, and a number of negatively regendered men, who remain biologically male but are refigured by occupational or other associations into subservient or subsidiary roles. This category includes many men who maintain, in one way or another, the functions of literature.

One should not overemphasize this condition. All male critics and writers cannot now expect by this logic to be recognized and respected as members of the oppressed classes, deserving only of sympathy instead of criticism. To propose this would be to mask the residual survival of a very considerable (white) male establishment within the

2   Lyotard, *Postmodern Condition*, 27.

subculture of the academy as well as outside it. It would also misrepresent the ongoing struggle for position among the various factions of the academy, a struggle by no means decided. But one can say that, relative to their gender peers in the other professions, male literary critics do occupy a feminized place, even where they have managed to maintain a position that is "above" that of their female colleagues. They are partly and generically feminized, as literary critics, even if they preserve a locally remasculinized place for themselves within their discipline. Traditionally, men have done this by recourse to philology, or New Criticism, or theory. Within the postmodern these options are no longer there, or at least not there in the same way. And within the academic postmodern, of course, white males are now very visibly on the discursive defensive even where they continue to hold on to considerable institutional power. Indeed, at the time of writing, there is a gap between the emergent discursive power, largely the possession of "non–white males" (a category that includes, for instance, gay men as well as women and minorities), and the institutional control still largely held by traditional persons. The tension between the two groups keeps alive the image of radical transformation within the profession.

There has been, I think, a shift within and around feminism even since 1986, when Andreas Huyssen could still find it "baffling that feminist criticism has so far largely stayed away from the postmodernism debate which is considered not to be pertinent to feminist concerns."[3] That debate was at first conducted very much in the mode of high theory, the most masculinized element of debate in the humanities. But theory has increasingly come to doubt its own adequacy as a rationalist stronghold, both through its general loss of credibility as posited by a postmodern condition and because of the redefinition of theory itself by feminist and other interests committed to an acknowledgment of their own situatedness. Feminism no longer ignores the debate about the postmodern: it is a full participant on all sides of that debate. Indeed, it seems now to be in a position to investigate the relation between feminism and feminization in a new way, and thus to contribute to the critical historicization of the academic postmodern for which I have been appealing.

Feminism has a long history, one that proves that even a history

3   Huyssen, *After the Great Divide*, 198.

written by the winners can record its deviant moments and roads not taken, or plowed over. In its rhetorical identity for us now *feminism* tends to serve as a description of very recent intellectual-political efforts, those mounted since the 1960s by and on behalf of women. But one can identify one or another kind of feminism as emerging in counterpoint to almost every shift in the dynamics of modernization since the Renaissance and perhaps earlier. As such, these feminisms have often attempted a resistance to *feminization*, to the gendering of certain undesirable or disavowed social and personal characteristics as the natural properties of women, and the imputed or acquired attributes of certain groups of negatively regendered men. The argument for the function of feminization within modernity has been made in at least two important books, for America and Britain respectively. Ann Douglas's *Feminization of American Culture* makes the case for a formative relation among sentimentalization, consumerism, and literature in the American nineteenth century as constitutive of the syndrome of feminization and of modern "mass" culture. She also proposes that the feminization of culture went along with an actual "feminine disestablishment" whereby women increasingly moved and were moved from being producers to being consumers.[4] Subsequently, Nancy Armstrong, in her *Desire and Domestic Fiction*, has found in eighteenth-century Britain a similar conjunction of social-textual energies whereby the very notion of the modern subjectivity came into being as a feminized entity: "the modern individual was first and foremost a woman."[5] Like Douglas, Armstrong specifies the new modern (and feminized) individual as middle-class, and partly formed by (as she is formative of) the cultural artefact called "British literature" (20–21).

These two books summarize a great deal of evidence for the coevolution of feminization and of the modern notions of literature and of subjectivity. That their respective samples are a century or so and an ocean apart does not matter, since they are exploring a long-durational syndrome whose credibility depends less on a precise moment of abso-

4   Ann Douglas, *The Feminization of American Culture* (New York: Knopf, 1977). In her sense of a disjunction between culture and its social-economic environment, Douglas opens the question of the relation between what I am calling feminisms and feminizations.

5   Nancy Armstrong, *Desire and Domestic Fiction: A Political History of the Novel* (New York: Oxford University Press, 1987), 8.

lute origin than on a general articulation of modernity. Philosophers have often looked to Montaigne and Descartes for modernity's exemplary expression (sometimes called an origin), while literary and cultural historians have tended to focus on what we recognize as the Renaissance for similar epitomes. [6] One could have, and others surely have, proposed earlier symptomatic moments. The emergence of capitalism and of consumerism, upon which the syndrome may well depend, has always required for its analysis a famously labile chronology.

This necessary largeness or looseness of focus allows us some broad but I think workable assertions: that feminization has been a dominant subject effect for the bourgeois or "middle" classes, upon and through whom the processes of modernization have been carried out; that feminisms have often arisen in critical reaction to that feminization; that our current notions of literature, and simultaneously of literary *criticism*, have developed within that same cultural evolution, as feminized media; so that those aspects of the postmodern that make central the literary are potentially continuing a long tradition of feminized subjection and subjectivity. The relation of femin*ism* to the (feminized) postmodern must then be inspected and perhaps contested; the desire to challenge must be set within a possible history of complicity, not to preempt the plausibility of challenge (in the manner of one kind of new historicism), but in hopes of plotting just where the mines are buried in the minefield, and thus in hopes for a better future. If any feminism, in other words, is to mount a critical alliance with the postmodern, it must beware of unacknowledged complicities with those postmodern priorities that are arguably the legacies of a traditional feminization process, legacies often apparent, I suggest, in the postmodern preference for the "literary" method.

The literary-centered postmodern is not, of course, the only postmodern. Cyborgs, computers, virtual-reality machines, and rewritten DNA models all seem at least to propose a technological postmodern that has on the surface little to do with the traditions of literary criticism. This "hard" postmodern seems to offer a world free of feeling,

---

6   See, among others, Joel Fineman, *Shakespeare's Perjured Eye: The Invention of Poetic Subjectivity in the Sonnets* (Berkeley and Los Angeles: University of California Press, 1986); Catherine Belsey, *The Subject of Tragedy: Identity and Difference in Renaissance Drama* (London and New York: Methuen, 1985); and Francis Barker, *The Tremulous Private Body: Essays on Subjection* (London and New York: Methuen, 1984).

introspection, and bewildering hermeneutic speculations about subject-object relations and responsibilities. And yet it might be suggested that the very appeal of these models, models declaring or assuming the death of the subject, is that they are dialectical formations, limit statements of the desire to be, finally and after all the promises, free of subjectivity. For in the nontechnological postmodern, subjectivity is everywhere, more than ever before. And the mode of subjectivity is *literary.* When Paul de Man called attention to literature as that which recognized the fictionality or language-bound identity of its own statements, he was repeating (albeit in the disguise of a technological ambition) the traditional understanding of literature as other than science, as dominated by a critical element of rhetoricity, and not by any assumption of systematic access to a world of natural things.

One can find, across a whole field of disciplines, instances of a common pattern of methodological and ethical priorities that read as analogues of the "new historicism" and/or feminism effect in literary criticism (an effect that, I have suggested, risks the attribution of deep familiarity). In political theory the massive appeal of Laclau and Mouffe may be attributed to their disinclination for the "Jacobin imaginary" of grand theory and their recommendation of an immersion in "that infinite intertextuality of emancipatory discourses in which the plurality of the social takes shape."[7] (Note the assumption that the social *is* plural, which is not the same as saying it ought to be.) In a similar spirit Judith Butler speaks of gender as "a complexity whose totality is permanently deferred," and of its social inscription as an "open coalition . . . an open assemblage that permits of multiple convergences and divergences without obedience to a normative telos of definitional closure."[8] And Evelyn Fox Keller writes about a scientific method called "dynamic objectivity" that is "not unlike empathy" in its assumption of a "connectivity with" the world, and tells about the "many worlds" quantum theorists for whom "the universe is seen as continually splitting into a multitude of mutually unobservable but equally real worlds."[9]

7   Ernesto Laclau and Chantal Mouffe, *Hegemony and Socialist Strategy: Towards a Radical Democratic Politics,* trans. Winston Moore and Paul Cammack (London: Verso, 1985), 2, 5.

8   Judith Butler, *Gender Trouble: Feminism and the Subversion of Identity* (New York and London: Routledge, 1990), 16.

9   Evelyn Fox Keller, *Reflections on Gender and Science* (New Haven and London: Yale University Press, 1985), 117, 147.

These instances stand for a multitude of others in their recognition of all knowledge as situated knowledge, and of the need to recognize the likely asymmetry of different persons' situatednesses. In some instances these recognitions can lead to a stringent despair or limitation on the claims made for knowledge (as with de Man and Derrida). In others, and at the moment they are in the majority, there is an affirmation of political-aesthetic possibility and a celebration of openness. [10] Feminist scientists like Keller and Donna Haraway are reluctant to give up completely on an objectivity that they still find potentially liberating albeit traditionally appropriated for masculine interests. But writers and scholars not working within a scientific tradition are often more relaxed about giving up on rationality and objectivity, hoping instead for some empirical resolution, in performed experience, of the tension between different interests. Their hope seems to be that the recognition of situatedness, and the admission thereof, can head off some of its more negative possible consequences, as if declaring that one has a position or an interest could be a way of achieving a useful methodological honesty, or at least a protective humility. It can also, of course, be a persuasive marketing tactic for a readership prone to conflating personal sincerity with analytic power.

I call these understandings literary not because they are always explicitly derived from a literary vocabulary but because they share with that vocabulary a recognition and celebration of the imprecision that comes from admitting one's subject positionality. And, as we have seen, the debt of the postmodern to the literary is sometimes quite explicit. It is so for Richard Rorty, the exemplary anglophone postmodern philosopher, who understands our present condition as lived within "the autonomy and supremacy of the literary culture," and who affirmatively infers from Nietzsche an understanding of history as "the history of successive metaphors" so that we should allow ourselves to "see the poet, in the generic sense of the maker of new words, the shaper of new languages, as the vanguard of the species."[11]

Modernity, then, for Rorty, devolves in and through the he-

10   This is what Teresa Ebert has called "ludic" feminism/postmodernism, against which she seeks to advance a "resistance" postmodernism ("Ludic Feminism, the Body, Performance, and Labor: Bringing *Materialism* Back into Feminist Cultural Studies," *Cultural Critique* 23 [1992–93]: 5–50).

11   Rorty, *Consequences of Pragmatism*, 150; Rorty, *Contingency, Irony, and Solidarity*, 20.

gemony of the literary, precisely at the point when philosophy and theology have failed to satisfy. One could propose a number of exemplary formulations of this shift: Hume, Rousseau, Friedrich Schlegel, Wordsworth, Kierkegaard, Nietzsche, Wittgenstein, would all suffice to illustrate some aspect of this emphasis. Hegel, however, would not quite do, since his solution to the unignorable problem of subjectivity, of situatedness, is designed certainly to acknowledge but also to defeat the sheer occasionality of historical experience. In this sense his work is the anticipatory antithesis to much of what is now recognized as the postmodern, in that it strives to preserve the (as we now say) master narrative marching through a sea of contingency and redundancy. Marx continues to be debated as falling on one side or the other (sometimes both) of this divide. Adorno elegantly articulated its existence, and his is, once again, a useful account for the disambiguation of feminism and feminization.

Adorno's *Negative Dialectics* "attempts by means of logical consistency to substitute for the unity principle, and for the paramountcy of the supra-ordinated concept, the idea of what would be outside the sway of such unity."[12] After Hegel, philosophy is obliged "ruthlessly to criticize itself," but it must do so by attention to everything in which Hegel was not interested (3, 8). Philosophy now must admit its inability to prescribe the particular, and to reduce what it interprets to "the concept"—a term (*Begriff*) having a specific history through Kant, Hegel, and beyond (11, 14). This imposes a "playful element" upon philosophy that is equivalent to the literary; thus the "element of the *homme de lettres*, disparaged by a petty bourgeois scientific ethos, is indispensable to thought" (14, 29).

Philosophy thus now knows "no fixed sequence of question and answer." Its questions are shaped by experience, so as to "catch up with the experience" (63). It would be wrong to assimilate lines like these to some strong identity with American pragmatism, of the sort that marks Rorty's project. Adorno remains, in complex but yet undeniable ways, a Marxist.[13] And thus the recognition of philosophy's necessary

---

12   Theodor W. Adorno, *Negative Dialectics*, trans. E. B. Ashton (New York: Continuum, 1973), xx.

13   Fredric Jameson's *Late Marxism: Adorno, or the Persistence of the Dialectic* (London and New York: Verso, 1990) attempts to adjust our focus to a poststructuralist component in Adorno's Marxism, which still "stands or falls with the concept of 'totality'" (9).

incoherence is not so much matter for celebration as for understanding. In other words, the kind of knowing that the familiarized subject lays claim to is a form of not knowing, or of denying an alternative knowledge.

How about the postmodern, and its apparently alternative replication of feminized positionalities? What does it mean to be free in response to a posited constraint, spontaneous in reaction to a perceived discipline, localized in the face of an attributed totalizing tendency? How can a critical feminism claim and define its place in this sea of traditionally feminized attributes? To endorse the values of mass culture, or to collapse the distinction between elite and mass culture is, as Andreas Huyssen's work has shown, to endorse that which has previously been feminized. [14] There is a dialectic here, and I suggest that it appears in the exemplary articulations of the whole period of capitalist modernization. Hegel will do for one side of this dialectic of modernity (and parts of him would even do for the other side): the master-narrative, masculinized version of the inevitable subjectivity of and in history. But the other side was there too, and its mode of self-representation was commonly the literary as such, before high modernism sought to remasculinize a part of the literary for elite identification. The oscillation between the two, the operation of the dialectic, may indeed be claimed as the very engine of bourgeois experience, always *between* interest and disinterest, ideology and science, nomadism and a sense of place. Between, again, feminine and masculine. And the languages within which the eighteenth-century middle class recognized itself were heavily marked by both the appeal and the fear of feminized cultural roles. Literature, incrementally gravitating toward the domestic, feminized sphere and away from the public sphere, has devised various ways of countering its subsumption (for instance, its projection of anarchist-erotic energies in the likes of Blake and Shelley), but it has never definitively escaped from the web. [15]

The eighteenth-century obsession with the feminization of culture and politics under capitalism is vividly apparent in the debates

14   Huyssen, *After the Great Divide*, 44–62.

15   Many of Terry Eagleton's writings describe this condition of literature: see, especially, *The Function of Criticism: From "The Spectator" to Poststructuralism* (London: Verso, 1984) and *The Ideology of the Aesthetic* (Oxford: Blackwell, 1990).

about commerce and luxury, about divided labor and surplus production, about the domestic and the colonialist economies—the debates within and alongside which the modern idea of literature was being defined. These debates had been ongoing in Western culture at least since Lycurgus wrote into the Spartan constitution a ban on commerce in the cause of preserving civic virtue. But various eighteenth-century commentators, faced with the social and political consequences of empire, capitalized agriculture, and imparkment, found themselves repeating the arguments with special conviction. As wealth came more and more from the colonies and the stock market, and as cultivation at home became more efficient, the defenders of a ruralist (and masculinist) political ideal became more and more defensive. Power was seen to be moving from country to city, and what came back to the country was the iconography of surplus wealth: parks and mansions occupied for half the year by stock-market millionaires, feminized personalities.

The increased concentration of surplus wealth in the hands of an aristocracy and a burgeoning middle class was seen as replacing an economy of need (masculinist subsistence) by an economy of desire (feminized superfluity). Once we have met our needs, we are free to develop desires, and desire is infinite. William Paley can stand for many others as he observes that trade does not depend on need: it does not matter "how superfluous the articles which it furnishes are; whether the want of them be real or imaginary; whether it be founded in nature or in opinion, in fashion, habit, or emulation; it is enough that they be actually desires and sought after."[16] Whig economists like Adam Smith thought that the luxury cycle (and all nonnecessities were defined as luxuries) would prove a creative stimulus for national wealth as well as a force for social bonding. Opponents predicted only the collapse of society itself. Luxury and desire together were the feminized components of social-economic life: unstable, unpredictable, superfluous, and experienced as constant process rather than as finished product. Smollett's Matthew Bramble saw unrestrained commerce as begetting "a spirit of licentiousness, insolence and faction, that keeps the community in continual ferment, and in time destroys all the distinctions of civil society; so that universal anarchy and uproar must ensue." Visiting old friends in the English countryside, Bramble discovers and

16 William Paley, *The Principles of Moral and Political Philosophy*, 20th ed. (London, 1814), 2:374.

relates three instances of "female vanity" having impoverished previously functional estates, turning them from production to consumption and display, and thence to bankruptcy.[17] The feminization of credit and luxury, versions of the traditional feminization of *fortuna*, was a commonplace in eighteenth-century moral and political philosophy and political economy.[18]

This was the field of reference within which modern literature took on shape and cultural definition. And literature was commonly cast as itself a luxury. Books designated as literature were, after all, expensive items, and required leisure for their consumption. The role of literature was in this way already feminized, and that feminization was exacerbated by the extraordinary and much discussed growth in the numbers of women writers and women readers. This situation brought about a visible tension between a masculinized literature, premised on the classics, on Milton, and on epic poetry and seeking to limit its availability by difficulty and high seriousness, and a feminized mode imaged in the vernacular and in the novel and lyric poetry. This tension explains why the major romantics were often so ambivalent about whether their work could or should have a common rather than a specialist reader. Rousseau, in one of his voices, made clear the relation between literature and national decline: "A taste for letters, for philosophy and the fine arts, enervates both body and soul. A confinement to the closet makes men delicate, and weakens their constitution; and the soul preserves with difficulty its vigour when that of the body is lost."[19] In other words, men become women when they develop a taste for literature.

Rousseau was not the first to think or to suggest this threatening regendering of the male reader. Sidney, it will be remembered, had worked hard to present poetry as an incentive to military valor in call-

17   Tobias Smollett, *Humphry Clinker*, ed. James L. Thorson (New York and London: Norton, 1983), 258, 271.

18   For extended treatments of this trope, see J. G. A. Pocock, *The Machiavellian Moment: Florentine Political Thought and the Atlantic Republican Tradition* (Princeton: Princeton University Press, 1975), especially 401–505; and John Sekora, *Luxury: The Concept in Western Thought, Eden to Smollett* (Baltimore: Johns Hopkins University Press, 1977).

19   Jean-Jacques Rousseau, preface to *Narcissus, or the Self-Admirer*, in *The Miscellaneous Works of Mr. J. J. Rousseau* (London, 1767), 2:135. See also my *Romanticism*, especially 126–71.

ing it "the companion of the camps";[20] but his very image seems to betray him into communicating a quite different companionship, one feminized and prostitute. Addison looked to the "rational and manly Beauties" of Milton to keep literature and its readers from inclining too far toward the feminized extreme always latent in the exercise of matters of taste.[21] Adam Smith deduced Shaftesbury's predilection for the fine arts from the "puny and weakly constitution" that made him unable to pursue "abstract reasoning and deep searches."[22] And Anna Barbauld further emphasized Sidney's case against the philosophers and the historians in commending the "partialities of particular affections" and "particular and personal" feelings that are proper to the encouragement of religion and—for Mary Wollstonecraft, who invoked her—especially apparent in good literature.[23]

The feminization of literature was not, of course, uncontested. Wordsworth's famous outcries against popular novels and plays, and high modernism's reaffirmation of sheer difficulty and massive intellectuality are just two instances of a masculinizing reaction. But the struggle has always occurred from within an already feminized general construction of the literary mode. Literary criticism, as an appendix or companion to literature, has experienced the same struggles. Its attempted diversions into theory have often been gestures of remasculinization and have been resisted by an establishment whose lexicon is dominantly feminized: intuition, exceptionality, sympathy, empathy, lived experience, and so forth.[24] (This is one part of an explanation of the contested relation between feminism and theory as traditionally understood, though the mix is now rather different.) Irving Babbitt, in 1908, thought that literature had become the provider of a "soothing

---

20 Sidney, *Apology for Poetry*, 127.

21 Addison, "Pleasures of the Imagination," 367.

22 Smith, *Lectures on Rhetoric and Belles Lettres*, 56.

23 Mary Wollstonecraft, preface to *The Female Reader*, in *The Works of Mary Wollstonecraft*, ed. Janet Todd and Marilyn Butler (New York: New York University Press, 1989), 4:57–58.

24 This is a more accurate summary of the British than of the American academy, where masculine or at least theoretical establishments have at least briefly been in place. But they have never been uncontested and have never achieved an enduring hegemony, despite the more general acceptance of professional-technical methods in America than in Britain. In both cultures, theory itself now stands against masculinization. The question is for whom will it be feminist and for whom merely feminized.

and mildly narcotic effect" for those who could not keep up the serious energies required for the pursuit of scientific knowledge.[25] He saw more and more women going into literature, creating a disciplinary culture of "effeminacy" (112) wherein even the stern philologian must have his "feminine or dilettante side" (115). Babbitt hoped for a literary training that might be "free from suspicion of softness or relaxation" (116). Subsequent generations of modernists, New Critics, deconstructionists, and other theorists have attempted to produce just this, but never with more than partial and short-lived success.

These long-standing connections among luxury, literature, and the feminization of culture are not, then, at all redundant for an analysis of the contemporary situation. Their dynamics are not categorically different from those adduced by theorists of the postmodern between political-aesthetic formations and the determinations of late capitalism. Junk bonds and simulacra may have replaced such terms as *commerce* and *desire*, but the same moral concerns exist in the same sorts of connection with analogous economic determinations. We are still having the argument about what, within the large range of things called postmodern, is merely a reproduction of ideology and what is a critique of it. I have suggested that in its enthusiastic embrace of the priorities of the literary mode, the postmodern gesture may also be inheriting a culturally sanctioned ethic of imprecision (as antitotality, local knowledge, conversation, or whatever) that is a function rather than a critique of feminization. This raises the question of a role for critical feminism, as that which must by definition or aspiration set out to critique feminization.

It seems unlikely that any answer to this predicament is to be had in general. Feminism is not a unitary movement defined by commonly agreed methods. On the contrary, it is as riven with disagreement as is the larger culture in which it functions, and it seems certain that a yet wider array of choices would open up to anyone who knows more than I do about what lies outside the narrow Anglo-American context, or what remains relatively unknown within it. Feminisms do arguably have a common goal in the liberation or improvement of the lives of women: their telos is as much in action as in theory. And this activist priority has been seen as visibly and at least superficially at odds with

25 Irving Babbitt, cited in Graff and Warner, *Origins of Literary Studies in America*, 111.

the postmodern predilection for the aesthetic and the discursive as its proper spheres of attention.[26] But even within activist feminisms there are radical disagreements about what will produce positive change, about what is revolution and what is mere reproduction. The problems raised by the postmodern rhetoric will likely reappear, in other words, in every feminist initiative that seeks to theorize itself at any level, though they are likely to remain less obsessive outside the academy than in it. Similarly and reciprocally, the postmodern has replicated many of feminism's internal debates in its own efforts at self-definition.[27]

The long-durational model I have sketched here might suggest that there are no ultimately separate histories for feminism(s) and for postmodernism(s). The rhetoric of academic self-definition functions with a strongly presentist and individualist emphasis. We set up "isms" and then go about the task of distinguishing them from other "isms," often on grounds that are improvisational rather than structural, and functions of competitive rather than historical categories. The exclusionary gestures still seem to come mostly from the men, it must be said, so that the syndrome of gendered disavowal Judith Lowder Newton saw in the new historicists may also describe the more general postmodern debate. David Harvey's *Condition of Postmodernity*, certainly one of the most important books in the field, is quite innocent of feminist work, and Jameson accords feminism only a single, albeit laudatory, mention, without discussion (*Postmodernism*, 107). If disavowal is one side of the coin, the other may well be uncritical espousal of the feminized, masquerading as the feminist. Sabina Lovibond has issued a timely reminder that the same Nietzsche who is for many commentators the founding father of the ethical-methodological emphases of the postmodernists also made a clear association between the emancipation from reason and a desired extinction of feminism.[28] She has ar-

---

26 See, for instance, Linda Hutcheon, *The Politics of Postmodernism* (London and New York: Routledge, 1989), 168, who notes feminism's commitment to "real social change" and contrasts postmodernism's downplaying of "strategies of resistance."

27 See Best and Kellner, *Postmodern Theory*, 205.

28 Sabina Lovibond, "Feminism and Postmodernism," *New Left Review* 178 (1989): 5–28, especially 16–18. See also her "Feminism and the 'Crisis of Rationality,'" *New Left Review* 207 (1994): 72–86.

gued from a feminist point of view against a simple rejection of the Enlightenment, and against any naive embrace of localism and of analysis merely within the "parish boundaries."[29]

A critical feminism, then, must search out a position within a culture of modernity that is still governed by a dialectic of masculinization and feminization. Given this, no simple assertion of spontaneity and empathy, and no mere abdication of authority, ought to be respected as by definition constructive. The methodological analogue is that no mere assertion of the repressive masculinity of totalities and grand theories is enough to constitute a real alternative. To repeat this language is just to repeat a traditional positionality: literary, feminized, against theory. To admit situatedness is not a solution, merely the beginning of the problem. Here is Gayatri Spivak making exactly this point: "I have invoked my positionality in this awkward way so as to accentuate the fact that calling the place of the investigator into question remains a meaningless piety in many recent critiques of the sovereign subject. Thus, although I will attempt to foreground the precariousness of my position throughout, I know such gestures can never suffice."[30] Not only does this not suffice, Spivak goes on to explain: it may actually inhibit, and subsist as "an interested desire to conserve the subject of the West." The confession of pluralized subject positions may serve to provide "a cover for this subject of knowledge" (271). This is no mere wordplay. For there is indeed a way in which the now monotonous reiteration of who one is and where one is coming from is accompanied by an almost audible sigh of relief, as if one is thereby exonerated from responsibility or culpability. If I speak only for and as myself, then I cannot go wrong, I do no damage. This gesture of authentication may be suspected on a number of grounds. When it functions to imply identity, then it displaces any encounter with the problems of poststructuralist theory; and when it implies recognition of the equality of all differences, then it mystifies, as Spivak aptly notices, the actual distinctions of power and opportunity distinguishing not only the "subject of the West" from others in the global

---

29   Lovibond, "Feminism and Postmodernism," 22.

30   Gayatri Chakravorty Spivak, "Can the Subaltern Speak?" in *Marxism and the Interpretation of Culture*, ed. Cary Nelson and Lawrence Grossberg (Urbana and Chicago: University of Illinois Press, 1988), 271. Spivak's writings are a model attempt at careful historical and theoretical specification of such terms as *feminism* and *postmodernism*.

sphere, but also the subject of the subculture from other subcultures. To propose situatedness as an alternative to theory is then to deprive ourselves of the one language through which situatedness itself might be understood. Situatedness above all things desperately requires theorization.

These paradoxes, and others like them, have led to some fairly significant divisions among those who seek a place for feminisms within the postmodern. The more self-conscious critics are, like Spivak, very much aware of the pitfalls of embracing a postmodernity founded in inherited feminization. They see that it is not enough to preach the value of detail against theory, of emotion against reason, of "community" against society. Patricia Waugh has argued, following Lovibond, that "if feminism can learn from Postmodernism it has finally to resist the logic of its arguments or at least to attempt to combine them with a modified adherence to an epistemological anchorage in the discourses of Enlightened modernity."[31] Nancy Fraser, coming from another direction, has supplemented Habermas's enlightened-modern project with its missing gender component, about which Habermas himself says "virtually nothing," and which significantly redefines the understanding of consumer and welfare culture that is to be gained from his work.[32] And, in the vast and as yet unmapped territory between subjectivism and objectivism, Ellen Messer-Davidow has proposed locating a "perspectivism" that would "bring together, in processes of knowing, the personal and cultural, subjective and objective— replacing dichotomies with a systemic understanding of how and what we see."[33]

The quest for an alliance between a critical feminism and a demystified postmodernism has thus been initiated. Lovibond looks forward to a "friendly relationship," though she insists on a place for reckoning with false consciousness and with the traditions of Enlight-

31   Patricia Waugh, *Practising Postmodernism, Reading Modernism* (London: Edward Arnold, 1992), 120.

32   Nancy Fraser, "What's Critical about Critical Theory? The Case of Habermas and Gender," in *Feminism as Critique: On the Politics of Gender,* ed. Seyla Benhabib and Drucilla Cornell (Minneapolis: University of Minnesota Press, 1987), 32.

33   Ellen Messer-Davidow, "The Philosophical Bases of Feminist Literary Criticism," in *Gender and Theory: Dialogues on Feminist Criticism,* ed. Linda Kauffman (New York and Oxford: Blackwell, 1989), 88.

enment modernism as components of her feminism.[34] Fraser and Nicholson propose a potential synthesis of a nonessentialist feminism with a postmodern theory that would produce a "pragmatic and fallibilistic" procedure based in alliances rather than in hypothetical unities and identities.[35] Others continue to stress the differences between what they see as feminism and as postmodernism. Waugh believes that feminism needs "coherent subjects" (125) in order to pursue an activist agenda, not least because women have never had them, have never been in control of the master subject whose viability is the object of the postmodern critique.

It seems to me that this debate might usefully be refigured within the long-durational perspective I have been advocating, and taken out of the oppositional moment of presentist perceptions. The crucial third term to be added to the discussion would then be *feminization*, which would be the important principle against which feminism would want to define itself. Some of what is called the postmodern would embody this feminization, while other of its attributions might not. To recast the debate in this way would be to deconstruct, or at least to investigate, such recourses as Waugh's to a notion of "western *patriarchal* grand narratives" (128), whose disappearance would leave an untroubled space for the constitution of integrally feminine subjects. I have suggested that the feminine subject has not been excluded from the Enlightenment project, so much as written in dialectically and subordinately, and thus made available to both women and men (literary men, for instance) in various, culturally mediated ways. Inclusion is a much more efficient form of repression than exclusion in these instances.

A long-durational history might not prove to be the ultimate history for the postmodern, or for critical feminism's place within or beside it. But it might at least toss the salad in some new way, and ask different questions of those who are searching for definitions of what they do or detest. I would not want to suggest (and I have to keep saying this) that there can in principle be nothing new about the postmodern. To do so would be to answer the reifications of presentism

---

34   Lovibond, "Feminism and Postmodernism," 11, 25–26, 28.

35   Nancy Fraser and Linda Nicholson, "Social Criticism without Philosophy: An Encounter between Feminism and Postmodernism," *Theory, Culture, and Society* 5 (1988): 373–94, 391.

with those of historicism. But it is when the postmodern ethic emerges as piety, as the way to go, as affirmative, as celebration, that I find it most suspicious. I return to Adorno, who notes the ubiquity of "the idol of a pure present" as an "endeavor to strip thought of its historic dimension" (*Negative Dialectics*, 53). Politicians are obliged to use the rhetoric of solutions. For us, the "intellectuals," analyses are all the better for being processed through thought and tested by skepticism, not with the result of disavowing all solutions (though that too is a besetting academic strategy), but in hopes of enabling the better ones. Much of what is called postmodern theory looks like affirmation, or its fellow traveler, despair. Between the two, there is a place for a skepticism that is not alienation but engagement. Adorno again:

> Thought as such, before all particular contents, is an act of negation, of resistance to that which is forced upon it; this is what thought has inherited from its archetype, the relation between labor and material. Today, when ideologues tend more than ever to encourage thought to be positive, they cleverly note that positivity runs precisely counter to thought and that it takes friendly persuasion by social authority to accustom thought to positivity. (19)

Thought, here, is critical action, "a revolt against being importuned to bow to every immediate thing" (19). Literary criticism, in its divorce from philology and from literary history, has always had about it a strong element of such importuning, whereby even the writings of the past are, as we have seen, voiced for the present and as if somehow original to the present. Its conventions are thus, in Adorno's sense, countercritical. This is as much of a problem for those of us trying to do leftish historical-political work as it is for the blind conservatives who, like Charles Hall Grandgent in 1913, attribute the indifference to the past to the misguided utopian claims of a misconceived "socialism" that would make the world anew.[36] If the schematic history I am here attempting is of any use, it will be because it *is* a history, not an immediate thing but a mediated tradition. And as such it is not readily available in the easeful, insouciant manner of so much of the new historicism, nor reducible to that other postmodern commitment to con-

36   Charles Hall Grandgent, cited in Graff and Warner, *Origins of Literary Studies in America*, 128.

tingent opportunism—to what is of use to us now, and at hand. This history has to be worked for and worked over. It does not determine either the possibility or the impossibility of a postmodern feminism that is not itself a version of the feminization of the postmodern. It simply asks us to think a little harder than usual about where we are coming from.

Five

LOCALISM, LOCAL KNOWLEDGE, AND LITERARY CRITICISM

The feminist moment in contemporary literary criticism, I have suggested, has been a significant contributor to the new culture of autobiography, even as it has given rise to a critical countercurrent within feminist criticism itself. The traditional cultural positionality of literary criticism as imprecise and sensibilitarian, and thus feminized, has been strengthened as such by the new emphasis on situatedness, which subtracts from general conviction precisely what it adds in locally situated, empirical credibility. The more convincing the message is as a statement in place and time and for an occasion and a person, the further it is from making any more general claim to interest or applicability. Consensus or disagreement here is a matter of empathy or declared difference: we endorse or dispute the statement according to who we think we are and where we think we stand.

I have suggested that literary criticism, in this current incarnation, is proving very marketable among other humanities and social-science disciplines, and that the result of this export trade might be called academic postmodernism. The marketing takes various forms, and in this chapter I examine one of them: the rhetoric of localism and local knowledge, a rhetoric traditional to literary criticism but not previously as identifiable or welcome among other disciplines as it now seems to be. The culture of domesticity that has been widely recognized as one of the conditions of emergence of a bourgeois private sphere is itself a form of localization, with its effort at keeping women in place. And subjectivity itself, as the signature of literature and literary criticism's place in the culture of modernity, has been described by Charles Taylor as a form of "strong localization." Thus he writes: "We can now think of ideas as being 'in' this independent being, because it makes sense to see them as here and *not elsewhere*. And reciprocally, the notion of a separation requires some new sense of locale. "¹ This moment of individualization is profoundly divisive. Liberal thinkers have celebrated it as the inception of authentically human theologies and moral systems, while others (including such otherwise antagonistic elements as Catholics and Marxists) have seen here only the end of organic society, common purpose, and communal faith. Nietzsche wrote of nineteenth-century Germans as "no longer secure in a unified subjectivity," and described the condition of the artist and intellectual as an acute version of this general alienation.² The writers and critics of literature must also fall under this analysis, so that the present embracing of the rhetoric of localism can look very like making virtue of necessity. Taking the long view of modernity as an epoch roughly initiated or signaled in the writings of Montaigne and Descartes, one can see various versions of this "new sense of locale," each of which has been subject to celebration or dissent. (The transition from Enlightenment to romanticism, as popularly recognized and described, is one instance; the tussle over the objectivity or subjectivity of "science" is another.) At the moment there is no doubt that the localists are winning hands down among avant-garde intellectuals. Lyotard has declared that with the demise of grand narratives and metanarratives one can only recognize the plurality of language games and the heterogeneity of elements, which "only give rise to institutions in patches—local determinism." The permanent institution is thus displaced by the "temporary contract."³

For some commentators the new localism is just a neutral fact of life. Edward Soja's postmodern geography is premised on the idea of social spatiality as "a spatial matrix of nested locales" whose academic outcome must be a flowering of "critical regional studies."⁴ In the practical sphere this leads to what John McGowan has called "a pragmatic politics that starts from particular issues at particular local sites, a position that has found its most influential expression in Foucault's descrip-

---

1   Charles Taylor, *Sources of the Self: The Making of the Modern Identity* (Cambridge: Harvard University Press, 1989), 188. Compare Macpherson, *Political Theory of Possessive Individualism*, which argues for the place of subjectivity in the ideology of property. Macpherson quotes Henry Ireton's concern about the money economy as leaving its participant with "nothing that doth locally fix him to this kingdom" (152).

2   Nietzsche, *Untimely Meditations*, 82.

3   Lyotard, *Postmodern Condition*, xxiv, 66.

4   Soja, *Postmodern Geographies*, 148, 189.

tion of the specific intellectual."[5] The task of the critic, then, comes to be that of bringing out the "local, political contingency" of whatever is being inspected, whether to destroy error or plead for imitation.[6] Commonly there is a strong ethical component to this position, whereby we are roundly informed that to try to transcend the local is a sort of moral sin as well as an epistemological error (the epistemological ammunition comes, as often as not, from the writings of Richard Rorty, as a case against epistemology itself), a (masculine) fantasy no longer acceptable in polite company. And in a spectacular way it has become very clear that the ethics of localism is no longer a matter of mere academic concern. European political parties in particular (and some American politicians) are very interested in Amitai Etzioni's doctrine of "communitarianism," with its reorganization of the hierarchy of responsibility as ascending from the individual to family to community and only in the last resort to society at large.[7] What the scholars celebrate as an epistemological revolution can thus become available as a political tool for the attack on the welfare state. Fredric Jameson, one of the exemplary critics of localism, has good reasons for his questioning of "small-group, nonclass political practices" as all too available for "the more obscene celebrations of contemporary capitalist pluralism and democracy" and all too prone to remain as "unrelated fuzzy sets and semiautonomous subsystems."[8]

Localism is of course an enduring fantasy component of modern life, as appealing to those who feel that they have lost or missed it as it is complex and ambivalent for those who actually (and always only partly) live it. W. B. Yeats wanted for his daughter what he had not had himself: the experience of living like "some green laurel / Rooted in one dear perpetual place."[9] One senses here, along with the wish for freedom from the anxieties of self-consciousness and self-making, a re-

5 McGowan, *Postmodernism and Its Critics*, 277.

6 The words are James Clifford's, in *The Predicament of Culture: Twentieth-Century Ethnography, Literature, and Art* (Cambridge and London: Harvard University Press, 1988), 13, but they are generic in the lexicon of the new historicism. On Clifford's move away from the defense of localism, see Robbins, *Secular Vocations*, 193–94.

7 See Norman Stone, "A Mad Scramble for the Centre," *Sunday Times* (London), 9 October 1994, sect. 3, 6–7.

8 Jameson, *Postmodernism*, 318, 320, 372.

9 "A Prayer for My Daughter," in *The Collected Poems of W. B. Yeats*, 2d ed. (London: Macmillan, 1969), 213.

ification and feminization of the child, a desire that she be, in Wordsworth's lines, "a thing that could not feel" the pleasures as well as the
pains of life. [10] At least since Adam Smith proposed that the health of
the capitalist economy depended upon the unencumbered movement
of the labor force, the industrial pastoral has purveyed a compensatory
image of preindustrial stability by way of a conjunction of the rural and
the domestic: happy families in fixed localities. And Smith himself was
probably making virtue of a mobility deemed somehow necessary
since the exit from Eden.

Most traditional incarnations of the localist ideal have declared or
implied an investment in fixing the position of women, whether within
the garden of Eden or within its postlapsarian analogues: home, family, and the domestic routine. Rural labor always did and still does
make use of women workers as indiscriminately as do the industrial and
service economies; but modernization's attributes of urbanization, literacy, and mobility have gained the reputation of dislocating home
and family, and licensed a corresponding romanticization of rural (local) life. And so, when localism has functioned as a nostalgic or utopian alternative to the rough facts of modern life, it has incorporated
into its ideological profile a fantasy about the function of the feminine
as a kind of foundational motif. Literature's conditioning affiliation
with the feminized component of modern culture (for which I have
previously argued) thus renders it identifiable also with the local. And,
indeed, Anglo-American and especially British literature and criticism
has had an abiding predilection for ethical and methodological localism. Literary critics have commonly prided themselves on being particular, and in speaking for particularity. Give them a theory or a
general idea, and they will show you the individual exception, the one
that does not so much make the rule as prove the implausibility of all
rules. They have thus functioned as the cautionary conscience, ignored at our collective peril, of a modernization process they and
others have defined as motivated principally by a dangerously instrumental reason aiming to level us all to the rank of automatons.

But this urgent exceptionalism has not, of course, been the result
of a merely abstract moral incentive. In the eighteenth century, where

---

10   William Wordsworth, "A Slumber Did My Spirit Seal," *"Lyrical Ballads" and Other*
Poems, 1797–1800, ed. James Butler and Karen Green (Ithaca and London: Cornell University Press, 1992), 164.

we may trace the origins of modern literary criticism, the emphasis upon individuality (strong localism) as typicality in the British national character (and for instance in the characters of Shakespeare's plays) functioned as the self-definition for a bourgeois readership that was increasingly formative of culture while remaining excluded from political power. Hume, for example, proposed that Britain's commitment to tolerance and mixed government produced a culture of individuals rather than of types.[11] One might see this emphasis on dispositional idiosyncrasy as a compensatory principle making up for the lack of a political franchise: one expresses one's claim to attention by forms of exceptionalism that are ultimately privatized and aestheticized and displayed in the personality rather than in the polis.

At the same time, the class-formation process in the complex commercial culture that surrounded and determined the coming into being of literary criticism *was* dependent upon increased social and geographic mobility of the sort that Smith had recommended, and its technologies required (or seemed to require) the mastery of general ideas rather than a preoccupation with local particularities. John Locke, one of the most important advocates of the new class configuration, made this priority very clear in his theorization of language. He pronounced it impossible that "every particular Thing should have a distinct peculiar name." The human mind cannot retain a distinct idea of every item it encounters, "every Bird, and Beast Men saw; every Tree, and Plant, that affected the Senses." We cannot function like this in a complex world, where classification by type and general idea is essential: it is for this reason that "Men have never attempted to give Names to each Sheep in their Flock."[12]

But of course the strongly localized pastoral ideal promises just this: a name for every sheep in the flock. And Locke himself is clear that, notwithstanding the need for general ideas in language, things themselves remain resolutely particular: "When therefore we quit Particulars, the Generals that rest, are only Creatures of our own making, their general Nature being nothing but the Capacity they are put into by the Understanding, of signifying or representing many particulars"

---

11 David Hume, "Of National Characters," in *Essays Moral, Political, and Literary*, ed. Eugene F. Miller (Indianapolis: Liberty Classics, 1985), 197–215.

12 John Locke, *An Essay concerning Human Understanding*, corr. ed. P. H. Nidditch (Oxford: Clarendon Press, 1979), 409.

(414). What Locke deems inevitable, Blake finds deplorable: "General Knowledge is Remote Knowledge it is in Particulars that Wisdom consists & Happiness too."[13] The modernizing generalities that characterize species designations in the utilitarian poetries of such as Dyer and Thomson—"woolly breeders" and "finny tribes"—are countered by the microscopically local nominations of romantics like Blake and Clare and by a number of Wordsworthian protagonists who have an eye for every tree and flower and for every minute change in the weather. These poets and personae point out to us what would otherwise go unnoticed, as of absolute significance; they perform the poetry of relocalization. And this gesture of relocalization is itself gendered, and gendered feminine, as well as classed. John Barrell has argued that Wordsworth's famous "Tintern Abbey" poem subsists by organizing a series of shifts between lofty abstractions and particular details, with the first intelligible to (and directed at) educated males within the republic of letters, and the second identified with unlettered females and the lower classes. Abstractions can be filled out into meanings only by acts of mind, while natural details are self-explanatory. Dorothy can enjoy what William enjoys only by promise or projection; in herself and in the poem's present, she can manage only mute delight.[14]

The bifocal address Barrell finds in Wordsworth's poem is, I think, symptomatic of an ambivalence fundamental to literature and its criticism then and since. On the one hand, both literature and literary criticism aspire to and can even seem to access the language of generalities, associated with the masculine (economically privileged and thus disinterested men of superior social standing), with the sublime, and with scientific theory. On the other hand, they depend upon the precise localization of detail and perspective that is most fully savored when one is *not* the master of general ideas, that is, when one is a woman or a feminized man. The same diadic coding informs Wordsworth's portrayals of rural folk, at times emblems of rugged (masculine) self-dependence, at other times structurally feminized, politically or rhe-

13　*The Complete Poetry and Prose of William Blake*, ed. David Erdman, rev. ed. (Berkeley and Los Angeles: University of California Press, 1982), 560.

14　John Barrell, "The Uses of Dorothy," in *Poetry, Language, and Politics* (Manchester: Manchester University Press, 1988), 137–67.

torically, as in the description of the "crowd" at the foot of Helvellyn counterpoised to the dangerously empowered city throng:

> Crowd seems it, solitary hill, to thee,
> Though but a little family of men—
> Twice twenty—with their children and their wives. [15]

As gender (and feudal) hierarchy is preserved within the group—men, children, wives—so the whole group is infantilized and/or feminized when seen from the perspective of the mountain (to which, on another occasion, Wordsworth compared himself). The local is the primitive: but there, we are to believe at least for the moment, lies happiness.

Literary criticism and the literature it invokes can be read in terms of a similarly diadic movement between theory and fact, the general and the particular, the abstract and the local; but the movement only takes place, I have argued, within an already-feminized cultural position that gives one option a head start over the other. Much of literary criticism's disciplinary energy has come from its efforts to impose restraints on the runaway tendencies of general ideas. At worst its commitment to minute particulars has produced an anti-intellectual rhetoric of exceptionalism, an imaginary stick with which to beat the philosophers and the scientists, evident for example in the face-off between F. R. Leavis and C. P. Snow in the early 1960s. Whatever the limitations of Snow's technological utopianism, Leavis's response showed once again that the cosmopolitan ethic was more conformable with science than with literary criticism, which traditionally resorts, as it here resorted, to vitalist particulars as a defense against general ideas. For much of the twentieth century, literary criticism has marketed itself as a mobile energy moving between everyone else's fixed approaches. We take what we want from history, philosophy, anthropology, and so on, but we never linger long enough to fall under the spell of systems and structures, which are often seen to be morally as well as methodologically improper, leading us away from the fecund temporality of the "lived experience" (to echo one of Raymond Williams's favorite phrases) and toward the mind-set of the bureaucrat or

15 William Wordsworth, *Prelude*, 268 (beginning of book 8).

the prison guard. When E. P. Thompson, in his notorious response to Althusser (who was doubly damned as both a theorist and a Frenchman), announced that "history knows no regular verbs," he took up the rhetoric of literary criticism, and thus revealed himself in at least this anticipatory sense as a postmodern historian.[16]

That the postmodern initiative has brought with it a revival of localist rhetoric is not, I think, in question. The local and the particular are now commonly identified as determining the only subject positions that are ethically and epistemologically allowable within a society whose fundamental fracturings are a sort of given. The postmodern moment thus necessitates a fairly radical qualification of Alvin Gouldner's description of the "new class" in which intellectuals belong. Gouldner saw public education and the communications revolution as cosmopolitan, delocalizing forces sponsoring the "situation-free language variants" of critical discourse. Students are increasingly educated away from home by professional intellectuals inculcating general standards of judgment adjudicated by superior minds—their own.[17] What we now see, it seems, is a backlash against cosmopolitanism within the very subculture that has traditionally had most to gain from delocalization. Hence, perhaps, the apparent paradox of a postmodernity that celebrates simultaneously the onset of global culture and the reactive localisms deemed necessary to our survival. It seems very clear that the traditional distinction between theory and particularity has collapsed: most theory now preaches the virtues of localization. Natalie Zemon Davis has spoken of the appeal of a "microhistory" that is "concrete, privileging fact and event along with local thought and habit," and this is also the disposition of the new historicism in literary studies.[18] We live with what Alan Liu has astutely termed the "romanticism of detail," with a "revisionary idea of culture whose full sweep could be conveniently analyzed as a cultural *empirics, pragmatics,* and *dialogics,*" to the point that "the local threatens to go transcendental."[19] This recrudescence of the local by no means excludes the fantasy lo-

---

16 E. P. Thompson, "The Poverty of Theory, or An Orrery of Errors," in *The Poverty of Theory and Other Essays* (New York and London: Monthly Review Press, 1978), 46.

17 See Gouldner, *Future of Intellectuals,* 3–4, 43, 65.

18 Natalie Zemon Davis, "Stories and the Hunger to Know," *Yale Journal of Criticism* 5, no. 2 (1992): 160.

19 Liu, "Local Transcendence," 80, 91.

calism traditional in antimodernization rhetoric of the sort typified by Yeats's prayer for his daughter, "rooted in one dear perpetual place." That tradition lingers on in a familiar identity politics and romanticization of "community," and it can sometimes be the source of a certain political challenge, or utopia. Even Nietzsche regarded this "clinging to . . . one's own bare mountainside" as a "very salutary ignorance" in the face of the obvious pressures of a nation "given over to a restless, cosmopolitan hunting after new and ever newer things." But, he goes on (or went on, as early as 1874) to make clear that the view from the tree is a limited one:

> [T]he tree is aware of its roots to a greater degree than it is able to see them; but this awareness judges how big they are from the size and strength of its visible branches. If, however, the tree is in error as to this, how greatly it will be in error regarding all the rest of the forest around it! . . . The antiquarian sense of a man, a community, a whole people, always possesses an extremely restricted field of vision; most of what exists it does not perceive at all, and the little it does see it sees much too close up and isolated; it cannot relate what it sees to anything else and it therefore accords everything it sees equal importance and therefore to each individual thing too great importance. [20]

One could cast Nietzsche here as at once the exponent and the critic of much of what is recognizable as the postmodern, for it seems that we have not yet escaped the compulsive repetition of this very debate. While we may seem to have moved beyond the affirmation of a pastoralized localism, we have certainly not come to agreement about the terms within which it is properly contained and by which it is most suitably contextualized and—dare I say it—theorized. The still urgent argument about totalization (most famously in and around Jameson's work) is ample evidence of that. Our prohibitions and recommendations wander (strategically or hopelessly) between ethics and epistemology, so that what we think we cannot know, or have great difficulty knowing, comes to be cast as what we must not try to know, or must not know in the inherited ways. On the one hand, postmodernism's critics worry that the current ethical imperatives are nothing more than the latest version of the psychopathology of divided labor: trying to get things right on a small scale and hoping for the best about the outcome. Bruce Robbins is convincing in his linkage of the appeal of localism with a desire to preserve the image of effective agency.[21] On the other hand, those same critics are unable to resort to the old ways by invoking traditional models of objectivity, rationality, and theory. We cannot deny that, in Linda Alcoff's words, "location *bears on* meaning and truth" even if we are not prepared to concede that it "*determines* meaning and truth."[22] This predicament of not knowing what to do, or how to know, leading us to register unease or dissent without the prospect of clear alternatives, may itself be a fully developed consequence of living within what Foucault called the "analytic of finitude," which he identified as constitutive of modernity and which always subsumes within its logic of uncertainty any efforts we might make at grasping the limits of our own historicality.[23]

It may yet be useful to hold out for some potential distinction between the ethical and the epistemological, between what we ought to be doing (according to one kind of persuasion) and what we can know/do (according to a different order of conviction), in this matter of postmodern localization. I will return to this. For the moment I want to examine some aspects of the rhetoric of localism in one of its most formative and exciting disciplinary incarnations: in anthropology. Anthropology and literary criticism have traded methods and metaphors at various points in their respective evolutions. On at least two significant occasions, literary criticism has been the borrower, as it turned first to Sir James Frazer and then to Claude Lévi-Strauss for a new lease on its analytical life. Each of these turns had a foundationalist ambition, looking for a latent and real content to the apparent contingencies and confusions of social and literary information. Through the rituals of sacrifice and renewal, and through the structures of kinship and the exchange of women, culture and literature could be made to seem to be about something very deep and very real. Objective sense appeared to have been made of the language of appearances.[24]

21 Robbins, *Secular Vocations*, 187–88.

22 Alcoff, "Problem of Speaking for Others," 16.

23 Foucault, *Order of Things*, 312–18.

24 For an account of the deep common traditions of anthropology and literary criticism, see Vincent P. Pecora, "The Sorcerer's Apprentices: Romance, Anthropology, and Literary Theory," *Modern Language Quarterly* 55, no. 4 (1994): 345–82.

Recent relations between anthropology and literary criticism have been the other way round: anthropologists have redesigned their discipline by turning to the imprecisions and confusions of literary criticism and looking to poetry rather than science as the appropriate paradigm for imitation. For at least twenty years now Clifford Geertz has been describing and celebrating a "refiguration of social thought" that subsists by "analogies drawn from the humanities," thus publicizing for anthropology the same shifts and migrations that Rorty announced for philosophy.[25] Geertz has been massively influential in his readiness to declare that anthropology, far from functioning as literary criticism's scientific "other," is itself already literary. The "local knowledge" that he publicizes is not at all foundational, and completely undermines the traditional associations of localism with some sort of experiential or intellectual confidence or security. If we imagine the anthropologist as one who immerses him or herself completely in some local culture, mastering the language, becoming one with the people, and learning the names of all the sheep, then Geertz's "local knowledge" will surprise us. For what it brings out is not the comfort of complete knowledge but the interactive instability of all knowledge claims. The more local and small-scale the analysis seeks to remain, the more undecidable and disquietingly dialectical it becomes. We may sense that we are in the presence of some important kind of difference, one that may matter, but we can never be quite sure what it is or how it works. If we sense that we understand some things about the stranger, then we have to worry about the motivations for our own understanding; and if we set out to correct a sense of not understanding, then we give rise to a similar discomfort about the tools we bring to the task. If the traditional localist paradigm, with its associations of pastoralized innocence and guilt-free intervention, holds out the fantasy of totally sufficient knowledge, then reading Geertz will turn that paradigm on its head. Geertz takes us to remote places, immerses us as totally as he can, and then shows us how little we have learned. Or does he?

Many of the exemplary Geertzian moves are made in his important essay of 1973, "Thick Description: Toward an Interpretive Theory of Culture." The title, borrowed from Gilbert Ryle, might seem to

25 Clifford Geertz, *Local Knowledge: Further Essays in Interpretive Anthropology* (New York: Basic Books, 1983), 19.

promise a traditional kind of localist gratification, an immersion in detail and content to the point of effective completion, total knowledge. After all, thick description seems to contrast itself with thin description, as adequate instead of superficial. But the key word is actually in Geertz's subtitle: "interpretive." Ethnography is indeed thick description, but it is ethno*graphy* and not ethno*logy*; it is an act of writing built upon and within an act of reading. As such it is "like trying to read . . . a manuscript," one full of "ellipses, incoherences, suspicious emendations," and written in a foreign language, that of "shaped behavior."[26] Given these circumstances, the validity of cultural description should not be measured by a maximum of "coherence," which is only the mark of "a paranoid's delusion or a swindler's story" (17–18). Some minimum coherence must be assumed (and Geertz glosses over the problem of what minimum coherence might be), but beyond that, ethnography is best understood as "guessing at meanings, assessing the guesses, and drawing explanatory conclusions from the better guesses" (20). Its attentions must be "microscopic" and committed to "exceedingly extended acquaintances with extremely small matters" (21). Like the literary critic, the anthropologist is heavily committed to detail. But Geertz never signs up with the "against theory" faction that has always been typical of literary criticism at one of its extremes. Rather, he finesses the relation between detail and theory in a way that renders him residually acceptable to social scientists even as he chips away at some of their traditional assumptions. Thus we "insinuate" the theories we cannot fully or confidently "state" (24).

One can see Geertz here as a loyal cold warrior in the fight against overarching theories, but one whose social-science commitments will not let him abandon completely the ambition for some general paradigms, or potential paradigms. Thus he argues that there might be a useful generality emerging from ethnographical work, as long as it comes from "the delicacy of its distinctions, not the sweep of its abstractions" (25). This reads as an odd enactment of the dilemma, as then perceived, between liberalism and communism, the one creating wholes out of the recognition of ineluctable differences, the other imposing repressive totalities from above. And Geertz resolves the tension in much the same way as Rorty does, by an appeal to the norms of polite conversation and debate. There is no grand theory to be hoped

---

26   Clifford Geertz, *The Interpretation of Cultures* (New York: Basic Books, 1973), 10.

for from cultural analysis, which is "essentially incomplete." So much so that "the more deeply it goes the less complete it is." But this does not produce in Geertz any radically postmodern (or poststructural) skepticism, a declaration of the impossibility of ever being satisfied that one knows anything at all. That possibility is touched upon but laid aside in favor of "a refinement of debate. What gets better is the precision with which we vex each other" (29). In other words, oddly enough, the satisfactions of localization that are no longer available in the field are resurrected in the seminar room. The moral and epistemological stresses produced by any scrupulous encounter with the world of the "other" are converted into conversational skill and, some might say, professional advantage.

But it would not be fair to Geertz to leave things here. Ten years later, in 1983, he published another influential volume of essays under the title *Local Knowledge*, a title whose subtle ironies his readers should have by then learned to anticipate. Here he observed that the acceptance among social scientists of an inexact or literary methodology had now become rather common. Anthropology in particular had proved compatible with an emphasis on the "ineluctably local" and on limited knowledge claims:

> Long one of the most homespun of disciplines, hostile to anything smacking of intellectual pretension and unnaturally proud of an outdoorsman image, anthropology has turned out, oddly enough, to have been preadapted to some of the most advanced varieties of modern opinion. The contextualist, antiformalist, relativizing tendencies of the bulk of that opinion, its turn toward examining the ways in which the world is talked about —depicted, charted, represented—rather than the way it intrinsically is, have been rather easily absorbed by adventurer scholars used to dealing with strange perceptions and stranger stories. They have, wonder of wonders, been speaking Wittgenstein all along. (4)

This passage is as deceptively partial as it is rhetorically persuasive—and Geertz *is* a great stylist. By presenting anthropology as always already there, it obscures the degree to which the discipline has been back and forth between scientific and humanist-textualist self-descriptions. And by attributing an "outdoorsman image" to anthropologists, it mystifies the process whereby the discipline's embrace of

these (post)modern "relativizing tendencies" has come not with the
proliferation of fieldwork but with its decline, that is, with the incremental unavailability of innocently remote alternative cultures for empirical, in-place study and their replacement with our own samples
(urban anthropology) or with theory in the seminar room. The
"adventurer scholars," in other words, may be used to dealing with
strangeness, but it is an increasingly prepackaged version of the
exotic—some might say a simulacrum. And it is at least arguable that
in the period of classic explorer anthropology the encounter with
strangeness was accompanied with less rather than more interest in
"the most advanced varieties of modern opinion." At the same time, we
must grant Geertz's point that the decade of the 1970s saw an increased acceptance of methodological imprecision among ethnographers, even as we might wish to dispute the larger history implicit in
his statement. Geertz's attitude to the handling of the tension between
microscopy and macroscopy does not seem to have changed substan-
tially. He still seeks a nontotalized play between the two, a method
achieving "what generality it can by orchestrating contrasts rather
than isolating regularities or abstracting types" (13). This can provide
an orientation but never a foundation (187). Ethnography, like all
the other disciplines to which it has at last confessed its kinship, is a
"somewhat catch-as-catch-can enterprise, one whose aim is to render
obscure matters intelligible by providing them with an informing context" (152). As literary criticism always has, ethnography too now joy-
fully produces its "intellectual poaching license" (21), not as a badge of
shame in the face of challenge by the enforcers of scientific law, but as a
sign of membership of an intellectual elite, those who know the way
things really are and must be. But how must they be? Geertz has been
very convincingly taken to task for remaining too localist in his local
knowledge, too incurious about the national and transnational pressures that make his cultures into what they are.[27] From this perspective
one might propose that Geertz's commitment to the microscopic is not
just a gesture against (Western) theoretical abstractions but a willed

27   See Vincent P. Pecora, "The Limits of Local Knowledge," in *The New Historicism*, ed.
H. Aram Veeser (London and New York: Routledge, 1989), 243–76. For a general critique of the loss of faith in objectivity in anthropology, see Johannes Fabian, "Ethnographic Objectivity Revisited: From Rigor to Vigor," in *Rethinking Objectivity*, ed. Allan
Megill (Durham and London: Duke University Press, 1994), 81–108. Fabian is worried
about "postmodern nihilism" and the power of "literary critique" (90, 92).

exclusion of the nonmicroscopic determinations affecting cultures already far more involved with Western interests than most ethnographers can afford to recognize, let alone analyze.

Leaving aside what Geertz is very obviously not doing—that is, providing any minimally adequate level of social or historical (as opposed to abstractly methodological) self-consciousness—it is still worth asking what he thinks he is doing, in his own terms. His project can be understood as a response to the basic dilemma of anthropology as John and Jean Comaroff have defined it:

> An important moment of choice is now upon us. If we take our task to be an exercise in intersubjective translation, in speaking for others and their point of view, our hubris will cause us no end of difficulties, moral and philosophical. And if we see it to lie in the formal analysis of social systems or cultural structures, statistically or logically conceived, we evade the issue of representation and experience altogether. [28]

The anthropologist, in other words, can project him- or herself neither as scientist nor as translator; nor, if we carry this train of thought into more recent incarnations, can she or he be plausibly comfortable with the role of shaman or activist, without incurring some of the same doubts and disabilities. Geertz's focus on this question is less than crystal clear, but it is at least bifocal: it is about "them," the objects of our attention, but it is also about "us," as well as us-and-them. Encountering another culture gives us directions "toward some of the defining characteristics, however various and ill-ordered, of what it is we want to grasp: a different sense of law" (187). This suggests a protoscientific ambition. But later he describes the value of encounter as that of "bringing incommensurable perspectives on things, dissimilar ways of registering experiences and phasing lives, into conceptual proximity such that, though our sense of their distinctiveness is not reduced (normally it is deepened), they seem somehow less enigmatical than they do when they are looked at apart" (233).

The difference between having a "sense of law" and things seeming "somehow less enigmatical" is fairly radical for anyone seeking a precise or precisely usable prescription for ethnographic knowledge. Eth-

28 John Comaroff and Jean Comaroff, *Ethnography and the Historical Imagination* (Boulder: Westview Press, 1992), 12.

nography is, of course, more visibly fraught with moral implications than is literary criticism—no critic worries overmuch about a bad or wrong reading, which can always be supplanted by a better one with no residual damage to the text. But the anthropologist acquires existential responsibilities as soon as he or she dons the safari gear, even if the evidence for this is largely now in the historical record. Pronouncements about the characteristics of other cultures can and do have consequences, especially if no one else has made them before.

This responsibility makes it all the more understandable that Geertz would fudge or finesse the question (for who among us has the answer?) of exactly what the "different sense of law" might amount to, even as it seems more important that he not do so. It is clear what he is not proposing: that there is some transcultural or universal structure to human societies or to human experience. This is not how we can expect to make things "less enigmatical." But he is equally clear and consistent in his refusal of a naive relativism. This, indeed, he locates as a besetting "academic neurosis," which worries itself that confronting the situatedness of knowledge means having nothing to say that is not trivial or tautological (153–54). In *The Interpretation of Cultures* Geertz had rejected the lazy response to epistemological frustration: "I have never been impressed by the argument that, as complete objectivity is impossible in these matters (as, of course, it is), one might as well let one's sentiments run loose. As Robert Solow has remarked, that is like saying that as a perfectly aseptic environment is impossible, one might as well conduct surgery in a sewer" (30). The analogy is interesting, and misleading. Faced with a life-threatening emergency, one would make do with the best surgical environment available, even while knowing full well that degrees of sepsis matter a great deal. This is a false—and intriguingly scientific—measure of the question in ethnography. Why might it matter to have some knowledge, however imperfect, of another culture, rather than none at all? Why is it better to make some knowledge claim, however imperfect, rather than to refuse to make such a claim? The necessities here are contingent and hence disputable. It is true that we all live on the same planet, but that is not the same as saying that we all live in the same world, or are obliged to understand each other. Geertz sometimes seems to be presenting the de facto existence of ethnography—that it exists—as a rationale for its existence—that we should entertain a different sense of law, or make things less enigmatical. And, it seems to me, Geertz is in the last analysis the exponent of a sense of value, and of a dimension of argumentation that is related to the epistemological problem—that of knowing the "other"—but is not identical to it, and should not be identified with it or inferred from it. Geertz recognizes that we have all become "more and more involved in each other's business" and that it is then important to ponder "how local knowledge and cosmopolitan intent may comport, or fail to, in the emerging world disorder" (*Local Knowledge*, 183). And in a humane way he wants to make it possible "for people inhabiting different worlds to have a genuine, and reciprocal, impact upon one another" (161). But the underlying methodological procedures he advises or implies are always performative and pragmatist: they can be known or deployed in place and time only by those in the place at the time. As such, they remain unanalyzable and unpredictable. There is no reproducible method and no foreseeable outcome. This can produce only a laissez-faire model, unless one resorts overtly to a recommendation of one's own social conditions as adequate to the demands of encounter—as Rorty does in his defense of Western, liberal values—or makes an appeal to foundational categories of conscience, sympathy, or tolerance (which, for Rorty, are precisely the historical forms of the Western, liberal tradition).

Geertz is much too cautious a writer to take that route, but much of what he says seems to imply or require it. The moral instrumentalism of his ethnography comes clearer precisely as its epistemological procedures become more obscure. It expresses a cosmopolitan ideal whose embeddedness in the traditions of Western liberalism is never entirely set aside but never stridently celebrated. Encounter with the other produces curiosity and sympathy with one who is incipiently similar to us but only in limited ways, different in total context even as partial contexts overlap, and never exactly definable at a precise point on the line from the familiar to the incomprehensible. Geertz speaks of the achievement of learning to see ourselves as "a local example of the forms human life has locally taken" as one of "largeness of mind," and thus replicates a familiar and still dignified Enlightenment aspiration (16). But what does not look like the Enlightenment is the tetchy, defensive censuring of the urge for theory: "If there is any message in what I have been saying here, it is that the world is a various place . . . and much is to be gained, scientifically and otherwise, by confronting that grand actuality rather than wishing it away in a haze of forceless generalities and false comforts" (234).

Not all generalities need be forceless; it is the antitheoretical climate of academic postmodernism that can allow the writer to ignore the interesting or potentially useful ones. At this point Geertz still seems to be fighting the cold war, dazzled (ideologically) by the sheer diversity of human life and personality and committed to its preservation from the reductive attentions of a totalitarian (Marxist) intelligentsia and their attendant state apparatus. He is also, of course, defending the secular liberal perspective against the fundamentalisms of religion and nationalism whose totalitarian inclinations have always been far more evident in American life than any Marxism, and whose continuing presence has so often had the odd effect of persuading the intellectuals into a massive act of displacement, whereby the enemy is imaged as foreign-Marxist-theorist instead of being recognized as an enemy within. One might similarly speculate about the contexts of the effort that the academic postmodernism of the 1990s is making at capturing or speaking for a popular culture that is disaggregated and carnivalesque rather than coopted and predetermined by popular fundamentalisms. The academic postmodern cannot, for some complex reason, seem to free itself into complete critical distance from the aura of nationalism (so much of what is seen to enact the postmodern is, after all, the product of American technology and global Americanization), and thus it cannot begin to resolve the question of the degree to which it serves the master it purports at other times to criticize. Why is it that Geertz's endorsement of "the power of the scientific imagination to bring us into touch with the lives of strangers" reads almost like a celebration of television?[29]

Geertz has recently come back to the matter of local knowledge, and he has reiterated his long-standing conviction that "universals" are either implausible or trivial, and made even clearer the degree to which he is satisfied with the "minimum damage" rationale for the kind of anthropological research he respects.[30] Universals, of course, were never the issue: between the local and the universal (and within the local), the question is one of workable theories and productive generalities, not transcendental norms. It is in that middle realm that historical models and their deviations do their work. But these were never at

29   Geertz, *Interpretation of Cultures*, 16.

30   Clifford Geertz, "'Local Knowledge' and Its Limits: Some *Obiter Dicta*," *Yale Journal of Criticism* 5, no. 2 (1992): 130–32.

the center of Geertz's interests, as they are at the center of Bourdieu's.[31] In fact, one might conclude that his efforts were all directed at heading off exactly this kind of analysis, given his emphasis on the promise and potential of cultural exchange rather than on its arguably precontaminated identity. His latest remarks endorse the "renunciation of authority" that he sees in the "direct and open acknowledgement of limits" of the best ethnographic research. But there is an aw-shucks tone to his sense of the value of the experience whereby he, "a middle-class, mid–twentieth-century American, more or less standard, male, went out to this place, talked to some people I could get to talk to me, and think things are sort of rather this way with them there" (132). And the irony is by no means completely ironic. This *is* what anthropologists do, and they had better admit it. In so doing, for Geertz, they free themselves from possible guilt or culpability. But only if they believe that the "renunciation of authority" is possible, or complete, or sufficient. Once again, Geertz has finessed the big question.

But he does at least, if only by these indirections and evasions, bring us to the big question. His positive and liberal polemic on behalf of a cosmopolitanism that does not resign us to "anarchy, grantsmanship and the higher solipsism" but rather leaves open the possibility that "people inhabiting different worlds" might have "a genuine, and reciprocal, impact upon one another" (*Local Knowledge*, 161) inevitably leads him into certain kinds of accountability about how, within what constraints, and with what consequences such reciprocity occurs. Thus his critics have continued to comment on his use of "the old dichotomy of the universal and the local" as insufficient unto a world in which "all theories of the middle range necessarily involve linking the particular and the general in some generative combination."[32]

Geertz nibbles at the inherited categories and seemingly decides between them without offering any coherent alternative in the sphere of either politics or method. That presumably goes some way toward

31 Bourdieu is dogged in his defense of a local-universal sequence in sociological research. Dense study of local situations *can*, he affirms, lead to "universal laws" and "transhistorical variants." See Bourdieu and Wacquant, *Invitation to Reflexive Sociology*, 75, 78.
32 Sara Suleri, "Local Knowledge and Its Limits," and Jack Goody, "Local Knowledge and Knowledge of Locality," (respectively), *Yale Journal of Criticism* 5, no. 2 (1992): 155, 146.

explaining his extraordinarily pervasive influence in the humanistic and social-science academy. Stephen Tyler's postmodern anthropology is much more confrontational, setting out to offer "the language of resistance to all totalizing ideologies that justify the repression of the commonsense world in the name of utopia, or that seek to theorize practice and judgement as the expression of theory."[33] Tyler's postmodernism is as antagonistic to the apparent academic norms of constructive conversation as Geertz's is compliant with those norms. Tyler's postmodernism "names no positive program nor system of concepts; it narrates no minatory tales, evokes no original allegories of past wholeness, and builds no foundations for future utopias" (3). For Tyler the model of dialogue, with its origins in the conventions of polite conversation and agreed reciprocity, is merely a mystification deployed in support of the "fable of participant observation" (98): there is no real dialogue in the ethnographic act. But despite his withering critique of liberal ethnography, Tyler too cannot resist the lapse into the language of solutions, and when he falls into it he reproduces just another version of the literary prototype as the preferred paradigm. Rorty looked to poetry as a model for the continual self and cultural creation that philosophy ought now to become, and Geertz appealed to the methods associated with literary criticism (and Wittgenstein) as renovating influences for ethnography. Tyler also calls for a "return to the original context and function of poetry which, by means of its performative break with everyday speech, evoked memories of the *ethos* of the community and thereby provoked hearers to act ethically" (202). The ethnographer does not read a text but takes part in the "cooperative story making" of a "polyphonic text" that has no final synthesis (203). It must be fragmentary because life is like that, at best "a collection of indexical anecdotes or telling particulars" (208). Like a poem, this ethnography "creates its own objects in its unfolding and the reader supplies the rest" (215).

What we see here, I think, is simply the superficially anarchistic poetic paradigm, not so far removed from the liberal-progressive poetic paradigm as Tyler's rhetorical bravado might lead us to think. He does not really lead us beyond "the theoretical and commonsense categories of the hegemonic western tradition" (206), as he promises to do, but rather offers a very traditional release and return cycle by way of

33 Tyler, *The Unspeakable*, xi.

the somatic, cathartic, and figurative resources of the aesthetic experience. Instead of agreeing that we agree or disagree about important interpretations, as we do in Rorty's poetic, we are here carried away by the power of utterance into a momentary suspension of disbelief that is at once powerful and phantasmagoric—as it has to be if it is to avoid precisely the processes of reification it sets out to critique. The difference is not between traditional and radical, Western and non-Western, but between good conversation and good rock and roll. Tyler says as much when he describes his postmodern ethnography as "an object of meditation which provokes a rupture with the commonsense world and evokes an aesthetic integration whose therapeutic effect is worked out in the restoration of the commonsense world" (211). The hope must be that the world will then be somewhat different from what it was, and this is the same hope that Lyotard, Rorty, and Geertz make explicit. But Tyler cannot afford to make ethnography an unacknowledged legislator for humankind, nor can he imagine the world's great age beginning anew, for to do so would be to engage, once again, the forbidden dialectic of local and general that caused such problems for Geertz and Rorty and that remains so firmly established in the received methodological traditions of "western hegemony" even as that hegemony seeks to pluralize itself from within. It is exactly this dialectic that poetry, with its willing suspensions of disbelief, can momentarily suspend. But we cannot read poetry all the time, or it would not be poetry.

I have said that the inspection of the rhetoric of localization that runs through so much of academic (and other) postmodernism often reflects a category confusion between ethics and epistemology, between questions about what we ought to do and questions about what we can know. The awareness that we are not supposed to speak for others, who are supposed to speak for themselves, is an ethical awareness, though one very troubled by its comfortable location within an ideology of equal opportunity. It is quite different from an argument that says that we cannot know others in ways that are not always already forms of ourselves; or (another version) that there are no forms of ourselves that are also forms for others. This second, epistemological argument raises enormously difficult questions, for which we arguably do not even have objectifiable resolutions. But it is quite different from the lazy, self-affirming gesture that is so often made to follow from it, which says that we *must* not speak for or as the other. This conviction might be, I have implied, quite convenient to and sufficient for a subculture in which everyone has an opportunity to speak for themselves—though I would question whether there is or has ever been such a subculture except in the ideological imaginary. But it will not do at all as either an epistemology *or* an ethics for a more differentiated world, in the face of which it can only look like a localist mystification. S. P. Mohanty has posed the question exactly as I would pose it: "It is necessary to assert our dense particularities, our lived and imagined differences; but could we afford to leave untheorized the question of how our differences are intertwined, and, indeed, hierarchically organized? Could we, in other words, afford to have *entirely* different histories, to see ourselves as living—and having lived—in entirely heterogeneous and discrete spaces?"[34] The problem with the academic postmodern, as I have here instanced it, is exactly that it does leave this question untheorized, as Mohanty puts it. Indeed, it can go so far as to pronounce that the ambition *to* theorize is itself illicit, itself a symptom of just what got us into trouble as Western imperialists or authors of grand narratives. But all narratives, even those of the minimally imagined "self," are potentially as grand as any other; all localities are potentially as intertwined as they are distinct. It seems obvious that we would get a more adequate ethics and epistemology by recognizing this. In fact the pretence that things are otherwise, or that we can fudge the question of theorization altogether, whether by catharsis or conversation, may itself come to be seen as nothing more than the shock condition of *precisely* the Western hegemonic mentality that cannot fully face its own history and current practice of complicity and responsibility without collapsing into sentimental guilt or existential (institutional?) panic. A similar reaction formation has been convincingly argued to be behind the current interest in "postcoloniality," which substitutes a model of new beginnings and diminished responsibilities for a confrontation with the very much in-place mechanics of colonialism.[35]

It is in the context of this particular crisis in the first-world imaginary that the contemporary appeal of various pragmatisms makes such eloquent sense, with their general adherence to a policy of "making it

34   S. P. Mohanty, "Us and Them: On the Philosophical Bases of Political Criticism," *Yale Journal of Criticism* 2, no. 2 (1989): 13.

35   See Miyoshi, "Borderless World?"

up as you go along." This has always been a tradition in literary criticism as it too has tried to negotiate difficult social-educational tensions within the national cultures of Britain and the United States without bringing those tensions to full theorization, since to do so would be to dislodge the illusory sufficiency of the aesthetic as any long-term solution to the problems of modernization. The paradigm is well formulated by the literary critic Leah Marcus in her advocacy of a local knowledge that is "a suspension of our ruling methodologies, insofar as that is possible, in favor of a more open and provisional stance toward what we read and the modes by which we interpret; it should be a process of continual negotiation between our own *place*, to the extent that we are able to identify it, and the local *places* of the texts we read."[36]

Surely no one would question the desirability of exactly such openness and flexibility in the difficult acts of reading, conversation, or international exchange. But the embedded (and unemphasized) qualifiers, "insofar as that is possible" and "to the extent that we are able to identify it," are at the very heart of the task of theorization, and not at all to be passed off as mere modesty. What appeals rhetorically, as it does in so much of Geertz's writing, is the disavowal of absolutist statements. But the disavowals are rhetorically subordinate to exactly the degree to which they are methodologically primary: *they*, and not the attributions of positive localization, are what require exposition. Otherwise we are trapped between the Scylla of unconscious self-projection and the Charybdis of what Mohanty has described as "sentimental ethical gestures" (24) in the direction of the other—which may, after all, be the same thing.

My case, then, is that literary criticism and its methods as traditionally expounded and more recently exported into neighboring disciplines is not so much a solution as a symptom of the problem. That does not, of course, make it worthless. But insofar as we passively replicate its long-standing tirade "against theory" and, by frequent association, against theorization, then we are certainly not in a learning mode! Significantly, the great ethical crises of our times that have visible international dimensions—torture, genocide, clitoridectomy, immiseration—manage to impinge upon our minds without seeming to trigger any collectively articulated response. In explaining this it

36 Leah Marcus, *Puzzling Shakespeare: Local Reading and Its Discontents* (Berkeley and Los Angeles: University of California Press, 1988), 36.

might not be impertinent to ponder other determinations than the numbing effect of television or the impotence of individual acts. In the academy, at least, these do not seem sufficient excuses for the failure of (or lack of interest in) a method. In explaining our inertias we might need to look very skeptically at the rhetoric of localism and the aesthetic gratifications it purveys.

Six

ROMANTICISM AND LOCALISM

The academic postmodern as I have so far described it contains among its affirmative gestures a variety of localisms and local knowledges. There is the localism of the self, of subjectivity, and of speaking personally; the localism of the anecdote and the situated locality (in place and time) intimated in the model of conversation; the "local knowledge" of Clifford Geertz, which is all we have even as it does not tell us very much, or very clearly; and, of course, there is the continued existence of the fantasized localism of the dear, perpetual place, no less powerful in the ideological imaginary just because it probably never existed, or disappeared at precisely the point at which it began to be invoked as an object of nostalgia.

Throughout this study I have been emphasizing the long-durational elements of modernity that continue to inform the articulation of the postmodern. In previous chapters I have sought to provide a history for the syndromes of anecdote and conversation that are so prominent in the academic postmodern. In this chapter I turn again to the late eighteenth and early nineteenth centuries, and to what we recognize as romanticism, in order to examine the phenomenon of localism as it is there apparent. I am not here proposing that romanticism is any kind of unique origin for the problematics of localism, and thereby of the entire paradigm of the postmodern, thus instigating a debate about absolute beginnings of the sort that Fredric Jameson has characterized, with who knows what degree of neutrality or hauteur, as "largely academic."[1] But I am suggesting, as I have throughout, that there is a continuity between then and now, one that is significant albeit inabsolute. In other words, we will find anticipatory formations in romanticism of the features of postmodernism, but we will also find distinctions and

1 Jameson, *Postmodernism*, 59.

differences. Platitudinous as this may sound, it is the key to any precise history of the postmodern, especially of the academic postmodern, whose rhetorical self-image depends so often on the denial of significant ancestry as a means of making itself seem new.

This said, it may be helpful to begin with a very trenchant case for absolute origins, that made by Philippe Lacoue-Labarthe and Jean-Luc Nancy in their book *The Literary Absolute*. The thesis here—and perhaps this is the sort of thesis Jameson had in mind—is that literature, philosophy, criticism, and theory were first and definitively synthesized as one and the same or each-in-all by the Schlegels and the Jena circle around 1800. When literature knows itself as the "production of its own theory," then we have the inception of "the critical age to which we still belong" (xxii). This is not so much a crisis or turn *in* literature as a sign of literature's being refigured by the pressures of a crisis in the entire system of modern history (6). That system then became *aesthetic* and *poetic*, that is, original, generational, temporal, situated within the orbit of the subject and knowing itself as such. Paul de Man and others have repeated or reproduced a similar model of "literature" and seen its exemplary articulation in romantic writing, or in the specific dynamics of Kant's third *Critique*, which has been a frequent sourcebook for postmodern theorists. [2]

There is something to this attribution of an origin. Friedrich Schlegel's *Critical Fragments* and *Athenaeum Fragments* are indeed, among other of his writings, histories of the postmodern by anticipation. One can find similar exemplary foreknowledges in the writings of Sterne and Diderot, as in Montaigne before them and Wittgenstein after them. All sorts of partial histories and disciplinary emphases announced the postmodern before its time, and items such as the following, from Schlegel, seem especially expressive: "The whole history of modern poetry is a running commentary on the following brief philosophical text: all art should become science and all science art; poetry and philosophy should be made one." [3] Readers of Schlegel (in this phase of his career) soon discover that what may look like a grand to-

---

2 That it has, in this process, been misunderstood, is the interesting argument of Christopher Norris in *The Truth about Postmodernism*, 29–99.

3 *Friedrich Schlegel's "Lucinde" and the Fragments*, trans. Peter Firchow (Minneapolis: University of Minnesota Press, 1971), 157, cited in Lacoue-Labarthe and Nancy, *Literary Absolute*, 13.

tality of everything is actually an ironic reduction to the parameters of temporality and subjectivity. And it is unlikely that one could find this said a hundred years earlier, or said in any way that attracted any heightened attention. Romanticism is, in other words, a worthwhile place to look for an increase in the density and frequency of anticipatory postmodernisms, and it may therefore contain clues to the residual determinations that are still in play around the postmodern. That the academy as we know it had not yet come into being with its academic postmodern makes the case of romanticism all the more interesting.

It can be seriously (if outrageously) suggested that the difference between Pope's villa at Twickenham and Wordsworth's cottage at Grasmere is the French Revolution. Pope's house is the antithesis of localization. Italianate to the last brick, it seems to belong somewhere else, by another river and under warmer skies. It is a cultured imposition, not a local emanation. In being what it is, it could be anywhere, and as such it speaks for a defiant cosmopolitanism, an international vernacular of polite living that transcends even as it advertises the achievements of a merely national state. By contrast William and Dorothy Wordsworth's Dove Cottage seems to signify an authentic localism, a valued piece of old England, and it has been relentlessly celebrated as such by the heritage industry that has grown up around such places, whatever it was to William and Dorothy themselves. In fact it was for them a complex dwelling, an interlude between the respective grandeurs of Alfoxden House and Rydal Mount, and an iconic simplification of and alternative to lives that had already been extraordinarily peripatetic and geographically unstable. Nor was it particularly comfortable, in the manner of today's centrally heated cottage hideaways. The upstairs room "smoked like a furnace," and the house, after five years, became so redolent with memories of the dear lost brother that they were glad to leave it. [4] But Dove Cottage has survived in literary history in a way that Alfoxden, Rydal Mount, Coleorton, and other Wordsworthian residences have not. The Wordsworths themselves seem to have felt the power of the myth, as they described

4 *The Letters of William and Dorothy Wordsworth: The Early Years, 1787–1805*, ed. E. de Selincourt, 2d ed., revised by Chester L. Shaver (Oxford: Clarendon Press, 1967), 274; *The Letters of Mary Wordsworth, 1800–1855*, ed. Mary E. Burton (Oxford: Clarendon Press, 1958), 2–3.

their "little domestic slip of mountain," their plans for a garden that will "make it more our own," and their neighbors "kind-hearted, frank and manly, prompt to serve without servility."[5]

The near-heroic pentameter of that last phrase, "prompt to serve without servility," brings the passage closer to Pope than the apparent difference in the two dwellings might seem to promise. Its literary elegance might suggest, at least, that we are not here dealing with the language of the local soil but with a sophisticated commentary incipiently conscious of its own literate distance from the neighbors here described. Over the years Wordsworth himself would take on the aura of a local zoning authority, pronouncing on the proper color for houses, the correct kinds of trees, and the bad effects of railways and tourists. But his bid to defend and represent the locals is always threatened in ways that are rhetorically clear even if they are unconscious. His own writing, as more and more critics have come to realize, records a series of acute psychological, social, and geographical dislocations, which become the more obvious the more strenuously he tries to put himself in place. He himself sought relief from this cultural peripateia, and literary criticism has worked hard on his behalf to remove its features from the cultural record. In this task Dove Cottage has figured as the residence most suitable for mythologizing as the favored locus of a domestic ideal open to the lower-middle ranks, who cannot aspire to the great house. Above poverty and below luxury, living in comfort while avoiding any appearance of conspicuous consumption, the cottage dweller bridges and dissolves the social and political chasm between rich and poor that was so frequently understood to have caused the French Revolution. The cottage, moreover, belongs in the country and is thus outside the sphere of metropolitan contagion in which revolutionary ferment was so often imagined to occur. In so subsisting, the cottage is the signature of localism, of belonging in place and through extended time, at a moment when space and time are being refigured by the fast mails and the newspapers—hence Wordsworth's analysis of the effects of "the rapid communication of intelligence"[6]—as many now think they are being refigured again by the computer and the satellite. After 1789, above all, the cot-

---

5   Wordsworth and Wordsworth, *Letters: Early Years*, 274–75.

6   *Prose Works of William Wordsworth*, 1: 128.

tage came to stand for everything that seemed most admirably and solidly British (and, in another historical sleight of hand, most *English*).

I will return to the legacies of 1789. That year did not originate the rhetoric of localization in British culture: Alan McKillop and Geoffrey Hartman among others have shown localism's importance in the classics and in their eighteenth-century imitators, with variously sacral and social-political associations.[7] But the French Revolution intensified localism, rendered it more resolutely particular, and brought it to a more explicit condition of crisis than it had previously displayed. In a similar way the events of 1789–93 did not originate the various crises of modernization, but they exemplified and signified them and made clear certain implications and consequences that had not previously been quite so unignorable. They also confirmed a long-standing tradition of anti-Gallicanism, and made possible the semiotic simplification of British culture into an us-and-them paradigm that is in some respects still with us. To many in Britain, the French Revolution seemed to be the disastrous result of a national obsession with theory, general ideas, and universalist ethics. In reaction the ideal Britishness came to be more and more defined in terms of particular instances and local rather than cosmopolitan attachments.[8] While the revolutionaries had made much of the iconography of public life in open spaces, the British nationalist media embraced the image of family values in small, self-sufficient communities. Pope's villa no longer fit the ideological picture.

That picture, however, was not easy to maintain, and most of its reproductions will not stand close scrutiny. Marx's notoriously confident mid-nineteenth-century declarations that the future of positive social life lay in embracing rather than in refusing industrialization represent an unusually clear acceptance of the processes of modernization, but related intuitions can be traced in many other writers, and almost no one manages to reproduce the pure language of

7   Alan McKillop, "Local Attachment and Cosmopolitanism: The Eighteenth Century Pattern," and Geoffrey Hartman, "Wordsworth, Inscriptions, and Romantic Nature Poetry," in *From Sensibility to Romanticism: Essays Presented to Frederick A. Pottle,* ed. Frederick W. Hilles and Harold Bloom (London: Oxford University Press, 1965), 191–218, 389–414; Geoffrey Hartman, "Romantic Poetry and the Genius Loci," in *Beyond Formalism: Literary Essays, 1958–1970* (New Haven and London: Yale University Press, 1970), 311–36.

8   This is one of the topics of my *Romanticism*.

achieved localism. In this sense, romantic localism is not very far from Geertzian local knowledge in its articulation of epistemological confusion and thwarted ethical gesturing—close enough, indeed, to suggest some continuity of cultural experience. Few were as confident as Marx was about the deficits of rural idiocy, but equally few managed to remain smugly in possession of a myth of rustic authenticity. One can see the struggle going on in the account given by William Cobbett of riding through Wiltshire one Sunday evening in August 1826:

> I got, at one time, a little out of my road, in, or near, a place called TANGLEY, I rode up to the garden-wicket of a cottage, and asked the woman, who had two children, and who seemed to be about thirty years old, which was the way to LUDGARSHALL, which I knew could not be more than about *four miles* off. She did *not know!* A very neat, smart, and pretty woman; but, she did not know the way to this rotten borough, which was, I am sure, only about four miles off! "Well, my dear good woman," said I, "but you *have been* at LUDGARSHALL?" "No." "Nor at ANDOVER?" (six miles another way). "No." "Nor at MARLBOROUGH?" (nine miles another way). "No." "Pray, were you born in this house?" "Yes." "And how far have you ever been from this house?" "Oh! I have been *up in the parish,* and over *to Chute.*" That is to say, the utmost extent of her voyages had been about *two and a half miles!* Let no one laugh at her, and, above all others, let not me, who am convinced, that the *facilities,* which now exist of *moving human bodies from place to place,* are amongst the *curses* of the country, the destroyers of industry, of morals, and of course, of happiness. It is a great error to suppose, that people are rendered stupid by remaining always in the same place. This was a very acute woman, and as well behaved as need to be. [9]

Cobbett deploys exactly the polite, cosmopolitan condescension ("the utmost extent of her voyages") he claims not to share; he laughs as he admonishes us not to laugh. As with the Wordsworths' description of their neighbors, "prompt to serve without servility," he inscribes social and educational distance in his very claims to common feeling and experience. The encounter with the local is at once de-

9   William Cobbett, *Rural Rides,* ed. George Woodcock (Harmondsworth: Penguin, 1967), 291–92.

sired, respected, and found wanting. Cobbett is emphatic that this is not rural idiocy, but it is certainly a narrowness of knowledge that is highly inconvenient for the flustered traveler. He describes the woman as "acute" and implies that she is happy. It is the happiness he himself does not have, prone as he is to the uncannily peripatetic life of a writer and chronicler whose utilitarian eye peers out from an oddly immaterial body and sees far more in the crops and soils than he does in the human faces he encounters. For Cobbett, like Wordsworth, is something of a Satan figure, condemned to roam the earth in search of home and shelter but never quite arriving there. He is proud of this woman as some kind of national ideal, the essence of rural England before its fall, but it is an ideal he cannot himself inhabit or experience. Like Wordsworth in his 1800 preface to *Lyrical Ballads*, he is sensitive to the negative consequences of urbanization and rapid transit, but he would still, after all, like to get to Ludgarshall, and fairly promptly. He has a commitment to the local but the habits of a cosmopolitan; he has, in other words, all the makings of a thoroughly postmodern personality. And, as if fully aware of the place of feminization in the syndrome of localization, he centers this meditation upon the pros and cons of travel and immobility on the figure of a near-inarticulate woman.

Similarly divided loyalties can be traced across much romantic writing, and they do not emanate simply from its authors being somehow confused about the French, though some of them were that. In fact, I would argue, the image of the French was produced quite purposively by the nationalist media as an attempt to paper over the divisions by simplifying them out into an us-and-them model of national identity. The strong sources of the divisions, then, were not so much international as within the borders of the nation-state, and they devolved from differences of class, economic and political opportunity, and (interactive with these others) gender. Indeed, it may be that it was only the power of these components that made possible the largely successful proliferation of francophobia, which functioned as a symbol of and release valve for pressures that were otherwise unspoken. Linda Colley has recently proposed a direct connection between patriotism—of which localism was a strong component—and self-interest, so that "being a patriot was a way of claiming the right to participate in British political life," a "highly rational" and "creative" response to historical opportunity and one eagerly embraced by such groups as the entrepreneurial middle ranks and the Scots.[10] Raising a toast to John Bull, strong ale, and roast beef does indeed seem to have been a way of forwarding oneself in the world. And, insofar as patriotism became available to those outside the ruling orders, it fell into a natural alliance with localism, whose ethic of staying in place marked off the vernacular speakers and the relatively immobile from the international travelers and cosmopolitans among the upper class. Localized economies were becoming less and less viable, as "The Deserted Village" and *Mansfield Park*, among other writings, made very clear. Enclosure and imparkment were financed by money made in the city and in the colonies; the owners of the land depended upon it less and less for their wealth and profit. For these reasons, to embrace localism, whether in the image of the owner-occupier or of the organically integrated Tory squire (the radical and traditional options, respectively), was to gesture against the new wealth, and against a subculture that liked to speak French, to travel, and to imagine itself as belonging to a worldwide citizenry. One of the great inhibitions against the French and British bourgeoisie's accepting the principle of universality for very long after 1789 was that the very same principle had already been coopted by the aristocracy against whom they were competing.

The soul of the bourgeoisie, of those thus competing for recognition, rights, and opportunities, was a divided soul, however. They could not simply collapse into a fantasized localism as the essence of their social identities, since the very modernization against which localism was in reaction was itself the condition of their emergence. This is the division of interest and awareness apparent in Cobbett's encounter with the cottage woman near Ludgarshall, and it is apparent also in much of Wordsworth's poetry as it describes encounters with peasants and itinerants. It is also a gendered division. I have argued in a previous chapter that the associations of the commercial and luxury economy were those of feminization, and that the new middle classes profiting from that same economy were generically feminized by it. The figure of the woman thus became critical in ways that it had perhaps not previously been critical; the threat and appeal of the feminine could no longer be imagined as open to merely subjective control, man and

10   Linda Colley, *Britons: Forging the Nation, 1707–1837* (New Haven and London: Yale University Press, 1992), 5.

woman, but came to inscribe a gender confusion that was pervasive because it was a condition of class formation itself.

Hence, I would suspect, the strong association between the feminine and the localized, enshrined by the Victorians as a cultural commonplace but present in anticipatory if unstable ways in romantic writing also. Domesticity is one strong ingredient here, and it contextualized both men and women, though women more completely than men. Cobbett's cottage woman is different from Wordsworth in his cottage, and closer to his sister, Dorothy, who did the chores. The ambivalence about the local that marks the writings of both Wordsworth and Cobbett is also (by a process between analogy and identity) an ambivalence about the gendering of the professional writer. These confusions made it very difficult for any writers to reproduce an unconditionally positive or negative representation of localization in the world they saw around and within them; they consigned unconditional approval to the languages of unacceptable sentimentality or nostalgia. The same confusions could also of course result in the specification of "rootedness" as the happy condition of those who had not yet begun the climb toward social or economic recognition, and thus function as a technique for keeping them in their place.[11]

Modernization worked against localism, and thus made localism available as a compensatory rhetoric to soften the processes and consequences of that same modernization. In the literature and literary criticism of the eighteenth and early nineteenth centuries, the same dialectic appears in the debate about the relative values of general and particular ideas. John Locke, as we saw in chapter 5, made clear the usefulness and the inevitability of general ideas when he pronounced it impossible that "every particular Thing should have a distinct, peculiar Name."[12] If we were unable to classify species and items with shared qualities under a single name, we would go mad in a sea of specificities. Above all we would be unable to make technological progress, to travel, or to cope with unpredictable human contact. We would have to live our lives on more or less the same spot within a minimal society of persons and things, and everyone else would have to do the same.

The opposite of this pastoral ideal is the dynamic of moderniza-

11 See Lucas, *England and Englishness*, 6.
12 Locke, *Essay concerning Human Understanding*, 409.

tion, requiring social and technological mobility and unpredictable effort—conditions that have been foundationally defined in Christian cultures as the very consequences of the Fall, so that absolute localism (life in the garden of Eden) is imagined as theologically improper even as it is deeply desired. What is played out in the writing and reception of British landscape poetry is exactly these economic and theological dilemmas, reproduced in the vocabulary of the aesthetic. Samuel Johnson proposed John Denham, the author of "Cooper's Hill," as the British originator "of a species of composition that may be denominated *local poetry*, of which the fundamental subject is some particular landscape."[13] Denham's Cooper's Hill, however, like Dyer's Grongar Hill, is only weakly localized. These locations are less important in and of themselves than as the sites of other meditations about eternity, mortality, royalty, and so forth. As such they are analogous to the minimal particularities of much eighteenth-century landscape poetry— for instance, the "silver eel" and "yellow carp" of Pope's "Windsor Forest"—which give each species one adjectival feature but are not meant to detain us into reflecting closely on individual identities or qualities. These items have use value and exchange value, but are of no real interest in themselves. They have a name, but no precisely imagined local habitation. Similarly, the villages and fields featured in this sort of poetry could be anywhere in Britain. John Scott's Amwell, Akenside's "dales of Tyne," and Goldsmith's Auburn are nominations unsupported by any significant local detail. I take it that these poems are thoroughly honest about the instrumentalism underlying the genre of the English georgic: we need to know enough to celebrate the uses and passing pleasures of nature, but not much more. A blushing rose is a blushing rose is a blushing rose. This is not just the aesthetic predilection of an aristocratic ruling class, but also an expression of the utilitarian priorities of the working farmer.

All of this is of course very far from the carefully specified localities of Clare and Wordsworth, and we can trace the emergence of different voices toward the end of the eighteenth century. Blair's *Rhetoric* of 1783, for instance, begins to find fault with the language of general attribution. Blair complains of the "unmeaning groups of violets and roses" that the "common pastoral-mongers throw together," and asks instead for objects that are "particularized." He contends that "no

13   *Complete Works of Samuel Johnson,* 9:77.

description, that rests in generals, can be good," because "every thing, in description, should be as marked and as particular as possible, in order to imprint on the mind a distinct and complete image."[14] Two years later John Scott takes fully to task the generalized rhetoric of the tradition of landscape poetry when he complains that in a poem like "Cooper's Hill" the place serves only "like the stand of a telescope, merely as a convenience for viewing other objects." It is wrong, he writes, to think that poetry cannot subsist "with any very minute specification of particulars," since it is exactly these particulars, these local details, that give us the greatest pleasure.[15]

One can see in this discussion an anticipation of the rhetoric of the postmodern. Using one's place merely "as a convenience for viewing other objects" has become the object of ethical disapproval; one should, instead, forswear the grand narrative and enter a local site or community with renewed commitment. And, in some articulations, one must do this because the local detail is all that is knowable without giving way to (usually ideological) fantasies of knowledge. The pleasures of localism also took on a philosophical rationale in the eighteenth century. Richard Polwhele, the celebrant of the old English gentleman and the antifeminist critic of those he saw as merely "unsex'd females," adapted Hume's categories of resemblance, contrast, and contiguity (which he renamed "vicinity") into an account of the psychological mechanisms of local attachment. In a passage that is an anticipatory schema for Wordsworth's "Tintern Abbey," he described how such attachment could be generated *"on the spot* where it originates," or *"during absence* from that spot," or *"on our return* to that spot, after absence."[16] These feelings, for Polwhele, explain and uphold the genesis of patriotism as well as of domestic virtue—for what should we care about if not the localities we know best? (26). And in one passage of the poem he makes explicit the class component of the localist ethic:

> Lo, St. John, in the pride of wisdom clad,
> Laughs at the local love, an empty name;

14   Blair, *Lectures on Rhetoric and Belles Lettres*, 436, 452, 456.

15   John Scott, *Critical Essays on Some of the Poems of Several English Poets* (London, 1785), 3, 315.

16   Richard Polwhele, *The Influence of Local Attachment with Respect to Home: A Poem* (London, 1796), 8, 25.

Scorns the craz'd wretch who wooes his kindred shade,
And deems to lucid sense each place the same. [17]

Henry St. John, first Viscount Bolingbroke, Tory foreign secretary to Queen Anne, aristocrat, and Jacobite, was exiled in 1715. He is the perfect target for Polwhele's polemic on behalf of the middle-class Protestant patriots of the 1790s. In his *Reflections upon Exile*, written in 1716, Bolingbroke explicitly disavowed the notion of any "secret affection, independent of our reason, and superiour to our reason, which we are supposed to have for our country; as if there were some physical virtue in every spot of ground, which necessarily produced this effect, in every one born upon it." Whether or not he is here making virtue of necessity, Bolingbroke offers a sustained critique of localism as a function of the ideology of nationalism. This notion of "secret affection," he says, "may have contributed to the security and grandeur of states. It has therefore been not unartfully cultivated, and the prejudice of education has been with care put on its side." In the face of these persuasions, the wise man should consider himself a "citizen of the world" whose true country is in "the heavens." Moreover, even in historical terms the localist identity is a myth, for "the families and nations of the world have been in a continual fluctuation, roaming about on the face of the globe, driving and driven out by turns." The small history of localities, in other words, is a history of grand narratives of migration, conquest, and exile. [18] If Bolingbroke were to participate in today's debate, one imagines him weighing in on the side of cosmopolitan theory against the defenders of the sufficiency of local knowledge.

One also imagines the rejoinder that these priorities are the privilege and consequence of living the life of a white male aristocrat. The case against Bolingbroke was made by Hume before it was made again by Polwhele. Hume argued that "nature has implanted in every one a superior affection to his own country," so that "we never expect any regard to distant nations, where a competition arises." [19] Patrio-

---

17   Richard Polwhele, *The Influence of Local Attachment with Respect to Home: A Poem in Seven Books: A New Edition, with Large Additions; and Odes, with Other Poems* (London, 1798), 1:58.

18   *The Works of the Late Rt. Hon. Henry St. John, Lord Viscount Bolingbroke* (London, 1809), 1:142–45.

19   David Hume, *Enquiries concerning Human Understanding and concerning the Principles of Morals*, ed. L. A. Selby-Bigge, 3d ed. revised by P. H. Nidditch (Oxford: Clarendon Press, 1975), 225.

tism, and thus perhaps racism, are natural, and not to be dislodged. Throughout the eighteenth century the argument between general ideas and particular specifications in poetry and philosophy parallels and interacts with that between cosmopolitanism and localism in ethics and politics. The anglophone middle class (and its imaginary proxy, the peasantry) stays home and tends its garden in the country, while the multilingual privileged ranks are at home everywhere. As the middle ranks of British society began to play a larger role in the creation of culture, they brought with them a comprehensive commitment to localization, explaining themselves to themselves in terms of long, locospecific evolutionary histories. Thomas Warton's *History of English Poetry* claimed to demonstrate the progress of the national muse from "a rude origin and obscure beginnings, to its perfection in a polished age, " and Percy's *Reliques* employed the same rhetoric of primitivism transcended.[20] But this confidently expressed sense of contemporary suprematism was by no means the only ingredient in the popularity of these books and others like them. They also offered a narrative of long-durational continuity to a generation increasingly conscious, as Wordsworth was, of the speed of cultural and political change: this is a fairly constant psychological response to modernization. They convinced people that, in some visible and recorded sense, "they" had always been "there, " against commentators like Bolingbroke who insisted that they had not. In this way they provided solace for those who had not, as some polemicists for the postmodern now say that they have, accepted the benefits of not having a past, of living only with a continuous present. And of course they served as reminders of times when some things were or seemed better for some people. Thomas Percy appeased the retrospective self-respect of professional writers in reminding them of a time when "the profession of oral itinerant Poet was held in the utmost reverence" (*Reliques*, xlix). This is perhaps the role that Wordsworth was unconsciously seeking in his wanderings around the Lake Country, and in his allusions to the happy former life of Simon Lee under a now-vanished aristocratic patronage.[21]

---

20   Thomas Warton, *The History of English Poetry*, ed. Richard Price (London, 1840), 1:4; Thomas Percy, *Reliques of Ancient English Poetry*, ed. Robert Aris Wilmott (London: Routledge, 1857), xlix.

21   See my *Wordsworth's Historical Imagination: The Poetry of Displacement* (London and New York: Methuen, 1987), 149–59.

As if to supplement the somewhat abstract designation of Gray's country churchyard, which could be any country churchyard and contained no historical names or dates, Gilbert White, postmodern before his time, provided a massively specific "parochial history" demonstrating the value of what might happen if "stationary men would pay some attention to the districts on which they reside, and would publish their thoughts respecting the objects that surround them."22 Gray's *image* of localization may have been precisely that, an image designed to satisfy the appetite for a perpetual place and for the extended lineage it represented (and graveyards are perfect for this in their juxtaposition of the living and the dead) without ever descending to the level of the irreversibly local in any way that might betray the universalism of his own buried class affiliations. In the preface to his *Popular Antiquities*, a version of which was first published in 1777, John Brand remembered Gray by way of licensing his own collection of folk memories that might otherwise have seemed beneath polite notice. Gray it was who gave immortality to "the little tombstones of the vulgar" and who opened the way for Brand himself to publish his book.23 But of course there were no details on Gray's tombstones: it is the *concept* of the dignity of the vulgar that is rendered into poetry. Brand seems to understand the paradox of eighteenth-century popular antiquarianism. On the one hand, the enduring or apparently enduring nature of popular culture seems to offer some stabilizing comfort to a dominant culture under stress from the changes brought about by modernization: "Things that are composed of such flimsy materials as the fancies of a multitude do not seem calculated for a long duration; yet have these survived shocks by which even empires have been overthrown, and preserved at least some form and colour of identity, during a repetition of changes both in the religious opinions and civil polity of states" (1:vii). The imagined endurance of these practices through time gives them the aura of a perpetual place, which survives as such by being beneath the notice of those who carry out the techniques of radical change. On the other hand, and in contrast to this apparently vol-

22   Gilbert White, *The Natural History of Selborne*, ed. Richard Mabey (Harmondsworth: Penguin, 1967), 3.

23   John Brand, *Observations on the Popular Antiquities of Great Britain*, 3d ed. (London: Bohn, 1853), 1:xvi.

untary embrace of folk culture, Brand is well aware of the specific history whereby the transition from Catholicism to Protestantism was managed not least by allowing or even encouraging the survival of residual folk practices in order to soften the perception of (and resistance to) such radical change: "it is not improbable, indeed, but that, in the infancy of Protestantism, the continuance of many of them was connived at by the state" (1:xi). Here he sides, implicitly, with Bolingbroke, in recognizing the political power of localist ideology as a mode of social discipline. And as such he anticipates the architects of late-twentieth-century theme parks and subdivisions; it would be hard to say for sure that we have not already begun the passage from representation to parody to pastiche that culminates, according to Fredric Jameson, in the postmodern identity.

Brand's ambivalence is like Cobbett's: both are aware of the limitations of the very localized qualities or entities they purport to celebrate. This instability can be traced throughout romantic writing, which is seldom able to reproduce the "patriotic" rhetoric of place in the straightforward way managed by Richard Polwhele. Sometimes the instability is more or less managed, and at other times it is quite out of control. Writers with firm religious commitments, like Blake and Cowper, could find eternity anywhere and at any time. Here is Cowper:

> Truth is not local, God alike pervades
> And fills the world of traffic and the shades,
> And may be fear'd amid the busiest scenes,
> Or scorn'd where business never intervenes.[24]

One can see why Cowper was so popular. He tells his reader that it is quite acceptable to be immersed in the commercial economy; good and evil are not to be limited to retirement and business, respectively. But the transcendence of the local is not here by way of the approval of secular, universalist ideals of the sort that would come to be associated with the French and the followers of Paine and Godwin. The ingenuity of God's grace is that it selects us one at a time, and thus preserves the stability of earthly society both literally and metaphorically. The criti-

24 Cowper, "Retirement," *Poems*, 1:264.

cal moment may come anytime, anywhere, even in the pulsation of an artery, but it will not destroy throne and altar.

A similar refusal to produce the poetry of strong localism helps explain the anachronism of George Crabbe. We might code this as proper Protestant piety, as a refusal to fetishize earthly sites and situations, or we might see it as a sign of Crabbe's imagined or actual affiliation with a utilitarian interest or aristocratic disinterest, each of which regards local detail as subsumable by a general view. For all the apparent locospecificity of so many of Crabbe's titles—"The Village," "The Borough," "The Parish Register," and so forth—and for all the "Chinese accuracy" and "Flemish minuteness" of which Jeffrey and Hazlitt complained, [25] his landscapes are oddly delocalized. For those who already know it, the Suffolk coast can be vividly imagined while reading Crabbe's poems, but there is little if any geographical localization— real place-names, real people, times, events. In his preface to "The Borough" (1809) Crabbe explains his use of an "imaginary personage" as intended to keep the reader "from view of any particular place."[26] He does not tell us why he does this. Certainly the power of his moral tales might be weakened by his offering them through the vehicle of a gallery of local grotesques. But he was working against the spirit of the age. His own son, in the role of editor, provided a series of localizing footnotes proving that the borough "is evidently that of Aldborough magnified"; and his editor was happy to offer *Finden's Landscape Illustrations* for the sum of 2s. 6d. as a supplement to the edition. [27]

Related tensions between the local and the general or generic can be found all over late-eighteenth-century and romantic writing. Goldsmith gave his deserted village a name but gave us no directions, thus initiating one of the great investigative efforts of literary history. "The Traveller" begins with an image of favored domesticity located in the poet's brother (not in a place) and goes on to chronicle the good and ill in everything and everywhere. Southey, who has been remembered as a great conservative, wrote obsessively international poetry. His epics are set all over the place, his "English Eclogues" confess themselves an imitation of the German, and his Spanish traveler comments ironically

25 Arthur Pollard, ed., *Crabbe: The Critical Heritage* (London and Boston: Routledge & Kegan Paul, 1972), 58, 74.

26 *The Poetical Works of the Rev. George Crabbe* (London: John Murray, 1834), 3:10.

27 Ibid., 3:10, 4: endpaper.

on the English fixation on the words *home* and *comfort*.[28] Byron, Keats, and Shelley, in reaction to a perceived Wordsworthian paradigm, have almost no patience with the poetry of localism and its potential for upholding an ideology of nationalism, and in this they anticipate a high Victorian reaction, embodied in the Brownings, against the culture of Little Englandism.

If there is in romantic writing no clearly hegemonic narrative of localism triumphant—and I do not think that there is, notwithstanding Richard Polwhele's efforts—then we cannot look to romanticism as some sort of foundational moment against which to measure the distance traveled by our own postmodernism. The same skepticism and conflict produced by an inspection of the Geertzian local knowledge syndrome can be found in a careful reading of much romantic writing about persons and places, and persons in place. This suggests that we should be looking for a common history rather than for a definitive epistemological break. Or rather—since my topic is the *academic* postmodern—it suggests that if such a break really has occurred then we are still in search of a language for describing it, and are in the meantime happily reproducing the languages we have inherited. The strenuous efforts at localization evident (and celebrated) in the poetry of Wordsworth and Coleridge are often undercut by ironies of temporality and of disposition. Wordsworth, who spent (or wrote that he spent) a lot of time on the road meeting people, was prone to radical misunderstanding, and can thus appear as the prototype of the modern anthropologist. And both of them are most vividly "there" in writing when they are not "there" in body. If this is true of all writing, then it is especially true of writing that dramatizes and describes the separation, as this writing does.

Thus the young Coleridge imagines his place of retirement, with its italicized *heres* and *theres*, all the more intensely for having left it, and for sensing that it can properly be reoccupied only when distribution shall have undone excess, and all men have such a favored spot. He is both there and not there; there in mind and heart, but far away in action and in moral imperative.[29] The "dear Cot" that must be left behind

28   Robert Southey, *Letters from England*, ed. Jack Simmons (London: Cresset Press, 1951), 93–94.

29   *Coleridge: Poetical Works*, ed. Ernest Hartley Coleridge (Oxford: Oxford University Press, 1974), 106.

is both gendered as feminine and is the repository of sexual and domestic happiness in the empirical life. The writer who moves out of retirement is also, in the desired world of the imaginary, remasculinizing himself. Coleridge's poems of the 1790s are full of exactly the sorts of particularities and local details of whose absence, in Denham and others, John Scott had complained. If Coleridge's narrator is not "climbing the left ascent of Brockley Coomb in May, 1795," then he is composing at Shurton Bars, "near Bridgewater," in September of the same year.[30] He puts himself in place, localizes himself, in a densely detailed way. He is never just there, but there at a certain time of day in a certain mood and seeing a certain slant of light. Like Ruth Behar interviewing Esperanza for *Translated Woman,* he records every incident as in its place and in no other. But the effect of this, as all readers educated in the poststructuralist (de)construction of subjectivity will aver, is the opposite of any conviction of presence, of really being there. Coleridge protests too much, and by an obsessively minute realism alerts us to the trompe l'oeil device that is realism itself. In other words, the more he asserts that he is there and seeing these things, the surer we are that he isn't; or, at the very best, that what he sees at one moment will not stand as any accurate description of the next, so that what commences is a Shandyan narrative instead of a Coleridgean landing place.

It is one of the ironies of literary history that a number of the poems that dramatize this situation (and situatedness) have come to be known as "conversation" poems. Most of them are monologues, and in this respect Coleridge anticipates the same problems of the conversation paradigm for which I have argued (in chapter 2) in its postmodern reincarnation. Coleridge's addressees—wife, daughter, friend—do not get a word in, if they are even present in the scene of the poem. I mention just one of these poems: "This Lime-Tree Bower My Prison" of 1797. The poem is a brilliant dismantling of the icon of cottage contentment, which it only partly reconstructs by a transcendentalizing sleight of hand (or mind), thus having to invoke the entire Kantian apparatus in its pursuit of presence.[31] The bower, which ought to be the locus either of companionable conversation or solitary peace, provides

30   Ibid., 94, 96.

31   For a full account of this, which I will not repeat here, see my *Wordsworth and the Figurings of the Real* (London: Macmillan, 1982), 1–12.

neither: it shelters the disgruntled and disabled narrator, who would prefer to be out walking with his friends. Gradually the imagined or recollected details of their itinerary enliven the poet's mood to the point where he appreciates the much smaller details of what is around him. Strenuous specifications of "this" and "that" jostle with the suspended belief of "perchance" in his narration of the imagined walk. It is only when, revivified, he turns to his immediate surroundings that the descriptions make the claim to full presence. The process is one of miniaturization, as he moves from the imagined landscape to the leaves and trees and shades that are now before him. Acceptance of the sufficiency of these images is a lesson in humility. But it is also the assertion of being, and being there. Coleridge is struggling for the same sort of authority as many of our contemporary academic autobiographers seem to be seeking. But his narrative reverts for its final consolation to the imagined landscape, the one he cannot see, in a postulation of transcendental consensus that would precisely *not* be available to the postmodern autobiographer, who must remain arrested at the point of local (self) description lest he or she commit the fall back into speaking for others, and thence into grand narrative or posited totality.

As an instance of one who remains in Coleridge's penultimate position, fascinated by and alive to the shadow and light of leaf and tree before his eyes, we may produce Borges's protagonist Ireneo Funes, whose condition of physical paralysis has allowed him to outfox John Locke and to register the absolute specificity of everything—and to remember it: "we, at one glance, can perceive three glasses on a table; Funes, all the leaves and tendrils and fruit that make up a grape vine."[32] This is the condition Coleridge was beginning to approach in his appreciation of the minutiae of nature that he had not registered before. Thus it is the condition he supplants or avoids by reintroducing the transcendental consensus with his absent friends. Sanity is restored, and the condition of paralysis and of a constantly original present is headed off. That is the condition Funes experiences, and Borges makes clear its philosophical associations:

> Locke, in the seventeenth century, postulated (and rejected) an
> impossible language in which each individual thing, each stone,

32   Jorge Luis Borges, *Labyrinths: Selected Stories and Other Writings*, ed. Donald A. Yates and James E. Irby (New York: New Directions, 1964), 63.

each bird and each branch, would have its own name; Funes
once projected an analogous language, but discarded it because
it seemed too general to him, too ambiguous. In fact, Funes remembered not only every leaf of every tree of every wood, but
also every one of the times he had perceived or imagined it . . . .
He was . . . . almost incapable of ideas of a general, Platonic sort.
Not only was it difficult for him to comprehend that the generic
symbol *dog* embraces so many unlike individuals of diverse size
and form; it bothered him that the dog at three fourteen (seen
from the side) should have the same name as the dog at three
fifteen (seen from the front). (65)

This is, in representational extremis, the postmodern condition of living without selective memory (here, too much memory) and hence
with no use for memory. History that is thus complete is the same as no
history: there is no usable narrative. No one could accuse Funes of
projecting an imperious subject position, of smothering vital detail, of
failing to see the marginal items in his world. Everything is there, always. But nothing matters more than anything else, so that opera-
tional consciousness is denied. Hence paralysis. Borges produces the
ethics of the "petit histoire" to its limit condition, which is also the
limit condition of that strand of localism I have been describing as central to the culture of modernization. Coleridge makes the move beyond stereoscopic particularity by way of a transcendental chiasmus.
This move is no longer available to Funes or to his postmodern com-
panions.

 After what has been said so far about the dynamics of romantic
localism, the typicality of Wordsworth's (in)famous lines written *near*
Tintern Abbey will be somewhat self-evident. Its long title, conveniently erased by a literary history that wants to remember this poem
as being written at Tintern Abbey as well as about it, is pseudospecific:
"Lines Written a Few Miles above Tintern Abbey, on Revisiting the
Banks of the Wye during a Tour, July 13, 1798." Or rather, the particularity of the date has functioned to insinuate the specificity of place
that the title explicitly refuses, as if space and time are scrambled together in an oxymoronic localism that seeks to be but can never be
quite "there." A reading of the lines beneath the title only confirm and
compound its intimation of geographical and physical displacement.
The political implications of this displacement have been the topic of

some timely analysis from such critics as Kenneth Johnston and Marjorie Levinson. [33] A related politics may well have more to do with the situation of the analogous postmodern subject than I have space to explore here. But for now I simply want to register the displacements themselves, which render the poem a magnificent defeat for the localist aspiration. Indeed, if one did not have a sense of the poet's struggle with this aspiration—and one does have that sense—then it might almost be proposed as a parody. (To the best of my knowledge, Wordsworth has yet to find his Anthony Hecht.)

Like Coleridge, Wordsworth is never quite "there" when he says he is there. We are given a date but no precise place, so that the narrator-writer stands outside the localization of map and compass just as he is outside the domestic communities—"these plots of cottage-ground" and "pastoral farms"—he observes or imagines. [34] It is now widely recognized that Wordsworth's effort at inscribing a present being by triangulating between past and future (both arguably as imaginary as real) is rhetorically unsuccessful, or at least ambiguous. The accumulation of subjunctives and conditionals does not produce a strong declaration of being or being in place, and the Lutheran "here I stand" (118) actually isolates the speaker from the landscape he is viewing, introducing a "picture of the mind" that is as much reflexive as descriptive. It is in this pure, abstract spot of time, between recollection ("recognitions dim and faint") and projection ("for future years"), that Wordsworth reveals himself to be *nowhere*. The best-known and best-loved of all romantic poets of place is, after close inspection, written as constantly out of place.

As such, he is of course reproducing the condition of exile from Eden that is the foundational myth of Christian and especially Protestant culture, and thus intimating the ultimate impropriety of ever allowing oneself to feel completely at home and in place. (The same dynamic informs Coleridge's "Reflections on Having Left a Place of Retirement.") He expresses the wish that he has been or will be effec-

---

33   Kenneth R. Johnston, "The Politics of Tintern Abbey,'" *Wordsworth Circle* 14 (1983): 6–14; Marjorie Levinson, *Wordsworth's Great Period Poems: Four Essays* (Cambridge: Cambridge University Press, 1986), 14–57.

34   William Wordsworth, "Lines Written a Few Miles above Tintern Abbey, on Revisiting the Banks of the Wye during a Tour, July 13, 1798," in *"Lyrical Ballads" and Other Poems*, 116.

tively made by nature, but he also admits to the inevitability ("while here I stand") of having to make himself in opposition to inheritance and orthodoxy and therefore also to tradition. And yet it is of course tradition to which Wordsworth constantly turns for the subjects of his poems. In "Tintern Abbey" there are no inscriptions, informative locals, or ideal communities; it is the figure of the sister, Dorothy, who bears the burden of tradition. She is imagined as the bearer of the message. And the medium is oral and gestural rather than written. It is her "voice" and "wild eyes" that register what he is (what he was), and it is in her "memory" that he will live on, if he is to live at all (119–20).[35]

Dorothy, in this way, has become the icon of the oral, folk tradition whose anachronism is formally announced in the very fact that this is a written poem. And it is of course written by a man, who at once romanticizes and disciplines the potentially unconstrained woman by positioning her as he does: the effort at localization goes with the effort at feminization. John Barrell, as I have previously noted, has argued that the poem relies upon the very language of abstraction and general ideas that was being theorized or assumed as unavailable to the female or uneducated reader, an observation that locates Wordsworth even farther from the imagined act of localization he seems to be trying to perform.[36] And it also divides him from the sister in whom he is purporting to find a prospect of memorization. The first and most local of all communities, that of the garden of Eden, had not lapsed into sexual or social division and had no need of writing. Just as Wordsworth cannot put himself "back" into the landscape he thinks he remembers, so he cannot bridge the historical, theological, and ideological prescriptions of the sex-gender system. Dorothy is his best hope, but, unlike Cobbett's cottage woman, she too is a wanderer. The effort to localize through gender is not supported by a social or geographical "perpetual place." And the effort is also disciplinary. What Dorothy must lose with the passage of time is her "wild ecstasies," traded in for the "sober pleasures" that come with making a "mansion" and a "dwelling place" of the *mind* (120). Dorothy is thus already, for

---

35   For an account of Wordsworth's formulation of the relation between oral and written culture, and of its political implications, see James Chandler, *Wordsworth's Second Nature: A Study of the Poetry and Politics* (Chicago and London: University of Chicago Press, 1984), 144–83.

36   Barrell, "Uses of Dorothy," 137–67.

William, the girl he left behind him. And her positioning at the very end of the poem negates whatever of transcendental solace (never very convincing) we might wish to specify in the earlier image of "something far more deeply interfused." The move from Coleridge to Wordsworth is also a move out of any confidence in the shared subjectivity provided by the transcendental model.

The example of "Tintern Abbey" will stand for much of Wordsworth in this respect. His poetry of place is always, at least in the early career, subject to the same radical strains. One can see them in the strident exclamations of "Home at Grasmere" and in the peregrinations of *The Prelude*. Like Cobbett, Wordsworth is a roamer, a satanically restless spirit whose exile is both social-historically and idiosyncratically determined.[37] His poems about the naming of places are poems of alienation, and his ideal country cottages are, like those of Margaret and Michael, paradises lost. The exaggerated precision of Wordsworth's directions at the beginning of "Michael"—"If from the public way you turn your steps / Up the tumultuous brook of Green-head Gill"[38]—suggests possession of a good deal of old-fashioned local knowledge. But the evolution of the narrative as a *story* about a world now lost makes the poem more credible as an instance of postmodern (Geertzian) local knowledge, where what is known is called into question even as it is articulated. In this way we may nominate Wordsworth as a precursor of our contemporary storytellers, those whose "return" I described in the introduction and chapter 1. He too is acutely anxious about his relation to his ethnographic subject, and he too seeks to at once confess that anxiety and limit its consequences by invoking the occasionality and explicit situatedness of the story, and of "literature" itself.

The poetical localism that Richard Polwhele recommended so aggressively in principal was, then, by no means easy to perform in practice. What the effort registers, in the writing of Coleridge and Wordsworth, is exactly that: effort. And the inscription of the poetical subject *making* this effort removes the poetry once and for all from any pretension to represent images of localized social sufficiency, commit-

---

37 See my accounts of "Gipsies" in *Wordsworth's Historical Imagination*, 22–55, and in "Figuring Sex, Class, and Gender: What Is the Subject of Wordsworth's 'Gipsies'?" *South Atlantic Quarterly* 88 (1989): 541–67.

38 William Wordsworth, "Michael," in *"Lyrical Ballads,"* 252.

ting it instead to the dramatization of subjectivity and situatedness that is the familiar signature of what we know as romanticism and of postmodernism. Robert Burns was commonly produced as the poet of Scotland, but it is diction rather than place that gives Burns's Scots poetry its sense of locale, and even the diction is miscegenated. The bonny Doon, like so many other eighteenth-century locations, could be more or less anywhere, and Burns's habit of "translating" his poems into polite English only firms up the degree to which the effect of localization is dependent upon language. John Clare, who is perhaps the English poet closest to Burns in his reputation as "local," did produce poetry that is localized in both diction and in subject, but John Barrell has suggested that the most emphatic localization came *after* locality itself and the stable subjectivity it provided were destroyed by enclosure. [39] The microscopic detail and immersion *in* place that mark Clare's poems are, as Barrell points out, a refusal of the aristocratic, wide survey so typical of landscape poetry, and thus they are a gesture of class affiliation. But they may also be read as the rhetoric of childhood, and thus as a nostalgic re-creation of a time before the onset of class consciousness itself. For reasons that are at once social-historical and ontogenetic, Clare's hallucinogenic particularity is almost always denoted as the inscription of loss:

> Een the old oak that crownd yon rifld dell
> Whose age had made it sacred to the view
> Not long was left his childerns fate to tell
> Where ignorance & wealth their course pursue
> Each tree must tumble down—old "lea close oak" adieu. [40]

The "local knowledge" that romantic writing adumbrates thus partakes as much of displacement as of placement, and in this way it predicts the Geertzian paradigm as described in chapter 5. Localism and localization in neither case provide any empirical certainties of being and belonging in place, but instead stimulate uncertainties of meaning and disposition. One might suppose here that there has been a continuum of radical transformations of communication and information

---

39 John Barrell, *The Idea of Landscape and the Sense of Place: An Approach to the Poetry of John Clare* (Cambridge: Cambridge University Press, 1972), especially 187–88.

40 John Clare, "The Village Minstrel," in *The Early Poems of John Clare, 1804–1822,* ed. Eric Robinson and David Powell (Oxford: Clarendon Press, 1989), 2: 170.

(newspapers, fast mails, railways, airplanes, satellites, computers) and of the economic matrix within which they have occurred (the stock market has been with us since the late seventeenth century), making it meaningful to describe a coherent, long-durational response to modernity, which has only recently come to be called *post*modern. David Harvey, who favors a quite recent origin for what he calls the postmodern, has described one of its symptoms as a new sensitivity to "vernacular traditions, local histories, particular wants, needs, and fancies."[41] This could be Gilbert White introducing his history of Selborne. And if we reply, with Baudrillard, that this appetite for the vernacular must be understood as already imaginary, or, with Jameson, as pastiche, then we can still find the origins of this displacement in the anxieties of romantic subjectivity, though admittedly not produced to the point of exuberant celebration. The strong component, within the sphere of culture, that holds together the long-term dynamic of modernization, is the location we know as "literature." I have argued that it is the reinvention of literature within the contemporary academy as an omnivalent method for the humanities and social sciences that has gone into the creation of an academic postmodern. We seek our inspiration in literature and turn to it for our solutions. This will be the subject of my final chapter.

41 Harvey, *Condition of Postmodernity*, 66.

Seven

THE URGE FOR SOLUTIONS AND
THE RELIEF OF FICTION

I know it is often the young who are most nostalgic
for the past they've yet to acquire,
and have a lively instinct for faking history.
Malcolm Bradbury, *Doctor Criminale*

I would guess that those of us who are professional intellectuals and teachers of the humanities have had the experience of giving a presentation before students and colleagues in which we have declared ourselves more right-minded and radical than the rest. And I would guess that we have also then had the experience of having our radical claims debunked as overtly or covertly reactionary and conformist by persons in the audience who think that they are far more radical than we are. Sometimes this comes in the form of an explicit counterclaim or rival formulation; sometimes it takes on a more confrontational rhetoric and asks us, in so many words, precisely how we imagine that our ten cents' worth is going to change the world, or affect the folks in Peoria. And the difficulty we have with this sort of challenge indicates, I think, that most of us still do imagine that we are changing the world, or should be changing the world. Few among us have the confidence to pronounce that the question is irrelevant.

The accusation of inertia can occur whether or not one has made any actual claim to be changing the world, which should lead us to suspect that its motivations are deeply determined and perhaps resident in the academic forum itself. For we are the inheritors of a mélange of (variously) activist traditions, among them those of the priest, the legislator, the "thirties" and "sixties" radical, and the writer or artist. The positioning of the humanist intellectual within modernity can be read as entailing a more or less constant uncertainty about what is effective and creative and what is inept or merely reproductive. Few of us can comfortably accept Veblen's diagnosis of our cultural function as entirely dependent upon our uselessness, our availability as luxury items for a consumer culture, or Nietzsche's sour pronouncement that "the scholar, the scientific average man, always rather resembles an old maid."[1] The sheer panic that we might indeed be old maids has only been heightened by the increase in skeptical self-consciousness that marks so much of the methodology of the postmodern. The skepticism, it seems, often serves to make the desire for real effectivity all the more powerful for having to work by negation. Fredric Jameson has described the "new" orthodoxy as one within which we must not "emit propositions" or give the "appearance of making primary statements or of having positive (or 'affirmative') content." Nothing can be true but everything can be false, so that "the mission of theoretical discourse thus becomes a kind of search-and-destroy operation in which linguistic misconceptions are remorselessly identified and stigmatized, in the hopes that a theoretical discourse negative and critical enough will not itself become the target of such linguistic demystification in its turn."[2]

But, as I have argued throughout, the scrupulous suspension of belief that Jameson here describes is by no means the only response to (or specification of) the postmodern to be found among professional intellectuals. The popularity of autobiography and the recrudescence of the storyteller, along with a new enthusiasm for the polite culture of anecdote and conversation, the rebirth of identity politics, and the appetite for localism and local knowledge, are signs of a more traditional and affirmative response to the times. We have seen a powerful reinvention of identity politics, of speaking confidently for oneself or one's subculture, as if the denial of universality has somehow entailed the integrity of the local. One might say, then, that we are between extremes, or (collectively) positioned at both extremes—denying and asserting foundations and foundationalism at the same time, or critiquing it in one place only to lapse immediately into it at another. Derrida puts it well in describing his own predicament: "This position of dual allegiance, in which I personally find myself, is one of perpetual uneasiness. I try where I can to act politically while recognizing that such action remains incommensurate with my intellectual project of deconstruction."[3] Many of us are possessed by the desire for a radi-

1   Nietzsche, *Beyond Good and Evil*, 315.

2   Jameson, *Postmodernism*, 392–93.

3   Richard Kearney, ed., *Dialogues with Contemporary Continental Thinkers* (Manchester: Manchester University Press, 1984), 120.

cal action while being burdened with a recognition that such action is either impossible or unknowable as such, should it ever occur. The moment of deconstruction was one that posited the prospect of a more or less complete disconnection between word and world, and it was therefore not long entertained by an academy still dominantly committed to the assertion of just such a connection. Those who have declared themselves quite happy without the prospect of radical action, like Paul de Man and Stanley Fish, have been judged threatening and even immoral.

Among academic theorists and critics the urge for a solution most often takes the form either of a proposed methodological breakthrough or of an overt moral exhortation. And sometimes the one can be seen in the disguise of the other, so that ethics and epistemology are packaged together in a comprehensive prohibition. At times the solution is to be imagined in destroying what we have, on the assumption that what comes next can be no worse. Baudrillard looks to a time when the "mirror of production" will have been broken, and to a "refusal, pure and simple, of production as the general axiomatic of social relations."[4] Lyotard places his hopes in the stochastic "unexpected" that can occur when the degree of displacement is at its maximum and held within the pretotalizing limits of the "local."[5] Jameson's interest in the utopian is less identified with the anarchistic turn than is Lyotard's hope for the future, but it too recognizes the difficulty or impossibility of describing that future with the terms available in the here and now.[6]

In its less absolute and more cheerfully affirmative incarnations, the urge for solutions takes the form of an enthusiasm for inclusiveness. If nothing is confidently to be excluded, then let us admit everything. In reference to the autobiographical moment that is so characteristic of the times, the editors of *The Intimate Critique* have put their faith in the power of "personal, political, and critical self-revelation" to resolve the problems of skepticism by a "capacity to express and construct multiple locations."[7] In a more historical-objectivist rhetoric, the "multi-

---

4   Baudrillard, *Mirror of Production*, 47, 141.

5   Lyotard, *Postmodern Condition*, 16, 66.

6   Jameson, *Postmodernism*, e.g. 159–80, 208.

7   Freedman, Frey, and Zauhar, *Intimate Critique*, 10.

dimensional critical theory" called for by Steven Best and Douglas Kellner does much the same, holding nothing alien to itself as it entertains "a broad range of perspectives on the domains of social reality and how they are constituted and interact."[8] This is very close to the last position I myself felt confident enough to articulate, and it has the obvious appeal of a continual openness.[9] But, appealing as it is, it threatens to collapse into the banal endorsement of our own continuing, collective professional relevance: whatever happens, we will be there to bring you the news and provide the interpretation. As such it risks dismissal as one massive empowerment project for academic criticism, premised on visibly reactive and post hoc intuitions rather than on any control of or insight into a present or future condition.

Empowerment is indeed the name of much of the game, and is what is going on in a good deal of what is known now as cultural studies. But this predicament affects us all and need not be completely disabling, even as it should never be ignored. The compulsion to action, or praxis (as it used to be called), is often produced as a prospective corrective to this feared professional insularity. Thus John McGowan, dissenting from Jameson's "inability to supply any model of action," sets out to "find for the intellectual a recognizable and constructive role in a society's politics."[10] The enormous question at issue here, which we can focus on more clearly thanks to the work of Pierre Bourdieu, is of course whether such a role is open to us at all, however hard we look for it. McGowan himself is well aware of the nuances required by any analysis of our situation in this respect. While committed to arguing against "political despair," he is well aware that intellectuals as a group do not practice a distinctive or coherent politics (273, 275). The universities work at least as efficiently to insulate us *from* the public sphere as they do to connect us with it, so that any politics we profess would be wise to "steer between the overvaluation and undervaluation of thought" (278).

In this passage between, we may explain the powerful appeal of pragmatism, with its positive evaluations of what Lyotard more cynically and skeptically specifies as the "temporary contract" he sees to be

---

8   Best and Kellner, *Postmodern Theory*, 263–64.

9   Simpson, "Moment of Materialism," 28–33.

10   McGowan, *Postmodernism and Its Critics*, 180, 210.

increasingly typical of "the professional, emotional, sexual, cultural, family and international domains."[11] Cornel West has suggested that the "distinctive appeal of American pragmatism in our postmodern moment is its unashamedly moral emphasis and its unequivocally ameliorative impulse." While well aware of the limits of this posture—which Michael Billig has recently shown to be, in the case of Richard Rorty, more or less synonymous with flying the flag[12]—West himself wants to rescue a "prophetic" pragmatism as a tool for encouraging "the flowering of many-sided personalities and the flourishing of more democracy and freedom," and one that remains a "particular American intervention."[13] Not all of those inspired by pragmatism are comfortable with the rhetoric of positive action, of course. Stanley Fish for one is adamant that our theoretical ruminations have no consequences and our problems no solutions in the sorts of terms we aspire to deploy in addressing them and in justifying ourselves.[14]

Academics do continue to offer solutions to what are perceived as world problems, even as many of us are compelled to admit that it is not a good time for us to try to do so. Some of our difficulties are surely to be explained in reference to the professionalized condition of the first-world intellectuals who are addressing these questions of reference and relevance. Because the empirical nature of our relation to the nonprofessional sectors is so mediated and etiolated, it is not difficult to conclude that there might be no such meaningful relation at all, or at least none that has any useful function. The openings provided by gender politics for making connections between the academy and the "public sphere" (as it is often called) have come as a great relief for many professional intellectuals starved of any sense of authentic political action. Others who have taken the road of autobiography have

11   Lyotard, *Postmodern Condition*, 66.

12   Billig, "Nationalism and Richard Rorty."

13   West, *American Evasion of Philosophy*, 4, 237. Compare Frank Lentricchia's case for the work of Kenneth Burke as a native alternative to Marxism in *Criticism and Social Change* (Chicago and London: University of Chicago Press, 1983). James Clifford has sought to "open space for cultural futures" (*Predicament of Culture*, 15); and Brook Thomas has advocated "pluralistic inclusion" as a way to "create a space in which to imagine a new future" (*New Historicism*, 50). The rhetoric of affirmation is everywhere.

14   Stanley Fish, "Consequences," in *Doing What Comes Naturally: Change, Rhetoric, and the Practice of Theory in Literary and Legal Studies* (Durham and London: Duke University Press, 1989), 315–41.

come to feel that the academy is no longer the place that makes them most comfortable, that they might feel better by getting out of it. [15]

There is of course a traditionally professional solution to the discontents of the profession: write their history. John Guillory, in arguing for a move away from exclusive attention to "the problematic of representation" and toward that of "the systematic constitution and distribution of cultural capital," is doing just that; and so is Alan Liu, in his important initiation of a history for the new historicism. [16] My own effort in this present study belongs in this camp, and it is not for me to say whether such effort is in fact a required preliminary to any useful "politics" or simply a traditional avoidance of the need to profess one. If progress really were to emerge from *understanding*, as many of our inherited philosophic radicalisms have claimed, then there would be no need to worry about the usefulness of good history. But this inheritance is of course one of the many put into question by the postmodern itself. Lyotard, in a language that is hard to define as either jest or earnest, speaks of the need to "save the honor of thinking" even or especially in the face of all that cannot now be said: "the time has come to philosophize." [17] Those of us who still think that it is not redundant to historicize have to do so with a certain suspension of belief about what exactly such historicizing can achieve. What has been lost—or at least I have lost it—is any firm faith that, in the words of one believer, "historical knowledges" are "necessary for the social struggle against oppression," or that the "struggle over theory" will produce "emancipatory knowledges." [18] I certainly hope that this might be the case, but I have no solid conviction that it is.

I have argued throughout that the definition of the postmodern moment within the academy has relied upon acceptance of the categories of literature and the literary as descriptive of syndromes and symptoms from which they had previously been excluded, principally by the rival disciplinary conventions of philosophy, history, and the social sciences. I have also reminded myself, at various points along the

---

15   See Adam Begley on Jane Tompkins in "The I's Have It: Duke's 'Moi' Critics Expose Themselves," *Lingua Franca* 4, no. 3 (1994): 55–56.

16   Guillory, *Cultural Capital*, 82; Liu, "Power of Formalism," especially 752–57.

17   Jean-François Lyotard, *The Differend: Phrases in Dispute*, trans. Georges Van Den Abbeele (Minneapolis: University of Minnesota Press, 1988), xii, xiii.

18   Ebert, "Ludic Feminism," 39, 32.

way, that the academic postmodern as I have been describing it is not the only postmodern, even within the academy itself. In particular, there is the alternative postmodernity imagined by the exponents of technoculture, who are seeking less to replicate than to resist the terminologies of the literary by recourse to the languages of science, the languages traditionally farthest from the literary. Before moving into an extended discussion of the relief of fiction as another important recent incarnation of the rule of literature—with which I will conclude this book—it is important to acknowledge the turn to technology, which I take to be a reaction (often apparently generational) against the tendencies I have been proposing as typical of the academic postmodern.

From a number of possible examples it seems most useful to select the best known and most influential: the work of Donna Haraway. In a sense Haraway's most famous statement, "A Cyborg Manifesto," inherits the scientific utopianism of C. P. Snow and his Enlightenment ancestors. It is a refusal of the familiar humanist distrust of technology (Haraway herself is a primatologist), but it is also a redefinition of what we have mostly thought of *as* science and technology. Its appeal is precisely in its bridging the gap between human and nonhuman by focusing on the cybernetic organism, both as a metaphor for a new concept of identity and as a literal description of what identity is more and more coming to be. Haraway's essay has had a tremendous impact on the imaginations of humanists and social scientists, especially for its polemical refiguring of traditional (and traditionally frustrating) gender models. When it proposes that "organisms have ceased to exist as objects of knowledge, giving way to biotic components, i.e., special kinds of information processing devices," it seems to offer not only a newly positive use for technology but a socialized and deindividuated model of the self: certainly something well clear of the rule of literature. [19]

But much of the manifesto is just that, a manifesto, a projection of a better world to come. And this "ironic political myth" is also a noticeably literary myth. The cyborg's commitments are to attitudes or attributes we can recognize as traditionally literary: "partiality, irony,

---

19 Donna J. Haraway, "A Cyborg Manifesto: Science, Technology, and Socialist Feminism in the Late Twentieth Century," in *Simians, Cyborgs, and Women: The Reinvention of Nature* (New York: Routledge, 1991), 164.

intimacy, and perversity" (149, 151). Disciplinary as well as ontological boundaries are indeed being breached here, but in directions we can now recognize as quite traditional. As Haraway breaks down the borders between animate and inanimate life (and human and animal life), she also brings together the languages of literature and those of science and technology. In an interview in which she discusses "A Cyborg Manifesto," Haraway recollects:

> I didn't set out to write a manifesto, or to write what turned out to be a heavily poetic and almost dream-state piece in places. But, in many ways, it turned out to be about language. As a result, the manifesto is not politically programmatic in the sense of proposing a priority of options; it's more about all kinds of linguistic possibilities for politics that I think we (or I) haven't been paying enough attention to.[20]

The technocultural incarnation of a positive postmodernity invokes, then, both the language of literature and its anarchistic-utopian orientation. Haraway's manifesto makes us ask how much of the literary continues to be refigured in cyberpunk, science fiction, and even cybernetics itself. I shall not pursue the question here, nor indeed imply that I know the answer. It is clear enough, I think, that both the biological and informational sciences require more than literary vocabularies for their adequate description, and that Haraway herself is not so much reproducing the rule of literature as including its elements within a more synthetic rhetoric for the imagining of positive political and social futures. In this way she and others like her represent a desire for more than the literary, and for more than the academic postmodern, but it is not clear that they do not still privilege the literary as a historical and perhaps ethical obligation. If modernity has indeed been accompanied and perhaps enabled by the masculinized industrial control of women's bodies and women's labor, then the reproduction of such feminized elements of culture as "literature" must be examined with particular scrutiny if we are not to end up as unwitting collaborators in a system that we recognize, with another part of our brains, as oppressive. Literature has traditionally been a friend to the alienated modern

20 Constance Penley and Andrew Ross, "Cyborgs at Large: Interview with Donna Haraway," in *Technoculture*, ed. Constance Penley and Andrew Ross (Minneapolis and Oxford: University of Minnesota Press, 1991), 14.

subject, but it can also be a friend that, like "poetry" for Oliver Gold-smith, "found'st me poor at first and keep'st me so."[21]

With Goldsmith's phrase in mind, in its questioning of the role of "poetry," I now turn by way of conclusion to another contemporary phenomenon, one fully expressive of the rule of literature: the return to fiction, and the relief of fiction. In the aftermath of those noto-riously formative and reflexive books like *Finnegans Wake*, *Gravity's Rain-bow*, and the French *nouveaux romans*, which many critics would find to be constitutive of the postmodern, there has emerged a recently rein-vigorated genre of novels in which the suggestion has been reaffirmed that life is literature, and literature life. This is the same chiasmic struc-ture that Brook Thomas has astutely located as typical of new histori-cist argumentation, and indeed similar gestures are apparent in both literary criticism and historical writing.[22] Anthropologist Ruth Behar embraces the Spanish word *historia* as useful for "making no distinction between history and story," and confesses (or celebrates) that she "no longer knew where I stood on the border between fiction and nonfic-tion."[23] As if in recognition of the incremental power of institutional determination in the recirculation of this idea (which is of course tradi-tional in traditional literary criticism), many of the new novels are about academics, and belong within a genre aptly defined by Adam Begley as that of the "postmodern postdoctoral romance."[24] Academic culture has been seen as a suitable site for fiction at least since *To the Lighthouse*, and in such classics as *Lucky Jim* it came to be figured fully within the comic-parodic mode, where it has firmly belonged ever since. Although there is more than an element of moral seriousness in such books as Alison Lurie's *War between the Tates* (1974) and David Lodge's *Changing Places* (1975), both of which are efforts at making sense of the cultural challenges we call the "sixties," the dominant mode remains comic, and it is this that has guaranteed their popu-larity.

The "postmodern postdoctoral romance" is rather different, even

21   Oliver Goldsmith, "The Deserted Village," line 414, in *The Poems of Thomas Gray, William Collins, Oliver Goldsmith*, ed. Roger Lonsdale (London and New York: Longman, 1989), 694.

22   See Thomas, *New Historicism*, especially 183–85, 193–96.

23   Behar, *Translated Woman*, 16.

24   Adam Begley, "Raiders of the Lost Archives," *Lingua Franca* 3, no. 5 (1993): 36.

as it is visibly continuous with its predecessors. It comes into being after the heyday of "theory" in the academy, and even when it takes a negative position about that "theory," its own fictional techniques are often unthinkable without it, and knowingly so. In the bibliographical information prefacing her 1987 novel, *Mary Swann*, Carol Shields reacts to the postmodern fiat about the death of the author by having printed the statement that "the Author asserts the moral right to be identified as the author of this work."[25] And Malcolm Bradbury's *Doctor Criminale* has as one of its key narrative elements the protagonist's recognition that the elusive Criminale is more than just a text, someone written "by language" or by his "sharp-eyed readers"; he is also a complex human being with complicated moral, political, and human needs and obligations.[26] The more crotchety conservatives, like David Lodge, take explicit swings at the poststructuralist nostrums in a rhetoric of gleeful realism. Lodge made his name in *Changing Places* with an acerbic if occasionally amiable critique of American professionalism in the figure of Morris Zapp, widely identified on the gossip circuit as Stanley Fish. In the more recent *Nice Work* (1988), the digs at contemporary theory are no longer disguised by efforts at humor, and stand out as opinionated asides or outbursts of bitterness. Lodge's theorists are sexless, or limited to sex in the head, and the best thing that can happen to them is that they will, like Robyn Penrose, find a way back to "life" and come to see themselves as part of "a classic realist text, full of causality and morality."[27] Deciding *not* to go to America, and joining in the new public sphere of small, entrepreneurial capitalism, are the making of the heroine in moral terms, whatever the outcome.

Lodge's novels appeal to academics who like to disavow their collective bad faith by rendering it the exclusive property of an overprofessionalized minority (though along the way he allows us all to laugh at ourselves) and to general readers who relish the exposure of the petty vanities and malices of the guardians of culture. His stories suggest the wish, fairly evidently, that the "sixties" had never happened, and when push comes to narrative shove, they haven't really happened in any way that matters. Lodge's topic is the shift in academic priorities known as "theory," one version of which is the post-

25   Carol Shields, *Mary Swann* (London: HarperCollins, 1993).

26   Malcolm Bradbury, *Dr. Criminale* (Harmondsworth: Penguin, 1993), 21–22.

27   David Lodge, *Nice Work* (Harmondsworth: Penguin, 1988), 218.

modern, but his novels do not incorporate theory in any way other than the polemical—it has not informed their technique. They do not, for this reason, fall within the definition of the "postmodern post-doctoral romance," though they address some of the same issues.

A new direction can be sensed in Umberto Eco's massively successful *The Name of the Rose* (1980). Eco's novel is an unashamedly literary book, full of allusions both to scholastic and theological controversies of the Middle Ages and to the paradigms of postmodernist fiction. It is a manuscript about manuscripts, and a book about the power of books; about "men who live among books, with books, from books," and who exercise upon and around them the entire range of human passions, positive and negative.[28] The medieval sense of the production of knowledge as carried on "through a glass darkly" and "in fragments" (3) is perfectly congruent with the postmodern predicament: "it is also true that in those dark times a wise man had to believe things that were in contradiction among themselves" (12). The hero, William of Baskerville, is a good detective, intellectually as well as physically dominant, and he occupies the pure serene of detection, where the narrative of suspense is wholly and deliberately removed from anything that might seem, on the face of it, pertinent to our day and age. Eco's (fictional) preface declares his own emancipation from the recent compulsions (again, the "sixties") of reference and relevance:

> I transcribe my text with no concern for timeliness. In the years when I discovered the Abbé Vallet volume, there was a widespread conviction that one should write only out of a commitment to the present, in order to change the world. Now, after ten years or more, the man of letters (restored to his loftiest dignity) can happily write out of pure love of writing. And so I now feel free to tell, for sheer narrative pleasure, the story of Adso of Melk, and I am comforted and consoled in finding it immeasurably remote in time (now that the waking of reason has dispelled all the monsters that its sleep had generated), gloriously lacking in any relevance for our day, atemporally alien to our hopes and our certainties. (xviii–xix)

28 Umberto Eco, *The Name of the Rose* (1980), trans. William Weaver (New York: Time Warner, 1986), 126.

The signals here are striking, and generic. The return of pleasure, and of pure pleasure in surfaces, is a familiar postmodern priority, announced by Susan Sontag in *Against Interpretation* and by many others since. And it is the commitment to surfaces, to the apparently unimportant or meaningless, that allows a heroic role for the liberated academic (of whom William of Baskerville is the prototype). When the world becomes a text, who better to guide us through it than the professional reader? Reading one's way through a textualized world now becomes an *act*, an instance of *praxis*, and since this is all that the world is, there need be no anxieties about other forms of action. In the image of extreme unworldliness, the lives of monks and monasteries, we find the maximum of available significance and legitimation for pure intellection and interpretation. The professional (or vocational) academic, in a way that he or she could never be for David Lodge, is heroic, and there is no world elsewhere.

The best-seller career of Eco's novel clearly depended upon a readership well beyond even the 800,000 or so college teachers employed in the United States and looking anxiously for a positive self-image that might allow them to celebrate rather than to feel defensive about their apparent distance from the public sphere. Alison Lurie has observed that "most professors are not especially strong or beautiful; and though they may appreciate or at least forgive these qualities in their students they do not much care for them in their peers."[29] Not for nothing is the academic romance populated with nubile young students (usually women) who fall hopelessly for their aging and unprepossessing professors (usually men). In fact, the normal range of beauty and deformity is probably to be found in the academy; but academics, I take Lurie to be suggesting, do not *think* of themselves this way, because they do not have the sure sense of significant action that goes with such positive self-images (or perhaps the modesty that accepts ordinariness). It is this that the "postmodern postdoctoral romance" puts right. In Lurie's *Truth about Lorin Jones* (1988), Polly Alter's biographical focus on the life of the painter Lorin Jones makes her own life seem not "serious or interesting" and that of her subject "realer to her than her own."[30] From a position in which her own potential creative career is sensed as blocked by the precursor, and sideswiped into

29   Alison Lurie, *Foreign Affairs* (New York: Avon Books, 1990), 29.

30   Alison Lurie, *The Truth about Lorin Jones* (New York: Avon Books, 1990), 41.

mere biography, Polly Alter *becomes* Lorin Jones, both in her "instinctive understanding" of her feelings (56) and in her relationship with Jones's former lover. Moments of coadunation are, however, succeeded by moments of complete alienation, so that Polly goes through a cycle of speaking with the dead, becoming the dead, and losing all contact with both Jones and herself. The academic quest does produce access to life, to that fantasized "other" we like to imagine as out there for the taking but not usually by us. If we just go deep enough into our narrow little specialties, we will emerge into satisfied citizenship of the world. (This is also the trajectory of the smart law student in another best-seller, John Grisham's *Pelican Brief* of 1992, though it figures there in a more conventionally real risk narrative.) Through literature, as it were, we will discover all there is of life. And there again is the chiasmus: literature is life, and life is literature.

This is the message of what is for me the masterpiece of the genre, A. S. Byatt's *Possession*, published in 1990 and worthy winner of the Booker Prize. *Possession* goes quite beyond the inherited parameters of the university novel as instanced by such writers as Amis and Lodge. That genre, as I have suggested, has subsisted on a high level of cynicism, setting out to show the dust on the ivory tower and the phoniness of today's Young Turks. It is usually described with the attribute "comic" and sometimes even "hilarious" or "uproarious." Byatt, in contrast, boldly calls her book a romance, and so indeed it is. It tells tales of lovers, past and present, and it is positively Terentian in its inclusiveness. Even the parodic literary theorist and the obligatory American academic are gentled into insignificance rather than being run down by rhetorical buses. The figure who begins the novel as a shabby unemployed graduate student, Roland Michell (Barthes-Foucault?), achieves professional success and human happiness simultaneously through possessing the virtues (previously thought of as afflictions) of dogged scholarship and worship of detail. His very lack of imagination, his devotion to the miniature facts of his subject, the Victorian poet Randolph Henry Ash, give him access to a new life within and beyond the imagination. Through his discovery of the passions of the past, he gets the girl of the present. Byatt's writing takes the conventions of postmodern pastiche and turns them inside out. She invents not just the poetry of both Ash and his lover, Christabel La Motte, but the letters between them, brilliant cornucopias of Victorian intellectual life and culture. She brings the past to life, and makes the present look pale in comparison. And she invents the framework for the invention, all held together—as it is for Eco—by the undeniable power of reading and imagining. As she puts it:

> Now and then there are readings that make the hairs on the neck, the non-existent pelt, stand on end and tremble, when every word burns and shines hard and clear and infinite and exact, like stones of fire, like points of stars in the dark—readings when the knowledge that we *shall know* the writing differently or better or satisfactorily, runs ahead of any capacity to say what we know, or how. In these readings, a sense that the text has appeared to be wholly new, never before seen, is followed, almost immediately, by the sense that it was *always there*, that we the readers, knew it was always there, and have *always known* it was as it was, though we have now for the first time recognised, become fully cognisant of, our knowledge.[31]

Thus the time-bound, imprecise, and unpredictable acts of scholarship and literary criticism become again foundational, in a way that we have been told, again and again, nothing any longer can be foundational. The religiose cadence of "that we *shall know*" indicates a reality once, after Paul de Man and his kind, thought lost forever. Of course the trick of it all is that Byatt is in charge of this writing *as* writing, and thus risks subjection to all the qualifications that a textualized self-consciousness now calls forth. But this is not, here, the occasion of any nostalgia for lost objects, but is instead a triumphant reintroduction to the quotidian world (of the academy), now transfigured into new harmonies and new possibilities. Byatt has healed the gap between the scholar and the object of scholarship, the mere critic and the real writer (and she herself lives out both careers). In a review of the novel aptly titled "At a Magic Threshold," Carolyn See makes the point: "If artists strive and pine and yearn to live on, through their work, into the future, it's the scholars, with equal tenderness and yearning, who lean and look, further and further back into the past, willing, finally, to lose themselves in the search for those lost artists. They meet on the threshold where knowledge is."[32] This is of course a traditional and

---

31   A. S. Byatt, *Possession* (New York: Vintage International, 1991), 512.

32   Carolyn See, "At a Magic Threshold," *Los Angeles Times Book Review*, 28 October 1990, 13.

even "humanist" model of what literary criticism is all about, and it speaks for the element of love (of self and/or other) that is at the heart of all identification with the figures of the past (hence the panic felt by many critics at negative criticism of their favorite writers). But Byatt's message is a little more artful than this, notwithstanding the clear position "against theory" that she takes in her narrative voice. It suggests that there is a history, whether we like it or not, and that while we can live without it, we would be much better by living with it, because of what it can do to transform the present. It suggests (with Lodge) that for all our professions of subject positionality, politicality, and theoretical integrity, we are really in search of some basic forms of happiness that have not changed much through time. And it demonstrates in its very narrative (unlike Lodge) how powerful the performance of these attempted connections can be. Editors, critics, and theorists of all genders, sexual preferences, and generations are captured by the spell of authentic passion and by the power of writing to bring it back to life. It is hard not to be possessed. It is hard not to want to speak with the dead.

Because, in this irresistible way, they are brought to life. Byatt's next book, *Angels and Insects*, is even more explicit in its topic of speaking with the dead. It (or half of it) is about the world of Victorian séances and spirit contacts. Emily Tennyson is trying to reach Arthur Hallam, and Lilias Papagay seeks her missing husband Arturo (as Papageno and Papagena go through tests of love and a passage through an underworld in *The Magic Flute*). Arturo Papagay affirms that the most important thing is "to be alive," but being alive seems to involve a constant need to try to reach the dead. Lilias Papagay replies later, to another, that it is "a natural aptitude of human beings in most societies to wish to speak with the dead."[33] Even as Lilias Papagay knows the whole business of contact with spirits to be "a parlour game, at one level, a kind of communal story-telling, or charade," Sophy Sheekhy (the medium) sees its deep necessity and compassion: "she thought of all the people in the world whose arms are aching and empty to hold the dead, and of how in stories, and very occasionally in sober fact, the cold and the sea give back what they have taken" (331, 336). For Alfred Tennyson, Hallam's death is the occasion of his greatest poem, a poem

---

33 A. S. Byatt, *Angels and Insects: Two Novellas* (New York: Random House, 1994), 183, 319.

"beautiful and alive and true" and enlivening not just the dead friend but the entire elegy tradition, "Dante and Theocritus, Milton and the lost Keats, whose language was their afterlife." This is a truth remaining even alongside Tennyson's recognition that "the world was a terrible lump of which his poem was a shining simulacrum" (311–12). Lilias Papagay herself is rewarded by the ultimate vindication of faith, a bringing back from the underworld, as her husband Arturo reappears to reward her love and steadfast fidelity.

Byatt's Victorians enter into something more than a mere conversation with today's scholar-readers, and in so doing they transform those scholar-readers into passionate beings for whom the skepticisms attendant upon respectable postmodern self-consciousness no longer much matter. Under the sway of passion—the passion of authentic knowledge as well as of sexual union—we are carried, Byatt suggests, beyond the rational fencing and parrying that is required by the academically proprietous effort at respecting difference and avoiding various kinds of incorrect self-projection. It is as if, for the space of at least this reading, we can step off the tightrope of self-control and self-censorship, and rectify the frustrations of epistemological omission without fearing sins of (epistemological) commission. We are released from the purely academic utopias promised by all those critics who hope (for that is all there is) that after their efforts the world *might* be a better place, into a fullness of imagination that is at once complete and completely fictional. We are released from the unsatisfactory assurance that we live entirely within the society of the spectacle—but only by the power of fiction and private imagination, themselves within the realm of the imaginary. And we are released also from the dilemmas and anxieties following from our knowledge of our professionalism, lifted out of the world in which we give grades and teach texts into one that we inhabit as a purely private space of reading and feeling and that can—the fiction tells us—have a transforming effect on even the most humdrum of lives. Byatt suggests that neither death nor life are ever in vain, and that no breath or jot of life is ever definitively lost or wasted. She is the fictional confirmation of Boswell's urge to write down everything (some of it already fictional). Randolph Henry Ash lives for the present generation in a way he never did for his own, so that the texts through which we recover that life become much more than objects of editorial antiquarianism or theories of interpretation. They become, in their secular way, sacred, and in this fashion Byatt fulfills her contract as a writer with the generations who have sought their metaphysical solace in a world without God; and, as Benjamin might have said, in a world without authentic (oral) stories. She shows that a godless world, without true stories, can yet be appeased by the brilliance of fiction and the powers of print.

Byatt's novels are in this respect consonant with a good deal of the work going on in the academy under the auspices of what I have been calling the academic postmodern. What are the autobiographies, the anecdotes, the conversations, the photographs (in even the most skeptical biographies), and the local knowledges of which I have been writing if not variations on the effort at giving life to what is otherwise threateningly (if also safely) dead? The academic postmodern, while it may purport to underwrite a technoculture that is beyond human sentiment (but also human frailty), a culture of hard surfaces, mechanized personalities, and insensible performances (one of the forms taken by high modernism, by the way), is at the same time engaged in a massive reaction against those very possibilities. It wants to bring things back to life, to speak with the dead. This is at once the desire for irresponsibility, for not being (perhaps criminally) responsible—thus James Clifford writes of the fictions of dialogue as converting the cultural text "into a speaking subject, who sees as well as is seen, who evades, argues, probes back"[34]—and the desire for the confirmations of the local habitations of body, touch, and voice, of the kind that Raymond Williams found, after all, in meeting (instead of just reading) Lucien Goldmann.[35] The remission narratives described by Natalie Zemon Davis in her *Fiction in the Archives* were engaged in showing rather than in telling: they "succeeded in creating a sense of the real" (47). And Simon Schama has written of the desire for a "communion with the dead."[36] It is the same desire for a sense of the real that conspicuously informs the standard new historicist narrative as it plays between hermeneutical skepticism and highly wrought empirical detail (dates, times, everyday trivia), juxtaposing the desire for each with that for the other without bringing the problem to the point of confrontational negation, and preserving thereby the warm-blooded temporality of the critical pre-

34   Clifford and Marcus, *Writing Culture*, 14.

35   See my "Raymond Williams: Feeling for Structures, Voicing History," *Social Text* 30 (1992): 9–26.

36   Schama, *Dead Certainties*, 319.

sent itself. The effort at giving voice to the previously silenced messages from the cultural-economic margins—the hope "to call forth more voices out of the void"[37]—is another form of bestowing life, of speaking with the dead.

Which brings us back, again, to Stephen Greenblatt, who has reinvented the motif of "speaking with the dead" for new historicists and humanities intellectuals in the present generation. Greenblatt told us (in 1988) that he wanted to speak with the dead, as if prescient of exactly the deep cultural desires Byatt was about to satisfy so richly.[38] If so, then he had perhaps earned the very relief of fiction that Byatt and his own "new historicism" provided. For his earlier book, *Renaissance Self-Fashioning*, recounted a meeting on a plane with a distraught father whose son had lost the power of speech and the will to live.[39] To prepare himself for the meeting, the father asked Greenblatt to mouth silently the words "I want to die." Greenblatt tells us that he could not do it. He thought that the man might be crazy and pull a gun; he feared wishing death upon himself; and he feared the loss of a belief in his own powers of free sentence formation—he resisted, in other words, the loss of a belief in self-fashioning. And this, he says, is the paradox of Renaissance (i. e. modern) man: that he understands that he is "remarkably unfree, the ideological product of the relations of power in a particular society" while still wishing to believe that he is "the principal maker" of his own identity.

Greenblatt's narrative is fascinating. It is itself such a literary slice of real life that one wonders if it might have been invented. The encounter with the man going to visit his "son who was in the hospital" repeats the drama of Wordsworth's "Old Man Travelling," while it repeats also Wordsworth's initial misunderstanding of what the man is feeling. As Wordsworth thinks the man serene who is in fact absorbed in grief, so Greenblatt picks his neighbor as the one "least likely to disturb me." What he then faces, like Wordsworth, is a sort of conversion narrative, a shocked eruption of the uncanny or metaphysical into the sphere of the ordinary. Greenblatt's plane trip is the modern world's and professional intellectual's version of Dante meeting Virgil

---

37   Freedman, Frey, and Zauhar, *Intimate Critique*, 10.

38   Greenblatt, *Shakespearean Negotiations*, 1.

39   Stephen Greenblatt, *Renaissance Self-Fashioning: More to Shakespeare* (Chicago and London: University of Chicago Press, 1980), 255–57.

or Christian meeting Evangelist. The mouthing of the death wish is an invitation to the underworld. The words he is asked to frame, "I want to die. I want to die," are an echo of the Cumaean Sibyl herself echoed (in Greek) in the epigraph to *The Waste Land*, that monument of modernism.[40]

Greenblatt in 1980 refused the journey and/or the conversion, and of course the risk; he did not perform the task laid upon him. He refused to become the Sibyl, she who (in Virgil if not in Eliot's source, Petronius) "chants from the shrine her dread enigmas and echoes from the cavern, wrapping truth in darkness."[41] He refused death: refused to face it and refused also to *be* death, to perform (as performative utterance) its rituals. If in 1988 he speaks of his professional identity as that of a "middle-class shaman" (*Shakespearean Negotiations*, 1), then he defines himself self-deprecatingly as something he has in fact (as told) refused to be, a conduit to the dead. The literariness of Greenblatt's encounter is therefore puzzling; it has not protected him from pain or risk. Life lived in the mold of Eliot and Wordsworth and all the journeyers to the underworld does not provide a protective, fictionalized screen for empirical experience; it may in fact make that experience all the more terrifying because of the knowledge of the literary tradition.

But Greenblatt releases himself, and his book, by telling us the story and by attempting to contain its moral within the more limited scholarly topic of the book itself, which is about the paradoxes of self-fashioning. Lyotard offers a brilliant insight into the culture of storytelling in which Greenblatt participates, and which I have argued to be one prominent component of the academic postmodern:

> By way of a simplifying fiction, we can hypothesize that, against all expectations, a collectivity that takes narrative as its key form of competence has no need to remember its past. It finds the raw material for its social bond not only in the meaning of the narratives it recounts, but also in the act of reciting them. The narratives' reference may seem to belong to the past, but in reality it is always contemporaneous with the act of recitation.[42]

40   T. S. Eliot, *The Waste Land*, in *The Complete Poems and Plays of T. S. Eliot* (London: Faber & Faber, 1969), 59.

41   *Aeneid*, 6.98–100, in *Virgil*, trans. H. Rushton Fairclough, rev. ed. (Cambridge: Harvard University Press; London: William Heinemann, 1978), 1:513.

42   Lyotard, *Postmodern Condition*, 22.

I think that this simplifying fiction is not so simple, for it explains the otherwise odd conjunction of an apparently traditional modality—that of the storyteller—as elemental to the syndrome of the (academic) postmodern. The re-creation of history—its facsimile, or simulacrum, in a process of performance (hence Greenblatt's tale appears to be at once reality and literature)—is what narrativity provides; so that one might well expect that it would become of critical importance to a generation obsessed with and perhaps convinced of the end of history as anything that is more than just performance. Literary time has always been performative time, at least since we moved from the allegorical and emblematic economy of the medieval to the realist and time-referenced representations of the modern. It has both imaged the lives of its readers and made those lives somehow more significant, more rounded, and more completed. The academic postmodern, of course, is a culture of openness, indeed of compulsive openness. It embraces the kinds of inchoate openness represented, for instance, by the *staging* of the Hill-Thomas debate, where everyone is invited to write their own story and where there is no prospect (as there was never any intention) of anyone being proven finally right or finally wrong. At the same time, as professional interpreters (and, in part, paid as such), few of us can live for long with the prospect of complete lability or absolute relativism. The satisfactions of the anecdote, the conversation, and the story are thus all the more powerful in that they provide temporary closures, places to rest (Coleridge used the phrase "landing place" in *The Friend*), momentarily consensual experiences that yet do not betray the fundamental commitment to time and process. This is, I have argued, one of the generic functions of literature within modernity. It is at once highly precise (concrete, specific, local) and unpredictable and surprising—methodologically quixotic, sensibilitarian, and above all beyond "theory." Just like a woman. If literature is thus traditionally feminized, and if the academic postmodern represents, as I have argued that it does, a reinvigoration of the rule of literature, then we should perhaps be aware of the various potentials latent in our embrace of this same academic postmodern. It would be stupid as well as churlish to claim that the "feminization" of the professional and corporate sectors evident in the acceptance of such practices as those of flextime and parental leave is a purely cynical and accommodationist policy; or that the academy's preference for subjectivist, antirationalist models of knowledge production is simply and entirely a response to a now inevitably subservient and compensatory cultural function. But we cannot reasonably avoid facing these questions, as we observe the uneasy correspondence between workplace policies of "site-based management" and "flexible task force formation" and academic exhortations toward the local, the subjective, and the miniature. Especially, I think, we cannot afford the mere celebrations of the literary as a new lease of cultural and political hope, in the manner of Rorty and of Brook Thomas, who sees in the very vagaries of the literary, "generated by a lack," a "source of potential strength."[43] If poets are indeed the unacknowledged legislators of the world, then we have accumulated remarkably little detailed information about the processes and results of their legislation. Literary criticism's history of literature (and of itself) is not short of bold proclamations about changed worldviews coming from the power of writing. But these are less and less adequate for more and more of us. The institution of literature in its modern form has, notwithstanding the efforts of various scholars to suggest otherwise, largely been active only aesthetically and in the sphere of private life. And it is private life that is the explicit priority in Rorty's ethics, as it is also the analyzed priority of the contemporary condition as theorized by such writers as Francis Fukuyama and Anthony Giddens.[44] The whole matter of oppositionality (traditionally a public gesture) is now, I think, in need of some serious investigation. Toward that effort, I have tried to begin a history for the academic postmodern, even as I am unsure both of the integrity of history itself and of the existence of any significant readership for it. Even the fear of death, or the desire to outface it, about which I have been writing at such length, is a partly and significantly historical condition: it has not always been so important, or so commonly articulated in this way. But to live within a historical condition, even when hoping to see outside it, is still to live in it. If I try to stand outside the consensus of the academic postmodern, I can hardly claim exemption from the uncertainties incumbent upon the postmodern academic. I too was possessed by *Possession*. But I end, as usual, with a commitment to historicizing—and with my footnotes.

43 Thomas, *New Historicism*, 216.

44 Rorty, *Contingency, Irony, and Solidarity*, 63–68; Francis Fukuyama, *The End of History and the Last Man* (New York: Avon Books, 1992), 283; Anthony Giddens, *Modernity and Self- Identity: Self and Society in the Late Modern Age* (Stanford: Stanford University Press, 1991), 9, and throughout.

BIBLIOGRAPHY

Addison, Joseph, and Richard Steele. *Selections from "The Tatler" and "The Spectator" of Steele and Addison*. Ed. Angus Ross. Harmondsworth: Penguin, 1982.

Adorno, Theodor W. *Minima Moralia: Reflections from Damaged Life*. Trans. E. F. N. Jephcott. London: Verso, 1985.

———. *Negative Dialectics*. Trans. E. B. Ashton. New York: Continuum, 1973.

Ahmad, Aijaz. *In Theory: Classes, Nations, Literatures*. London and New York: Verso, 1992.

Alcoff, Linda. "The Problem of Speaking for Others." *Cultural Critique* 20 (1991–92): 5–32.

Althusser, Louis. *The Future Lasts Forever: A Memoir*. Trans. Richard Veasey. New York: New Press, 1993.

Armstrong, Nancy. *Desire and Domestic Fiction: A Political History of the Novel*. New York: Oxford University Press, 1987.

Barker, Francis. *The Tremulous Private Body: Essays on Subjection*. London and New York: Methuen, 1984.

Barrell, John. *The Idea of Landscape and the Sense of Place: An Approach to the Poetry of John Clare*. Cambridge: Cambridge University Press, 1972.

———. "The Uses of Dorothy." In *Poetry, Language, and Politics*, 137–67. Manchester: Manchester University Press, 1988.

Barthes, Roland. *The Grain of the Voice: Interviews, 1969–1980*. Trans. Linda Coverdale. Berkeley and Los Angeles: University of California Press, 1991.

———. *Roland Barthes by Roland Barthes*. Trans. Richard Howard. New York: Farrar, Strauss & Giroux, 1989.

Baudrillard, Jean. *For a Critique of the Political Economy of the Sign*. Trans. Charles Levin. St. Louis: Telos Press, 1981.

———. *The Mirror of Production*. Trans. Mark Poster. St. Louis: Telos Press, 1975.

Bauman, Zygmunt. *Legislators and Interpreters: On Modernity, Post-Modernity, and Intellectuals*. Ithaca: Cornell University Press, 1987.

Begley, Adam. "The I's Have It: Duke's 'Moi' Critics Expose Themselves." *Lingua Franca* 4, no. 3 (1994): 54–59.

———. "Raiders of the Lost Archives." *Lingua Franca* 3, no. 5 (1993): 36–40.

Behar, Ruth. *Translated Woman: Crossing the Border with Esperanza's Story.* Boston: Beacon Press, 1993.

Belsey, Catherine. *The Subject of Tragedy: Identity and Difference in Renaissance Drama.* London and New York: Methuen, 1985.

Benjamin, Walter. "The Storyteller: Reflections on the Works of Nikolai Leskov." In *Illuminations*, ed. Hannah Arendt, trans. Harry Zohn, 83–109. New York: Schocken, 1969.

Bennington, Geoffrey, and Jacques Derrida. *Jacques Derrida.* Trans. Geoffrey Bennington. Chicago and London: University of Chicago Press, 1993.

Berman, Marshall. *All That Is Solid Melts into Air: The Experience of Modernity.* 2d ed. Harmondsworth: Penguin, 1988.

Best, Steven, and Douglas Kellner. *Postmodern Theory: Critical Interrogations.* New York: Guilford Press, 1991.

Bhaskar, Roy. *Reclaiming Reality: A Critical Introduction to Contemporary Philosophy.* London and New York: Verso, 1989.

Billig, Michael. "Nationalism and Richard Rorty: The Text as a Flag for *Pax Americana.*" *New Left Review* 202 (1993): 69–83.

Blair, Hugh. *Lectures on Rhetoric and Belles Lettres.* Philadelphia: Troutman & Hayes, 1853.

Blake, William. *The Complete Poetry and Prose of William Blake.* Ed. David Erdman. Rev. ed. Berkeley and Los Angeles: University of California Press, 1982.

Bolingbroke, Henry St. John. *The Works of the Late Rt. Hon. Henry St. John, Lord Viscount Bolingbroke.* 8 vols. London, 1809.

Booth, Wayne. *The Company We Keep: An Ethics of Fiction.* Berkeley and Los Angeles: University of California Press, 1988.

Borges, Jorge Luis. *Labyrinths: Selected Stories and Other Writings.* Ed. Donald A. Yates and James E. Irby. New York: New Directions, 1964.

Boswell, James. *Boswell's Life of Samuel Johnson, Including a Journal of His Tour to the Hebrides etc.* Ed. John Wilson Croker. 10 vols. London: John Murray, 1839.

———. *Life of Johnson.* Ed. R. W. Chapman. Corrected by J. D. Fleeman. London: Oxford University Press, 1970.

Bourdieu, Pierre. *Homo Academicus.* Trans. Peter Collier. Stanford: Stanford University Press, 1988.

Bourdieu, Pierre, and Jean-Claude Passeron. *Reproduction in Education, Society, and Culture.* Trans. Richard Nice. 2d ed. London: Sage Publications, 1990.

Bourdieu, Pierre, and Loïc J. D. Wacquant. *An Invitation to Reflexive Sociology.* Chicago and London: University of Chicago Press, 1992.

Bradbury, Malcolm. *Dr. Criminale.* Harmondsworth: Penguin, 1993.

Brand, John. *Observations on the Popular Antiquities of Great Britain.* 3d ed. 3 vols. London: Bohn, 1853.

Bürger, Peter. "The Disappearance of Meaning: Essay at a Postmodern Reading of Michel Tournier, Botho Strauss, and Peter Handke." In *Modernity and Identity*, ed. Scott Lash and Jonathan Friedman, 94–111. Oxford: Blackwell, 1992.

Burke, Kenneth. *A Grammar of Motives*. 1945. Reprint. Berkeley and Los Angeles: University of California Press, 1969.

Butler, Judith. *Gender Trouble: Feminism and the Subversion of Identity*. New York and London: Routledge, 1990.

Byatt, A. S. *Angels and Insects: Two Novellas*. New York: Random House, 1994.

———. *Possession*. New York: Vintage International, 1991.

Castiglione, Baldasar. *The Book of the Courtier*. Trans. George Bull. Harmondsworth: Penguin Books, 1976.

Chandler, James. *Wordsworth's Second Nature: A Study of the Poetry and Politics*. Chicago and London: University of Chicago Press, 1984.

Clare, John. *The Early Poems of John Clare, 1804–1822*. Ed. Eric Robinson and David Powell. 2 vols. Oxford: Clarendon Press, 1989.

Clifford, James. *The Predicament of Culture: Twentieth-Century Ethnography, Literature, and Art*. Cambridge and London: Harvard University Press, 1988.

Clifford, James, and George E. Marcus, eds. *Writing Culture: The Poetics and Politics of Ethnography*. Berkeley and Los Angeles: University of California Press, 1986.

Cobbett, William. *Rural Rides*. Ed. George Woodcock. Harmondsworth: Penguin, 1967.

Cohen, Walter. "Political Criticism of Shakespeare." In *Shakespeare Reproduced: The Text in History and Ideology*, ed. Jean E. Howard and Marion F. O'Connor, 18–46. London: Methuen, 1987.

Coleridge, Samuel Taylor. *Biographia Literaria*. Ed. James Engell and W. J. Bate. 2 vols. Princeton: Princeton University Press; London: Routledge & Kegan Paul, 1983.

———. *Coleridge: Poetical Works*. Ed. Ernest Hartley Coleridge. Oxford: Oxford University Press, 1974.

———. *Table Talk*. Ed. Carl Woodring. 2 vols. Princeton: Princeton University Press, 1990.

Colley, Linda. *Britons: Forging the Nation, 1707–1837*. New Haven and London: Yale University Press, 1992.

———. "Vengeful Susan." *London Review of Books*, 22 September 1994.

Comaroff, John, and Jean Comaroff. *Ethnography and the Historical Imagination*. Boulder, CO: Westview Press, 1992.

Cowper, William. *Poems*. 3d ed. 2 vols. London, 1787.

Crabbe, George. *The Poetical Works of the Rev. George Crabbe*. 8 vols. London: John Murray, 1834.

Daston, Lorraine. "Baconian Facts, Academic Civility, and the Prehistory of Objectivity." *Annals of Scholarship* 8, nos. 3–4 (1991): 337–63.

Davis, Lennard. *Factual Fictions: The Origins of the English Novel.* New York: Columbia University Press, 1983.

Davis, Natalie Zemon. *Fiction in the Archives: Pardon Tales and Their Tellers in Sixteenth-Century France.* Stanford: Stanford University Press, 1987.

————. "Stories and the Hunger to Know." *Yale Journal of Criticism* 5, no. 2 (1992): 159–63.

Derrida, Jacques. See Bennington, Geoffrey, and Jacques Derrida.

D'Israeli, Isaac. *A Dissertation on Anecdotes.* London, 1793. Reprint. New York: Garland, 1972.

Douglas, Ann. *The Feminization of American Culture.* New York: Knopf, 1977.

Eagleton, Terry. "Base and Superstructure in Raymond Williams." In *Raymond Williams: Critical Perspectives,* ed. Terry Eagleton, 165–75. Boston: Northeastern University Press, 1989.

————. "Fredric Jameson: The Politics of Style." In *Against the Grain: Essays, 1975–1985,* 65–78. London: Verso, 1986.

————. *The Function of Criticism: From "The Spectator" to Poststructuralism.* London: Verso, 1984.

————. *The Ideology of the Aesthetic.* Oxford: Blackwell, 1990.

Ebert, Teresa L. "Ludic Feminism, the Body, Performance, and Labor: Bringing *Materialism* Back into Feminist Cultural Studies." *Cultural Critique* 23 (1992–93): 5–50.

Eco, Umberto. *The Name of the Rose.* 1980. Trans. William Weaver. New York: Time Warner, 1986.

Elias, Norbert. *The History of Manners: The Civilizing Process.* Vol. 1. Trans. Edmund Jephcott. New York: Pantheon, 1978.

Eliot, T. S. *The Complete Poems and Plays of T. S. Eliot.* London: Faber & Faber, 1969.

Fabian, Johannes. "Ethnographic Objectivity Revisited: From Rigor to Vigor." In *Rethinking Objectivity,* ed. Allan Megill, 81–108. Durham and London: Duke University Press, 1994.

Ferguson, Margaret W. *Trials of Desire: Renaissance Defenses of Poetry.* New Haven and London: Yale University Press, 1983.

Ferguson, Margaret, and Jennifer Wicke, eds. *Feminism and Postmodernism.* Durham and London: Duke University Press, 1994.

Fineman, Joel. "The History of the Anecdote." In *The Subjectivity Effect in Western Literary Tradition: Essays toward the Release of Shakespeare's Will,* 59–87. Cambridge: MIT Press, 1991.

————. *Shakespeare's Perjured Eye: The Invention of Poetic Subjectivity in the Sonnets.* Berkeley and Los Angeles: University of California Press, 1986.

Fischer, Michael. *Stanley Cavell and Literary Skepticism.* Chicago and London: University of Chicago Press, 1989.

Fish, Stanley. "Consequences." In *Doing What Comes Naturally: Change, Rhetoric, and the Practice of Theory in Literary and Legal Studies*, 315–41. Durham and London: Duke University Press, 1989.

———. *Is There a Text in This Class? The Authority of Interpretive Communities.* Cambridge and London: Harvard University Press, 1980.

Foucault, Michel. *The Order of Things: An Archaeology of the Human Sciences.* New York: Random House, 1973.

Fraser, Nancy. "What's Critical about Critical Theory? The Case of Habermas and Gender." In *Feminism as Critique: On the Politics of Gender,* ed. Seyla Benhabib and Drucilla Cornell, 31–56. Minneapolis: University of Minnesota Press, 1987.

Fraser, Nancy, and Linda Nicholson. "Social Criticism without Philosophy: An Encounter between Feminism and Postmodernism." *Theory, Culture, and Society* 5 (1988): 373–94.

Freedman, Diane P., Olivia Frey, and Frances Murphy Zauhar, eds. *The Intimate Critique: Autobiographical Literary Criticism.* Durham and London: Duke University Press, 1993.

Fukuyama, Francis. *The End of History and the Last Man.* New York: Avon Books, 1992.

Gadamer, Hans-Georg. *Truth and Method.* New York: Seabury Press, 1975.

Gallop, Jane. "Knot a Love Story." *Yale Journal of Criticism* 5, no. 3 (1992): 209–18.

Geertz, Clifford. *The Interpretation of Cultures.* New York: Basic Books, 1973.

———. "'Local Knowledge' and Its Limits: Some *Obiter Dicta.*" *Yale Journal of Criticism* 5, no. 2 (1992): 130–32.

———. *Local Knowledge: Further Essays in Interpretive Anthropology.* New York: Basic Books, 1983.

Giddens, Anthony. *Modernity and Self-Identity: Self and Society in the Late Modern Age.* Stanford: Stanford University Press, 1991.

Gilbert, Martin. *The Holocaust: A History of the Jews of Europe during the Second World War.* New York: Holt, Rinehart & Winston, 1986.

Goody, Jack. "Local Knowledge and Knowledge of Locality: The Desirability of Frames." *Yale Journal of Criticism* 5, no. 2 (1992): 137–47.

Gouldner, Alvin W. *The Future of Intellectuals and the Rise of the New Class.* Oxford and Toronto: Oxford University Press, 1982.

Graff, Gerald. *Beyond the Culture Wars: How Teaching the Conflicts Can Revitalize American Education.* New York and London: Norton, 1992.

Graff, Gerald, and Michael Warner, eds. *The Origins of Literary Studies in America: A Documentary Anthology.* New York and London: Routledge, 1989.

Greenblatt, Stephen. *Renaissance Self-Fashioning: More to Shakespeare.* Chicago and London: University of Chicago Press, 1980.

———. *Shakespearean Negotiations: The Circulation of Social Energy in Renaissance England.* Berkeley and Los Angeles: University of California Press, 1988.

Guillory, John. *Cultural Capital: The Problem of Literary Canon Formation.* Chicago and London: University of Chicago Press, 1993.

Habermas, Jürgen. *The Philosophical Discourse of Modernity.* Trans. Frederick Lawrence. Cambridge: MIT Press, 1990.

Haraway, Donna J. "A Cyborg Manifesto: Science, Technology, and Socialist Feminism in the Late Twentieth Century." In *Simians, Cyborgs, and Women: The Reinvention of Nature,* 149–81. New York: Routledge, 1991.

Hartman, Geoffrey. "Romantic Poetry and the Genius Loci." In *Beyond Formalism: Literary Essays, 1958–1970,* 311–36. New Haven and London: Yale University Press, 1970.

———. "Wordsworth, Inscriptions, and Romantic Nature Poetry." In *From Sensibility to Romanticism: Essays Presented to Frederick A. Pottle,* ed. Frederick W. Hilles and Harold Bloom, 389–414. London: Oxford University Press, 1965.

Harvey, David. *The Condition of Postmodernity: An Enquiry into the Origins of Cultural Change.* Cambridge, MA, and Oxford: Blackwell, 1990.

Hegel, G. W. F. *Phenomenology of Spirit.* Trans. A. V. Miller. Oxford: Clarendon Press, 1979.

Heller, Scott. "Experience and Expertise Meet in New Brand of Scholarship." *Chronicle of Higher Education,* 6 May 1992, A7–9.

Howard, Jean E. "The New Historicism in Renaissance Studies." *English Literary Renaissance* 16 (1986): 13–43.

Hume, David. *Enquiries concerning Human Understanding and concerning the Principles of Morals.* Ed. L. A. Selby-Bigge. 3d ed. Revised by P. H. Nidditch. Oxford: Clarendon Press, 1975.

———. "Of National Characters." In *Essays Moral, Political, and Literary,* ed. Eugene F. Miller, 197–215. Indianapolis: Liberty Classics, 1985.

———. *A Treatise of Human Nature.* Ed. L. A. Selby-Bigge. Oxford: Clarendon Press, 1973.

Hutcheon, Linda. *The Politics of Postmodernism.* London and New York: Routledge, 1989.

Huyssen, Andreas. *After the Great Divide: Modernism, Mass Culture, Postmodernism.* Bloomington and Indianapolis: University of Indiana Press, 1986.

Jameson, Fredric. *Late Marxism: Adorno, or the Persistence of the Dialectic.* London and New York: Verso, 1990.

———. *The Political Unconscious: Narrative as a Socially Symbolic Act.* Ithaca: Cornell University Press, 1981.

———. "Postmodernism and Consumer Society." In *The Anti-Aesthetic: Essays on Postmodern Culture,* ed. Hal Foster, 111–25. Port Townsend, WA: Bay Press, 1983.

———. *Postmodernism, or The Cultural Logic of Late Capitalism.* Durham: Duke University Press, 1991.

Johnson, Samuel. *The Complete Works of Samuel Johnson.* Ed. Arthur Murphy. 12 vols. London, 1824.

———. "The Rambler, no. 60." In *Essays from the "Rambler," "Adventurer," and "Idler,"* ed. W. J. Bate, 109–14. New Haven and London: Yale University Press, 1968.

Johnston, Kenneth R. "The Politics of 'Tintern Abbey.'" *Wordsworth Circle* 14 (1983): 6–14.

Kaplan, Alice. *French Lessons: A Memoir.* Chicago and London: University of Chicago Press, 1993.

Kearney, Richard, ed. *Dialogues with Contemporary Continental Thinkers.* Manchester: Manchester University Press, 1984.

Keats, John. *John Keats: Complete Poems.* Ed. Jack Stillinger. Cambridge and London: Harvard University Press, Belknap Press, 1978.

Keller, Evelyn Fox. *Reflections on Gender and Science.* New Haven and London: Yale University Press, 1985.

Laclau, Ernesto, and Chantal Mouffe. *Hegemony and Socialist Strategy: Towards a Radical Democratic Politics.* Trans. Winston Moore and Paul Cammack. London: Verso, 1985.

Lacoue-Labarthe, Philippe, and Jean-Luc Nancy. *The Literary Absolute: The Theory of Literature in German Romanticism.* Trans. Philip Barnard and Cheryl Lester. Albany: State University of New York Press, 1988.

Lasch, Christopher. *The Culture of Narcissism: American Life in an Age of Diminishing Expectations.* New York: Norton, 1978.

Leavis, F. R. *Education and the University: A Sketch for an "English School."* New ed. London: Chatto & Windus, 1948.

———. *Revaluation: Tradition and Development in English Poetry.* 1936. Reprint. Harmondsworth: Penguin, 1967.

Lentricchia, Frank. *Ariel and the Police: Michel Foucault, William James, Wallace Stevens.* Madison: University of Wisconsin Press, 1988.

———. *Criticism and Social Change.* Chicago and London: University of Chicago Press, 1983.

Levinson, Marjorie. *Wordsworth's Great Period Poems: Four Essays.* Cambridge: Cambridge University Press, 1986.

Liu, Alan. "Local Transcendence: Cultural Criticism, Postmodernism, and the Romanticism of Detail." *Representations* 32 (1990): 75–113.

———. "The Power of Formalism: The New Historicism." *English Literary History* 56 (1989): 721–71.

Locke, John. *An Essay concerning Human Understanding.* Edited and corrected by P. H. Nidditch. Oxford: Clarendon Press, 1979.

Lodge, David. *Nice Work.* Harmondsworth: Penguin, 1988.

Lonsdale, Roger, ed. *The Poems of Thomas Gray, William Collins, Oliver Goldsmith.* London and New York: Longman, 1989.

Lovibond, Sabina. "Feminism and Postmodernism." *New Left Review* 178 (1989): 5–28.

———. "Feminism and Pragmatism." *New Left Review* 193 (1992): 56–74.

———. "Feminism and the 'Crisis of Rationality.'" *New Left Review* 207 (1994): 72–86.

Lucas, John. *England and Englishness: Ideas of Nationhood in English Poetry, 1688–1900.* Iowa City: University of Iowa Press, 1990.

Lukács, Georg. *The Destruction of Reason.* Trans. Peter Palmer. Atlantic Highlands, NJ: Humanities Press, 1981.

Lurie, Alison. *Foreign Affairs.* New York: Avon Books, 1990.

———. *The Truth about Lorin Jones.* New York: Avon Books, 1990.

Lyotard, Jean-François. *The Differend: Phrases in Dispute.* Trans. Georges Van Den Abbeele. Minneapolis: University of Minnesota Press, 1988.

———. *The Postmodern Condition: A Report on Knowledge.* Trans. Geoff Bennington and Brian Massumi. Minneapolis: University of Minnesota Press, 1984.

MacClean, Gerald. "Citing the Subject." In *Gender and Theory: Dialogues in Feminist Criticism,* ed. Linda Kauffman, 140–57. New York and Oxford: Blackwell, 1989.

McGowan, John. *Postmodernism and Its Critics.* Ithaca and London: Cornell University Press, 1991.

McKillop, Alan. "Local Attachment and Cosmopolitanism: The Eighteenth Century Pattern." In *From Sensibility to Romanticism: Essays Presented to Frederick A. Pottle,* ed. Frederick W. Hilles and Harold Bloom, 191–218. London: Oxford University Press, 1965.

McMillen, Liz. "A Passion for French." *Chronicle of Higher Education,* 9 February 1994, A8.

Macpherson, C. B. *The Political Theory of Possessive Individualism: Hobbes to Locke.* 1962. Reprint. Oxford: Oxford University Press, 1983.

Marcus, Leah. *Puzzling Shakespeare: Local Reading and Its Discontents.* Berkeley and Los Angeles: University of California Press, 1988.

Marx, Karl, and Frederick Engels. *Collected Works.* Vol. 6. New York: International Publishers, 1976.

———. *Collected Works.* Vol. 11. Moscow: Progress Publishers, 1979.

Messer-Davidow, Ellen. "The Philosophical Bases of Feminist Literary Criticism." In *Gender and Theory: Dialogues in Feminist Criticism,* ed. Linda Kauffman, 63–106. New York and Oxford: Blackwell, 1989.

Miller, Nancy K. *Getting Personal: Feminist Occasions and Other Autobiographical Acts.* New York and London: Routledge, 1991.

Miyoshi, Masao. "A Borderless World? From Colonialism to Transnationalism and the Decline of the Nation-State." *Critical Inquiry* 19 (1992–93): 726–51.

Mohanty, S. P. "Us and Them: On the Philosophical Bases of Political Criticism." *Yale Journal of Criticism* 2, no. 2 (1989): 1–31.

Nelson, William. *Fact or Fiction: The Dilemma of the Renaissance Storyteller.* Cambridge: Harvard University Press, 1973.

Newman, John Henry. *The Idea of a University.* Ed. Martin J. Svaglic. Notre Dame, IN: University of Notre Dame Press, 1982.

Newton, Judith Lowder. "History as Usual? Feminism and the 'New Historicism.'" In *The New Historicism,* ed. H. Aram Veeser, 152–67. New York and London: Routledge, 1989.

Nichols, John. *Literary Anecdotes of the Eighteenth Century.* Ed. Colin Clair. Carbondale: Southern Illinois University Press, 1967.

Nietzsche, Friedrich. *Basic Writings of Nietzsche.* Trans. Walter Kaufmann. New York: Random House, 1966.

———. *Untimely Meditations.* Trans. R. J. Hollingdale. Cambridge: Cambridge University Press, 1983.

Norris, Christopher. *The Contest of Faculties: Philosophy and Theory after Deconstruction.* London and New York: Methuen, 1985.

———. *The Truth about Postmodernism.* Oxford: Blackwell, 1993.

Nussbaum, Martha. "The Literary Imagination in Public Life." *New Literary History* 22 (1991): 877–910.

Oakeshott, Michael. "The Voice of Poetry in the Conversation of Mankind." In *Rationalism in Politics and Other Essays,* 197–247. London: Methuen, 1962.

Paley, William. *The Principles of Moral and Political Philosophy.* 20th ed. 2 vols. London, 1814.

Patai, Daphne. "Sick and Tired of Scholars' Nouveau Solipsism." *Chronicle of Higher Education,* 23 February 1994, A52.

Pecora, Vincent P. "The Limits of Local Knowledge." In *The New Historicism,* ed. H. Aram Veeser, 243–76. New York and London: Routledge, 1989.

———. "The Sorcerer's Apprentices: Romance, Anthropology, and Literary Theory." *Modern Language Quarterly* 55, no. 4 (1994): 345–82.

Penley, Constance, and Andrew Ross. "Cyborgs at Large: Interview with Donna Haraway." In *Technoculture,* ed. Constance Penley and Andrew Ross, 1–26. Minneapolis and Oxford: University of Minnesota Press, 1991.

Percy, Thomas. *Reliques of Ancient English Poetry.* Ed. Robert Aris Wilmott. London: Routledge, 1857.

Pocock, J. G. A. *The Machiavellian Moment: Florentine Political Thought and the Atlantic Republican Tradition.* Princeton: Princeton University Press, 1975.

Pollard, Arthur, ed. *Crabbe: The Critical Heritage.* London and Boston: Routledge & Kegan Paul, 1972.

Polwhele, Richard. *The Influence of Local Attachment with Respect to Home: A Poem.* London, 1796.

———. *The Influence of Local Attachment with Respect to Home: A Poem in Seven Books: A New Edition, with Large Additions; and Odes, with Other Poems.* 2 vols. London, 1798.

Richards, I. A. *Science and Poetry.* New York: Norton, 1926.

Robbins, Bruce. *Secular Vocations: Intellectuals, Professionalism, Culture.* London and New York: Verso, 1993.

—————, ed. *Intellectuals: Aesthetics, Politics, Academics.* Minneapolis: University of Minnesota Press, 1990.

Rorty, Richard. *Consequences of Pragmatism: Essays, 1972–1980.* Minneapolis: University of Minnesota Press, 1982.

—————. *Contingency, Irony, and Solidarity.* Cambridge: Cambridge University Press, 1989.

—————. *Philosophy and the Mirror of Nature.* Corrected ed. Princeton: Princeton University Press, 1980.

Rose, Margaret A. *The Post-Modern and the Post-Industrial: A Critical Analysis.* Cambridge: Cambridge University Press, 1991.

Rousseau, Jean-Jacques. Preface to *Narcissus, or the Self-Admirer.* In *The Miscellaneous Works of Mr. J. J. Rousseau,* 2: 121–48. London, 1767.

Said, Edward. *Beginnings: Intention and Method.* New York: Columbia University Press, 1985.

Schama, Simon. *Dead Certainties (Unwarranted Speculations).* New York: Knopf, 1991.

Schlegel, Friedrich. *Friedrich Schlegel's "Lucinde" and the Fragments.* Trans. Peter Firchow. Minneapolis: University of Minnesota Press, 1971.

Scott, Joan. "The Evidence of Experience." *Critical Inquiry* 17 (1990–91): 773–97.

Scott, John. *Critical Essays on Some of the Poems of Several English Poets.* London, 1785.

Sedgwick, Eve Kosovsky. "A Poem Is Being Written." *Representations* 17 (1987): 110–43.

—————. "White Glasses." *Yale Journal of Criticism* 5, no. 3 (1992): 193–208.

See, Carolyn. "At a Magic Threshold." *Los Angeles Times Book Review,* 28 October 1990, 13.

Sekora, John. *Luxury: The Concept in Western Thought, Eden to Smollett.* Baltimore: Johns Hopkins University Press, 1977.

Shapin, Steven. *A Social History of Truth: Civility and Science in Seventeenth-Century England.* Chicago and London: University of Chicago Press, 1994.

Sheringham, Michael. *French Autobiography: Devices and Desires.* Oxford: Clarendon Press, 1994.

Shields, Carol. *Mary Swann.* London: HarperCollins, 1993.

Shklovsky, Victor. *Theory of Prose.* Trans. Benjamin Sher. Elmwood Park, IL: Dalkey Archive, 1990.

Sidney, Sir Philip. *An Apology for Poetry, or The Defence of Poetry.* Ed. Geoffrey Shepherd. Edinburgh and London: Thomas Nelson, 1965.

Simpson, David. "Figuring Sex, Class, and Gender: What Is the Subject of Wordsworth's 'Gipsies'?" *South Atlantic Quarterly* 88 (1989): 541–67.

———. *Irony and Authority in Romantic Poetry.* London: Macmillan, 1979.

———. "The Moment of Materialism." In *Subject to History: Ideology, Class, Gender,* ed. David Simpson, 1–33. Ithaca and London: Cornell University Press, 1991.

———. "Public Virtues, Private Vices: Reading between the Lines of Wordsworth's 'Anecdote for Fathers.'" In *Subject to History: Ideology, Class, Gender,* ed. David Simpson, 163–90. Ithaca and London: Cornell University Press, 1991.

———. "Putting One's House in Order: The Career of the Self in Descartes' Method." *New Literary History* 9 (1977): 83–101.

———. "Raymond Williams: Feeling for Structures, Voicing History." *Social Text* 30 (1992): 9–26.

———. *Romanticism, Nationalism, and the Revolt against Theory.* Chicago and London: University of Chicago Press, 1993.

———. *Wordsworth and the Figurings of the Real.* London: Macmillan, 1982.

———. *Wordsworth's Historical Imagination: The Poetry of Displacement.* London and New York: Methuen, 1987.

Smith, Adam. *Lectures on Rhetoric and Belles Lettres.* Ed. J. C. Bryce. Oxford: Clarendon Press, 1983.

Smollett, Tobias. *Humphry Clinker.* Ed. James L. Thorson. New York and London: Norton, 1983.

Soja, Edward W. *Postmodern Geographies: The Reassertion of Space in Critical Social Theory.* London and New York: Verso, 1989.

Southey, Robert. *Letters from England.* Ed. Jack Simmons. London: Cresset Press, 1951.

Spence, Joseph. *Observations, Anecdotes, and Characters of Books and Men, Collected from Conversation.* Ed. James M. Osborn. 2 vols. Oxford: Clarendon Press, 1966.

Spivak, Gayatri Chakravorty. "Can the Subaltern Speak?" In *Marxism and the Interpretation of Culture,* ed. Cary Nelson and Lawrence Grossberg, 271–313. Urbana and Chicago: University of Illinois Press, 1988.

Stone, Norman. "A Mad Scramble for the Centre." *Sunday Times* (London), sect. 3, 9 October 1994, 6–7.

Suleri, Sara. "Local Knowledge and Its Limits: Responses." *Yale Journal of Criticism* 5, no. 2 (1992): 155–57.

Taylor, Charles. *Sources of the Self: The Making of the Modern Identity.* Cambridge: Harvard University Press, 1989.

Thomas, Brook. *The New Historicism and Other Old-Fashioned Topics.* Princeton: Princeton University Press, 1991.

Thompson, E. P. "The Poverty of Theory, or An Orrery of Errors." In *The Poverty of Theory and Other Essays,* 1–205. New York and London: Monthly Review Press, 1978.

Tompkins, Jane. "Me and My Shadow." In *Gender and Theory: Dialogues on Feminist Criticism*, ed. Linda Kauffman, 121–39. New York and Oxford: Blackwell, 1989.

———. "Pedagogy of the Distressed." *College English* 52, no. 6 (1990): 653–61.

Toulmin, Stephen. *Cosmopolis: The Hidden Agenda of Modernity.* Chicago: University of Chicago Press, 1992.

Tyler, Stephen. *The Unspeakable: Discourse, Dialogue, and Rhetoric in the Postmodern World.* Madison: University of Wisconsin Press, 1987.

Ulrich, Laurel Thatcher. *A Midwife's Tale.* New York: Vintage, 1990.

Vattimo, Gianni. *The End of Modernity: Nihilism and Hermeneutics in Postmodern Culture.* Trans. Jon R. Snyder. Baltimore: Johns Hopkins University Press, 1991.

Veblen, Thorstein. *The Theory of the Leisure Class: An Economic Study of Institutions.* New York: Macmillan, 1899.

Virgil. *Aeneid.* In *Virgil.* Trans. H. Rushton Fairclough. Rev. ed. 2 vols. Cambridge: Harvard University Press; London: William Heinemann, 1978.

Warton, Thomas. *The History of English Poetry.* Ed. Richard Price. 3 vols. London, 1840.

Watkins, Evan. *Work Time: English Departments and the Circulation of Cultural Value.* Stanford: Stanford University Press, 1989.

Waugh, Patricia. *Practising Postmodernism, Reading Modernism.* London: Edward Arnold, 1992.

Wellek, René, and Austin Warren. *Theory of Literature.* 3d ed. Harmondsworth: Penguin Books, 1963.

West, Cornel. *The American Evasion of Philosophy: A Genealogy of Pragmatism.* Madison: University of Wisconsin Press, 1989.

White, Gilbert. *The Natural History of Selborne.* Ed. Richard Mabey. Harmondsworth: Penguin, 1967.

White, Hayden. *Metahistory: The Historical Imagination in Nineteenth-Century Europe.* Baltimore and London: Johns Hopkins University Press, 1975.

Wilson, F. P. "Table Talk." *Huntington Library Quarterly* 4 (1940–41): 27–46.

Wilson, R. Jackson. *Figures of Speech: American Writers and the Literary Marketplace, from Benjamin Franklin to Emily Dickinson.* New York: Knopf, 1989.

Wollstonecraft, Mary. Preface to *The Female Reader.* In *The Works of Mary Wollstonecraft*, ed. Janet Todd and Marilyn Butler, 4:55–60. New York: New York University Press, 1989.

Wordsworth, Mary. *The Letters of Mary Wordsworth, 1800–1855.* Ed. Mary E. Burton. Oxford: Clarendon Press, 1958.

Wordsworth, William. *"Lyrical Ballads" and Other Poems, 1797–1800.* Ed. James Butler and Karen Green. Ithaca and London: Cornell University Press, 1992.

———. *The Prelude.* Ed. Jonathan Wordsworth, M. H. Abrams, and Stephen Gill. London and New York: Norton, 1979.

———. *The Prose Works of William Wordsworth.* Ed. W. J. B. Owen and Jane Worthington Smyser. 3 vols. Oxford: Clarendon Press, 1974.

Wordsworth, William, and Dorothy Wordsworth. *The Letters of William and Dorothy Wordsworth: The Early Years, 1787–1805.* Ed. E. de Selincourt. 2d ed. Revised by Chester L. Shaver. Oxford: Clarendon Press, 1967.

Yeats, William Butler. *The Collected Poems of W. B. Yeats.* 2d ed. London: Macmillan, 1969.

INDEX